Football's War &

The Tumultuous Season of

DESERT ISLAND FOOTBALL HISTORIES

CLUB HISTORIES

Aberdeen: A Centenary History 1903-2003	1-874287-49-X
Aberdeen: Champions of Scotland 1954-55	1-874287-65-1
Aberdeen: The European Era – A Complete Record	1-874287-11-2
Bristol City: The Modern Era – A Complete Record	1-874287-28-7
Bristol City: The Early Years 1894-1915	1-874287-74-0
Cambridge United: The League Era – A Complete Record	1-874287-32-5
Cambridge United: 101 Golden Greats	1-874287-58-9
The Story of the Celtic 1888-1938	1-874287-15-5
Colchester United: Graham to Whitton – A Complete Record	1-874287-27-9
Coventry City: The Elite Era – A Complete Record	1-874287-51-1
Coventry City: An Illustrated History	1-874287-59-7
Dundee: Champions of Scotland 1961-62	1-874287-72-4
Dundee United: Champions of Scotland 1982-83	1-874287-71-6
History of the Everton Football Club 1878-1928	1-874287-14-7
Halifax Town: From Ball to Lillis – A Complete Record	1-874287-26-0
Hereford United: The League Era – A Complete Record	1-874287-18-X
Huddersfield Town: Champions of England 1923-1926	1-874287-66-X
Ipswich Town: The Modern Era – A Complete Record	1-874287-43-0
Ipswich Town: Champions of England 1961-62	1-874287-56-2
Luton Town: The Modern Era – A Complete Record	1-874287-05-8
Luton Town: An Illustrated History	1-874287-37-6
Matt Busby: A Complete Man U record 1945-1971	1-874287-53-8
Motherwell: Champions of Scotland 1931-32	1-874287-73-2
Norwich City: The Modern Era – A Complete Record	1-874287-67-8
Peterborough United: The Modern Era – A Complete Record	1-874287-33-3
Peterborough United: Who's Who?	1-874287-48-1
Plymouth Argyle: The Modern Era – A Complete Record	1-874287-54-6
Plymouth Argyle: 101 Golden Greats	1-874287-64-3
Portsmouth: From Tindall to Ball – A Complete Record	1-874287-25-2
Portsmouth: Champions of England – 1948-49 & 1949-50	1-874287-38-4
The Story of the Rangers 1873-1923	1-874287-16-3
The Romance of the Wednesday 1867-1926	1-874287-17-1
Stoke City: The Modern Era – A Complete Record	1-874287-39-2
Stoke City: 101 Golden Greats	1-874287-55-4
West Ham: From Greenwood to Redknapp	1-874287-19-8
West Ham: The Elite Era – A Complete Record	1-874287-31-7
Wimbledon: From Southern League to Premiership	1-874287-09-0
Wimbledon: From Wembley to Selhurst	1-874287-20-1
Wimbledon: The Premiership Years	1-874287-40-6
Wrexham: The European Era – A Complete Record	1-874287-52-X

WORLD CUP HISTORIES

England's Quest for the World Cup – A Complete Record	1-874287-61-9
Scotland: The Quest for the World Cup – A Complete Record	1-897850-50-6
Ireland: The Quest for the World Cup – A Complete Record	1-897850-80-8

MISCELLANEOUS

Red Dragons in Europe – A Complete Record	1-874287-01-5
The Book of Football: A History to 1905-06	1-874287-13-9

FOOTBALL'S WAR & PEACE

THE TUMULTUOUS SEASON OF 1946-47

Series Editor: Clive Leatherdale

Thomas Taw

DESERT ISLAND BOOKS

First published in 2003
(second impression)
by
DESERT ISLAND BOOKS LIMITED
89 Park Street, Westcliff-on-Sea, Essex SS0 7PD
United Kingdom
www.desertislandbooks.com

British Library Cataloguing-in-Publication Data
A catalogue record for this book is available from the British Library

ISBN 1-874287-70-8

1 3 5 7 9 10 8 6 4 2

Printed in Great Britain
by
Antony Rowe Ltd

Contents

Introduction

Was there ever such a football season?

When I was born, in December 1946, George Stobbart had already made his mark on that football season. George was a typical wartime footballer, scoring 129 goals for Middlesbrough whilst working night shifts in the mine, and on Saturdays rushing for his train to away matches. By September 1946, George was supplanted by returning war heroes like Wilf Mannion. With a growing young family, George sought security by moving to Newcastle. There he became the filling in a sandwich of two ground-breaking football transfers. George's arrival stimulated an unseemly rush for United's wartime discovery, Albert Stubbins. The eventual fee, the second highest ever and a colossal amount of money in an age of enduring austerity, caused a sensation. George was immediately injured, so ambitious Newcastle spent the entire Stubbins fee on another young England star, Len Shackleton. George disappeared, to re-emerge to devastating effect in a 1947 FA Cup semi-final.

In later years George drifted to London and finished a career of wholehearted enthusiasm with Brentford. He took a pub and of course captained its Sunday morning team. There it was in 1964, by now 40-odd, that George, at inside-right, supplied beautifully weighted passes to your author, then a callow 17-year-old on the wing, who more often than not stumbled clumsily in his efforts to do them justice. George tried showing the same fortitude he demonstrated in going from coal face to wartime football pitch, although he did not always succeed. Sorry, George.

This is the story of an English football season. After 'the match', 'the season' is the most satisfying unit of organised football, a competitive test over an autumn, winter, and spring. All the elements of any season are here: early hopes, final disappointments; individual successes and failures; controversies and disputes; innumerable might-have-beens. In 1946-47 the League Championship was decided on the last day of a uniquely prolonged season, in mid-June, a cliff-hanger whereby the champion is not revealed until the last page.

1946-47 had lasting influence. It shaped England's managers until 1982 – Winterbottom, Ramsey, Mercer, Revie and Ron Greenwood. Matt Busby started out as a manager, and Bill Shankly's experiences coloured his future. Its players boasted a 'true classic breed': Stan Matthews and Tom Finney, Peter Doherty and Raich Carter, Tom Lawton and Wilf Mannion.

In traditional histories football's resumption after the war is just something that happened: inevitable, commonplace and insignificant. Or it appears unfathomable, an aberration, an inexplicable mix of vast crowds watching rough house play; of unprecedented profits on the backs of footballers paid a pittance. Recent accounts have acknowledged this economic injustice, yet depicted the players' attitude as docile, in keeping with an accepting age in which the referee's decision, like all authority, was unquestioned.

All wrong. The reality is the opposite. 1946-47 was the 'most momentous' season. It was no less than football starting again, the first of the modern era. It was tumultuous from start to finish, an unceasing clamour of voices – players, officials, commentators, politicians, and fans. Football was never so central to the life and decisive events in a troubled and despondent country.

It was far from inevitable. Real football had not existed for seven years: it was a struggle to get started, and it almost packed in unfinished. A regular, national competition depended on good travel facilities: yet the war left the transport infrastructure exhausted and chaotic. It needed equipment – balls, boots, kit, safe grounds – when there were shortages, rationing and higher priorities. Real football needed enough players: players able to escape the Forces, the mines, or the Essential Work of industrial reconstruction; and players who 'belonged' to a club, not the ubiquitous wartime 'guests'. That these obstacles were overcame is a tribute to the everyday achievement of football folk, but it also signals how important it was, to the country, to its government, that it did so.

It was a season of discontent, conflict between those who wanted change, and others, powerful voices, who needed a return to the past. Its most overt manifestation was the season-long industrial dispute by the Players' Union. But players also fought players, and they fought referees. Football authorities fought with each other, and all were lambasted by the loudest, most intimidating and conservative voice of all, the crowds.

So the football here is clothed in the sounds and images of its time, creating a texture and fragmentary glimpses of how the game touched the life of Britain. The football itself is vividly recreated with passion and poetry. The special qualities of the great players reoccur again and again, not abstractly, but influencing matches that counted. But others, many who would not appear in a conventional account, also feature: journeymen pros like George Stobbart; even anonymous trialists, ancient figures of the past; referees, managers and directors, groundsmen and gatemen; those whose working lives were touched by football – railway porters, hotel waiters, typists – and both named and unnamed members of the hordes who scrambled to see them play.

The story has a further backcloth: the weather. This had given British football a special character, and now the century's worst winter ultimately shaped its reconstruction and thus the nature of the postwar game. Football had always played through anything, but 1946-47 was different again. August's opening day carried primeval portents: 'to the accompaniment of sunshine, thunder, lightning, floods and a roar from a total crowd of nearly a million.'

The Shakespearean omens continued in September gales and rainstorms, and a wet November that turned war-damaged grounds into black-brown, impassable mud heaps. Still the crowds came, as many outside fighting to get in as there was inside, struggling for a view. After Christmas, the country came to a shivery stop for weeks on end: football was almost the only thing that kept going – on snow, ice, slush, sometimes all three; in blizzards, on the coldest days ever known for playing football. The season started 'crazy' and it ended 'weird': it was truly the most dramatic and important, ever.

This story is told primarily through the medium of contemporary papers. It was the only way you could find out what was going on. It was only the next day, reading his Sunday paper that the most famous footballer found out that 33 people had been killed attending a match in which he played. Hundreds waited outside local newspaper offices for midweek results. 'Phenomenal scenes' greeted the arrival of specialist Saturday evening football papers. Newsboys were overwhelmed by the swollen crowds – 'couldn't have been worse if we'd been giving away beer'. Sales were 50 per cent up on prewar levels even though newsprint restrictions kept production so low: 'I heard of one hostelry where on Saturday night last there were about 50 customers, all of whom had to share one *Green 'Un*, which was passed from one to the other.'

Newspapers travelled far and wide, to servicemen and others scattered throughout the world in the aftermath of war. Papers demonstrated their appeal by printing photographs of conscript servicemen reading their Saturday Football Special in Austria, Yugoslavia, Italy, Palestine, India – Lahore, Calcutta, New Delhi, Punjab, the North-West Frontier – Kenya, Southern Rhodesia, the Suez Canal, Aden, George Cross Island, Singapore, Sierra Leone, Egypt, Sudan, Iraq, Japan, Burma, Crete, Gibraltar, Greece, Mandalay, and Hong Kong.

'The press has to strike resonances with its audiences immediately,' and the sum of these resonances could be 'used to gauge the mood of the country' (Wilkinson, 1995). 1946-47 was a hard time of dark moods. This football season cannot be fully understood without an appreciation of the world outside the football gates, because it too often broke in.

Newspapers were football's medium. They provided immediacy: that day's match. They were disputatious, poetic and funny. Local papers were passionately committed to their town, a pride important to assert at a time of many reunions and more frustrations. The football club carried that pride and related expectations onto a national stage, and failures were roundly condemned. But commentators could also be reflective, and appreciative of history. There were after all 'two ways to write about a football match': you could stay in its immediacy, or 'relate the match to all the football preceding it' (Ledbrooke and Turner, 1950).

There was an important need to explain football in 1946, because a generation had grown up without the real thing. Its history reminded the British that football was their game, they were Pioneerland. And that too was timely, because just as Britain's Empire came under postwar threat, so England as Pioneerland was quickly assailed. The two, Empire and Pioneerland, were entrapped within an anxiety about Britain's place in the world.

The newspapers did not just talk football. They went beyond footballers at their football business – playing, training, changing clubs – to footballers in the course of their ordinary lives. Footballers who needed permission, from an Army Officer or a colliery's Absentee Board before they could play before 60,000 people. Footballers doing all sorts of other jobs. Footballers with homes, and those without. Doing the same things as other working people during the reconstruction. Trying to get on, or get by.

EXPLANATORY NOTE:
In 1946-47 there was no Premier League: rather a national First and Second Division, and a Third Division divided into Northern and Southern Sections. All four divisions contained 22 clubs who played 42 league games. There were two points for a win, and one for a draw. The FA Cup had no limit on replays. There were no substitutes, apart from by arrangement in internationals. The players largely occupied a distinctive position on the field, described by his perceived role – back, half-back, forward – and area of the field – left, right, centre. The centre-half was the middle of a defensive line of three, who were generally in direct opposition to two 'extreme wingers' and a centre-forward. Half-backs and inside-forwards were midfield players. The Football League comprised:

First Division:
Arsenal, Aston Villa, Blackburn Rovers, Blackpool, Bolton Wanderers, Brentford, Charlton Athletic, Chelsea, Derby County, Everton, Grimsby Town, Huddersfield Town, Leeds United, Liverpool, Manchester United, Middlesbrough, Portsmouth, Preston North End, Sheffield United, Stoke City, Sunderland, Wolverhampton Wanderers.

Second Division:
Barnsley, Birmingham City, Bradford Park Avenue, Burnley, Bury, Chesterfield, Coventry City, Fulham, Leicester City, Luton Town, Manchester City, Millwall, Newcastle United, Newport County, Nottingham Forest, Plymouth Argyle, Sheffield Wednesday, Southampton, Swansea Town, Tottenham Hotspur, West Bromwich Albion, West Ham United.

Third Division (South):
Aldershot, Bournemouth and Boscombe Athletic, Brighton and Hove Albion, Bristol City, Bristol Rovers, Cardiff City, Crystal Palace, Exeter City, Ipswich Town, Leyton Orient (although there was initial confusion regarding whether Orient were using their pre-war Clapton affiliation), Mansfield Town, Northampton Town, Norwich City, Notts County, Port Vale, Queen's Park Rangers, Reading, Southend United, Swindon Town, Torquay United, Walsall, Watford.

Third Division (North):
Accrington Stanley, Barrow, Bradford City, Carlisle United, Chester, Crewe Alexandra, Darlington, Doncaster Rovers, Gateshead, Hartlepools United, Halifax Town, Hull City, Lincoln City, New Brighton, Oldham Athletic, Rochdale, Rotherham United, Southport, Stockport County, Tranmere Rovers, Wrexham, York City.

ACKNOWLEDGEMENTS:
Many thanks to my family – Geoffrina, Robert, Stephen, Judith, Susannah and Holly – for their forbearance; to friends, especially Richard Purver, for their support; to Robin Moore and the Kenchels (veteranos) Football Club for their encouragement; and to the many fine newspaper writers during the 1946-47 season, especially Charles Mann, for their inspiration. Apologies to those whose material has been used in this book where copyright has not been identified, and who are invited to contact the author and publishers.

Photographs of Wilf Mannion (page 25), Tom Finney (page 125), Tommy Walker (page 223), and Frank Swift (page 226) are from *Football Stars*, published by Fore Publications. Illustrations on page 124 are from Kiddy's Cigarette Cards.

DEDICATION:
For all those footballers, and the journalists who wrote about them, and those like my parents who watched them, and showed faith in the future by having children in the tough years after the war.

1

The Football Commandos

'[Derby v Villa was] like a pitched battle, but it had as much argument as a peace conference. In between banging away at each other, like commandos meeting panzer troops, the players engaged in wordy warfare, and were as ready to argue with the referee as Molotov is to bandy words with Bevin and Byrnes ... biggest blowup since the night the bomb shattered the Osmaston stand ... it became a siege, the Villa behind their Maginot line and Derby battering away with their heaviest artillery.'

The peace might have begun, but life in Britain still reverberated with warlike echoes. Football in particular bristled with martial images. Teams commonly adopted 'blitzkrieg tactics' and suffered 'whole battalions', not just 'single spies', of misfortune; goals 'divebombed' into the net, and 'commando-fit' players made 'charges heavy enough to buckle a submarine'.

The imagery was acute. Collisions were especially violent; footballers and crowds competed over the fierceness of their intensity. Beneath the surface too there was turmoil. Reforging football was a passionate affair. Players, clubs and crowds alike resembled one of the autumn's centre-forwards; irresistible, but combustible – 'a blond bombshell who was always dangerous but never exploded'.

It was also a world of reconstruction, and peace conferences going wrong. The Cold War was intensifying by the month.

Football had no peace conference, just a series of forces searching for a new war. The Football Association (FA) had a patrician's internationalist vision, in which Britain would return to the fold of world football, and would embrace coaching and modernity. The clubs wanted a return to the past, to the disciplines and class relations of the Football League's first 50 years. The players remembered being 'thrown out of their jobs' in 1939. The war had changed their lives and now football would change. And change must come, for the country was mad for football: 'there is scarcely a home in the land wherein the game does not exert its sway.'

In public imagination, the war was survived by sticking together. Collectivity defined the country when it elected a landslide Labour Government to plan a new society. Collectivity also sent people to holiday camps, cinemas, and football matches. Football had contributed mightily to the maintenance of war morale, home and abroad. Afterwards the local club was a focus for revived communal pride, the reassertion of identity and togetherness. The public, the League and the Government needed real football – traditional, competitive, national – back, quickly.

However, spectating was so popular that it replicated the symbol of shortages and rationing – queuing. And queuing brought frustration. So instead of exorcising the lost years, football became embroiled in the convulsions of peacetime. High hopes faded as deprivations actually worsened: shelter, food and fuel all became scarcer. There was work, and there were diversions. Football was a means to get out, spend some money, shout a bit and keep depression at bay. The FA thought it 'a queer age in which people cannot spend on bread and clothing and are turning to sport'.

Football did not trust its vast crowds: in the 'midst of a soccer boom' maybe, but 'is it sure to be lasting?' When the players wanted to share the bounty, clubs feared they risked disaster later. Players were in a bind. So much expected, so little received. Seen as tin gods in public, they shared their public's private deprivations and insecurities. They wanted a truer reward. But what was that? Footballers were both heroes and villains: pursued and worshipped, but as fervently vilified and barracked. What they did on the field was rarely good enough. What they had done during the war was enduringly suspect.

What was the value of professional football after the war? The country was devastated and on the verge of bankruptcy. It needed fit young men for the reconstruction. If football boomed, and players got rich, they would need no other work. Was that OK? What was the value of their work? Were footballers skilled craftsmen, like many of those watching? Not according to their watchers who knew better and constantly denigrated these skills. Or was it the classic 'dead-end' job, the antithesis of what everyone valued in the postwar world, security? Or were footballers entertainers allowed to opt out of the work-a-day world – after all 'a variety artiste is not expected to drive a milk float?' And how could only the stars benefit from the boom, when football was the very expression of collectivity, a team, each relying on the others, and representing a proud but suffering community, and its working people?

The outcome would reflect the ancient tension between players and watchers. They had shared a war, and returned to a shared world. They had escaped from torpedoed ships and burning bombers; they had been prisoners-of-war and had received medals for bravery. How would their paths now separate?

2

The Front Line was their Touchline

'[Brentford's Harry Oliver] served as third engineer on a troopship in the Merchant Navy. It once broke down en route to Italy. She arrived a day late in Bari to find 17 ships sinking as a result of a dive bombing attack. If it hadn't been ...'

The English Channel was a sad place on 8 June 1940. The miracle of deliverance of 335,000 soldiers had given way to a realisation that Dunkirk had been a colossal military disaster. The Low Countries had been overrun and 'the fate of civilisation' depended on the fight for France. At home, industry, fuelled by its mines, would need to make good the loss of war material through intense production: 'the country understands at long last that we are fighting for our lives.'

Dunkirk had been 'hot as hell'. Rescue from the howitzers and mortars on the beaches meant surviving a 'merciless rain of machine gun bullets and shrapnel from dive bombers'. Thirty vessels were sunk, with many casualties. There were still boats in the Channel and still seamen pulling people out of the water. But they were no longer rescuers. Not everyone made it. These seamen were in the bitter business of fishing for dead bodies. And bitterness turned to anger when they heard the ship's radio. Something was out of place with their grim task and the nation's grimmer fate. The radio was broadcasting football's War Cup final, kicking off at Wembley at 6pm.

This tension overshadowed football's reconstruction. Officially football had a good war, symbolising what was good about the British way of life. But footballers fought, died, survived. Roy White of Spurs was in that Channel for hours after his rescue boat was sunk. The 19-year-old sergeant ended the war as a major and, along with other stars, joined touring circuses which took football to British Forces across the world. Twenty-one-year-old Joe Carr was killed at Dunkirk. Joe played all three fixtures of Sheffield United's 1939-40 First Division season before it was abandoned, with United lying second. He immediately joined the Army and played his last recorded match, a Sheffield derby, on 30 March 1940 whilst he was on embarkation leave. So football suffered its first casualty. There would be other heroes who did not live to see its return in 1946.

West Ham and Blackburn contested the 1940 War Cup final. The police set a limit of 50,000 on their final-with-the-frills-missing, and the players were on a £1 win bonus. In the Rovers team that so affronted the seamen fishing for dead servicemen were two players who would lose their lives. That Saturday 'rough-hewn' left-half Frank Chivers mined in Barnburgh Colliery near Doncaster until 4am, then dashed to London. In April 1942 this 'honest-to-goodness, broad-speaking Yorkshireman' would be killed instantly when a girder and a block of stone fell upon him, five minutes before the end of his shift. He left a widow and two small children. This Wembley final meant the break up of Blackburn's 1939 promotion team: 'Albert Clarke was the first to go, his colleagues seeing him off soon after the match when he left to join his unit.'

Albert Clarke had scored 23 goals in 1938-39: he was killed in Normandy, ten days after D-Day, while serving with airborne troops – his wife was expecting their second child.

At least 75 footballers died serving in the Forces. England lost two internationals and the prewar giants, Arsenal, eight. Yet footballers were tarred with the brush of avoiding real danger. Those seamen in the Channel echoed complaints in Parliament that players were too easily excused military duties, and too often absorbed into the Physical Training (PT) Corps. Choosing PT or conventional soldiering could have moral overtones. Following conscription, prewar golden boy Wilf Mannion and Middlesbrough teammate Harold Shepherdson were offered transfer to PT. Neither were keen, but Shepherdson saw the chance to develop new skills, initiating an honourable career which culminated in training England's 1966 World Cup winners – 'the best thing that ever happened to me'. Wilf, the greater footballer and therefore the more vulnerable to criticism, preferred to 'stay with the boys' (Varley, 1997, p.53).

Another international, Liverpool's Matt Busby, watched U-Boats sink the next ship in line of troop convoy, then had to defend himself against jibes that he was being kept safe. Flight also involved near misses: when the fourteen-strong Services team returned from playing in Belgium in October 1944, their aeroplane emerged from cloud to find another not twenty feet away. Twenty feet: otherwise the English postwar football scene would have been without Busby, Stan Matthews, Frank Swift, Joe Mercer, George Hardwick and Raich Carter.

The charge of avoidance endured. In 1950, on the brink of the Korean War, Bolton MP Alfred Booth attacked: 'nothing grieves me more every time Britain goes to war ... that able-bodied men, because they played for Bolton Wanderers or some other team, were kept out of it and never got nearer than 40 kilometres to it. That was their touchline.'

It was extraordinary because Wanderers were a model case of doing their duty. Of Bolton's 35 players in 1939, 32 went into uniform. The desperate retreat of soldier-footballers at Dunkirk was likened to England's champion runner: 'You rave about Syd Wooderson. Believe me, I could have given him a start on that last lap to Dunkirk.'

The dangers were real, even if the legend of the unit containing thirteen Wanderers entertaining the demoralised troops with a daring impromptu game – 'while the German dive bombers wheeled round for another attack'

(Franklin, 1956, p.41) – is mythic. Bolton eventually lost their footballing captain and war leader, Lieutenant Harry Goslin: the wartime international was killed by a shell-burst in Italy in December 1943. A younger Wanderer, Walter Sidebottom, was drowned in the Channel when his ship was torpedoed. So if this exemplary club could be charged with avoiding danger, how much more vulnerable were the 98 Crystal Palace players who served in the Forces, or 91 Wolves, or 76 from Liverpool? In postwar seasons, references to what players did during the war abounded. The description was always morally charged.

Resentment about special treatment eventually focused on the proliferating circus tours. Officially they were remarkably successful: a commanding officer claimed 'one soccer party was worth five ENSA [i.e. variety shows] in battle areas' (Rollin, 1985, p.173). But even stars like Denis Compton and Scotland's Tommy Walker risked being barracked as 'D-Day dodgers'. Tours could be exhausting: day after day travelling in hard Army trucks on unmade roads was no easy ride. Walker's three Asian tours covered 25,000 miles, whilst another comprised 120 games and 30,000 miles in one year. They spawned stories, apocryphal or otherwise, like that of a battery team about to lose its sixth Army cup final in India and Burma: 'a stranger walked into the dressing room and asked if he could have a game, but as the lads didn't like bringing in an outsider they said no politely. It wasn't until later that we found the stranger was Tommy Walker.'

Earlier, before Dunkirk, before the FA equipped the Forces, the football was simple, urgent and very British: 'both sides played in battle dress complete with Army boots. I asked one of the goalkeepers how he could tell his team. "That's easy," he said, "Them with the hats on are kicking up. Them with 'em off are kicking down".'

The unit football team strengthened solidarity and maintained the British way of life in foreign parts. Later it became more complicated, an uneasy mix of the sporting and the martial; of sentimental attachment to an English past and the uncomfortable reality of a clash of cultures overseas. In every theatre of war replica Football Leagues sprang up and did battle, for example the RAF Gaza and District League. 'For security reasons,' teams adopted famous names. Thus Cairo's Military Police were Aston Villa, and an Air Force unit, 'quartered in the parquet-floored splendour of flats overlooking the Nile, entered the League with a team of glossily-coiffured clerks styling themselves the Corinthians.'

The quality of pitches differed. Usually sand. 'Arsenal' typically managed to find both real turf and a big stand; 'Bournemouth' struggled in the desert along the scorching Suez road; and 'Millwall' on a rock-hard parade ground. 'York City' played below a temple celebrating where Samson cast down the gates of Gaza. 'Liverpool,' an RAF unit stationed in an Arab area, attracted so much local support that eight players turned up, in full football kit, for one match mounted on steeds lent them by their desert followers. Shades of Lawrence of Arabia.

A unit of Greek nationals supporting the RAF adopted English ways, at least to the extent of styling themselves 'Watford'. However when they conceded two quick goals and experienced 'an honest Anglo-Saxon shoulder charge' all hell broke loose: 'Onto the pitch streamed the lathi-corps, whacking right and left. It was a battle royal ... two of the Greeks had decided on a motorised assault for the honour of Watford. Climbing into the lorry which had brought them to the match, they bore down on our side of the scrum.' Only to be headed off by their opponents' MT truck and its Polish driver: 'The two vehicles met head-on, in a cloud of sand. There was another fight over that. There was a fight when the police arrived. There was a mother-and-father of a fight over all the fights in the towns that night. And a month later we had another cup-tie with Watford for the non-existent cup.'

Representative football could be a busy business. Jimmy Logie rarely played for Arsenal, but regularly six times a week in the Royal Navy. Blackpool's Eric Hayward remembered one spell of 82 days when he played 65 games. Representative football could also be arduous. In August 1944 an artillery division in Italy was confronted by the River Arno swollen and flooded by unseasonable rain. The intended ford seemed impassable but the division had to provide a representative to the regimental team playing in a knockout competition on the other side of the river the next morning. As darkness fell, and the flood not abating, the officer in charge 'ordered the luckless footballer to pack his blankets and his kit, and get across the river' by means of the only vehicle which might make it: a Matador, a huge diesel-engined carrier of ack-ack artillery. Once across he bedded down, and in the 'wee small hours' made his way to a road where a truck whizzed him fifteen miles to where the match was played, at breakfast time, because there was only one pitch in the area for all the Forces who wanted to play. When the player recrossed the river he brought news of an Artillery team defeat.

Professional footballers felt the heat of many frontlines. The career of George Hardwick, England's football captain during 1946-47, survived an early blow: aged seventeen, he had put through his own goal with his first kick in Division One. Then, in RAF service George 'got in the way of a few Nazi bombs, was badly crocked', and later was 'buried under a house during the London blitz'. Similarly England's Stan Mortensen was almost strangled in a parachute training jump and then his Wellington bomber crashed: the pilot and bomb-aimer were killed and the navigator lost a leg. Pilot Reg Foulkes, mainstay of Walsall's postwar defence, was told to forget football after his bomber crashed. Others given similar pessimistic messages included Jim Sanders and Jack Stamps. Goalkeeper Sanders, an RAF gunner, was badly wounded by an enemy fighter after nearly 200 operational flights; miner Stamps, wounded at Dunkirk, would score twice in Derby's 1946 FA Cup final win.

Golden boys suffered the trauma of battle. After escaping from Dunkirk, Wilf Mannion played four wartime internationals, and then resumed four years of real war. During heavy fighting in Italy in 1943, Wilf was the 'runner' for the company commander, England spin bowler Hedley Verity. The day Captain Verity received fatal wounds Wilf remembered 'we lost half the company'. On another day, 80 were killed. Wilf Mannion had shipped out before Bob Paisley's 'first glimpse of Rome through the dusty windscreen of a 15cwt. Army truck' (Paisley, 1983, p.1). Famously his second was as manager of Liverpool when they first won the European Cup in 1977. Bob Paisley was one of many whose careers might have ended before it began. A teenage Amateur Cup winner in 1939, he had little opportunity to impress his new club Liverpool before going overseas, fighting across North Africa and up Italy.

Footballers as seamen and aircrew survived near escapes. Ipswich's Bob Smythe was twice torpedoed and Southampton's Bill Bevis, a Royal Navy gunner on Merchant Navy ships, was mined once and torpedoed three times – he was once adrift for several days. Arthur Turner, a rear gunner with Coastal Command, was hunting U-boat submarines when his plane was shot down in the Bay of Biscay. The only survivor, he floated in a rubber dinghy in heavy seas until spotted by keen eyes aboard a rescue plane. Turner would top-score in Charlton Athletic's successful 1945-46 season and became the only amateur to play centre-forward in a Wembley FA Cup final. Laurence Cunningham of Barnsley was mentioned in dispatches with the famous Dambusters.

Some were shot down: a few were rescued by the French Resistance, more became prisoners. Luton had two returnee PoWs: Allan Steen, the 16-year-old who played in Wolves' 1939 double-challenging side, went missing in a bombing raid in 1943; and Doug Gardiner, who jumped from his damaged bomber at 16,000 feet. On landing in a back garden he was captured by German civilians who pushed him into an air-raid shelter until the raid was over. Gardiner was then rescued from lynching by passing Gestapo troops. Understandably years in a prison camp were not easily shrugged off. Luton created a stir when they sent Steen, Gardiner and Spencer Kettley, who had lost two stone serving in the Far East, to Ireland. The two or three months 'fattening up' there on Irish farm produce reflected badly upon the British food shortage, as critical Tory MPs observed.

Footballers numbered among the 50,000 Allied dead of the three-month D-Day campaign, like Fusilier William Bryan, ex-Sunderland, and Lieutenant Arthur Keeley, 27, formerly with Wolves: his brother Walter was Accrington Stanley's best forward during 1946-47. Another Accrington player lost both his legs to a land mine. But Manchester United's much-maligned defender Allenby Chilton would be one of many to find a campaign wound provided no protection against supporters' blame. Matt Busby later recalled: 'in those early days, Allen had to endure more than most players would tolerate, in fact he was invariably branded scapegoat' (Busby, 1957, p.94).

Bob Thyne played for Scotland against England in front of 90,000 people at Wembley, only four months after a mine blew him up. Thyne returned to Scotland in the autumn of 1946 when the Darlington club could not find the war veteran a place to live. Tom Cheetham (Lincoln) and Tom Burden (Chester) were both Normandy casualties, and both scored 28 league goals in 1946-47. Future England internationals (Tim Ward of Derby) and prewar (Newcastle's Doug Wright, winner of the Military Medal) were also wounded – twice Wright was told he would not play again. Aston Villa's Arthur Hickman, a Bofors Gun Sergeant, fought in the fierce battle for Caen, recovered from shrapnel wounds, crossed the Rhine and reached the concentration camps, where he guarded the captured commandant, the 'Beast of Belsen'.

Before then, paratroopers Cyril Williams and Don Dorman both fought to the last ditch at Arnhem, being wounded and taken prisoner. Both would be promotion challengers during 1946-47: Dorman for Second Division Birmingham, and Williams in Bristol City's vibrant Third Division forward line. There were other footballing prisoners, including both Southampton's goalkeepers. Royal Marine George Ephgrave, the tallest in the League at 6ft 4in, was captured on Crete; and Len Stansbridge was among the Army Medical Corps drawing lots at Dunkirk to decide who should remain with the wounded. He lost.

In Germany a single camp like the M-Stammlager IVB could put together an entire team of top pros, including Allan Steen. Prisoners of the Japanese could not play football: before the war Billy Jones had been on the verge of the Welsh international team. After a hard time in captivity, made nearly blind from malnutrition, Billy had to be led around Cardiff. Table tennis so assisted his recovery that he was able to show clever touches in City's public trial, although his eyes were 'still troublesome'.

The Cardiff team that attracted 50,000 crowds in the Third Division included three captured at Singapore. Southend's Cyril Thompson survived forced marches as a Japanese prisoner, yet returned to score five hat-tricks before Christmas 1946. Spurs' Albert Hall suffered particular hardships: taken at Singapore, his prison ship was then sunk by an American submarine. After hours in the water he was recaptured, but his 1946-47 season was marred by malaria.

Periods in captivity varied. Arsenal's Ted Platt was captured, suffering from battle fatigue, by the Italians in Tunisia but was soon rescued by a British advance. Similarly Alex McIntosh, of Wolves' 1939 Cup final team, 'drove into enemy lines by mistake' but the war ended a fortnight later. Centre-forward Jack Kirkham (who scored three of Bournemouth's ten goals against Northampton in the last prewar League match) was a 'Houdini' of the PoW camps. Jack escaped from Italian camps three times in eighteen months, and eventually joined guerrillas in the mountains.

It was not all one way. Liverpool's Edwin Spicer, a marine lieutenant, captured an enemy sergeant-major. The German had suffered leg wounds in a minefield, and surrendered by putting up his hands and shouting in English, 'Don't shoot, I am a Soccer International.' Spicer wrote to his mother: 'he was a professional footballer back in the Fatherland and had played against several English touring sides. He mentioned many well-known English players ...

with whom he corresponded. We had quite an interesting chat while he was being patched up a bit and you would have thought we were the best of friends.'

Eddie Spicer became one of six decorated Liverpool players. Berry Nieuwenhuys strangely won the Czech Medal of Merit, and Military Medals were awarded to goalkeeper Minshull and versatile Bill Jones, for rescuing a wounded comrade under heavy fire. Len Carney won the Military Cross at Monte Cassino: the amateur schoolteacher scored the winner amid thunder and lightning on 1946-47's opening day. Commando Jim Harley was mentioned in dispatches at Dunkirk and Dieppe. Harley escaped punishment for being sent off in the last prewar match, but the reprieve was shortlived: injury would end his career abruptly in 1948. Footballers from Blackpool, Coventry and Portsmouth were beribboned airmen: Arsenal's Ian McPherson twice won the DSO. He found it strange to play football in Cologne, which earlier he had helped 'prang' – then scored a hat-trick. Goalkeeper Jack Frost was twice rewarded for bravery, and centre-forward Jack Search, Lieutenant-Colonel, Royal Artillery, won the George Medal for fighting a fire in an ammunition dump. George (father of later England captain Ray) Wilkins 'would have won' the Victoria Cross, if there had been enough surviving witnesses.

Footballing failures in 1946-47 were blamed on 'too much soldiering'. Huddersfield's Bill Price hardly added to his 198 wartime goals; RAF service left Charlton's Charlie Revell a 'shadow of his former self'; Brentford's captain left his 'old assertiveness on the banks of the Nile'. Captivity prevented Allan Steen from fulfilling his precocious potential, and managers complained that their returning players had 'all their former ability practically kicked out of them'.

However, Jesse Pye had been told by Sheffield United to stick to being a joiner because he was not 'forceful enough', but participating in the Desert War cured him of his 'shyness'. Once, when officially confined to barracks for misdemeanours, Pye scored a goal against England's Frank Swift and he toured Italy with Stan Cullis's circus. Wolves thus won the race for his transfer and Pye scored a hat-trick in their 6-1 win over Arsenal on opening day. However his army release was conditional on returning to be a ... joiner.

The Army wrought another transformation, to the career of Swansea tyro Trevor Ford. When his Regimental Sergeant Major started picking the unit's team, Trevor volunteered: 'I am a full-back with Swansea Town.' Clearly a mite too forward, as the RSM delivered the put-down: 'Who's Swansea Town? Never 'eard of 'em.' But he also had vacancies elsewhere. 'Right. You will turn out at centre-forward tomorrow. We haven't got one,' (Ford, 1957, p.30) – words which changed Trevor's fate. In 1945-46 Ford scored over 40 goals, and by 1950 he was regarded as the best centre-forward in Britain.

The Army allowed Ossie Evans to get too heavy. Bury scored seven against Fulham's 17-stone-plus goalkeeper on opening day and Ossie never played again. Eddie Kilshaw, who scored Bury's first goal, had his own weight problems, putting on a stone of weight 'sitting in a cockpit for long hours at a stretch'. Once, flying in zero visibility, Kilshaw hit a hillside on a remote Scottish island, killing three crew members. He battled across the icy, windswept wastes until he arrived at the cottage of the island's only inhabitant. By Christmas Kilshaw's recovery was complete enough to attract record bids for an English winger. Bury later sold him for twice that, but he would be another whose career was suddenly cut down by injury.

Footballers raced to get back home. Tankman George Ashall drove from D-Day into Germany, but in late August he was demobbed from Trieste. He made it but, still 'to be fitted with a new pair of football boots', started with Coventry's juniors. By November, Ashall had scored a Second Division hat-trick. John Morris also crossed the Rhine in the tank corps before playing in India with Tommy Walker's Circus: the October demob of Manchester United's wartime discovery was eagerly anticipated. War damage meant United would play at Maine Road, so their true home was described with charming anachronism: 'in the quiet Old Trafford backwater ... they tend to lapse into poetry about this little man.'

Returnees faced an uncertain reception. Stoke had mourned the death in fighting of Harry Meakin, and were surprised when he reported back for training – with a Military Medal. As the papers insensitively explained: 'a man bearing the same name, from the same town unwittingly caused the confusion.' Tom Grimley, who 'kept goal for the Eighth Army during the dark years,' surprised West Brom – 'Well, here I am' – before playing his first game for a club he had joined eight years previously. Southampton manager Bill Dodgin needed a centre-half when a young man walked into The Dell and said 'I was your reserve centre-half before the war'.

There were others unable to start again: 'I have one in mind. He was 24 when the war began and all England rang with his praises. Sensational! Wonderful! A bagful of caps awaited him, and an honourable career. He is thirty now. For six years he has been right out of the game, his muscles and sinews stiffening, his eye and his judgement losing that uncanny "click" that used to make the fans scream with delight. He has done hard service in a part of the world that takes it out of a man and puts two years on his age for every one that he tears off his calendar. This boy is only one of dozens to whom football holds out no hope.'

Jimmy Denmark was another. Injury to this rock of Newcastle's defence had cost United promotion in 1938-39. On 9 February 1946, just demobbed, he had a 'try out'. Verdict: he was not the Denmark of old, although 'criticism would be unfair in view of his long spell out of the game'. Jimmy did not get another chance.

The war could leave deep mental scars. Wilf Mannion survived the killing in Italy but it left him exhausted, 'a shadow of the easy-going lad of 1939'. A combination of trauma and recurrent malaria diminished his interest in football. Wilf was gradually nursed back to reassert his genius before returning home in the spring of 1946. But returning footballers were changed men. Between appearances for England in February 1942 and September 1946,

Wilf had aged from 23 to 28, an inside-forward's best years. But he had also gone from being a footballer, 'nothing more and nothing less,' to being a survivor who 'had spent years fighting for his country's future, yet his own was uncertain ... he couldn't play forever ... With no skills or trade, he had nothing to mark him out for anything but labouring' (Varley, 1997, pp.61-67).

Mannion's anger focused on his club, who had paid no retainer but, through the power of registration, could command his return, as if nothing had happened: 'against this soccer serfdom, even the Army seemed to be a haven of freedom.' Such men were on a collision course. But those who had stayed at home also had their reasons not to welcome the return of real football.

Wally Fielding parachuted into trouble when he 'got a bit under the table' to join Everton

After the ersatz wartime games, crowds demanded the fierce competition of real, national football

Top row, left: Tommy Lawton, goalscorer par excellence
Top row, middle: 'Capocannieri' Dennis Westcott, the First Division's top goalscorer
Top row, right: Football League top goalscorer/miner/pigeon fancier Clarrie Jordan
Bottom row, left: Ronnie Rooke – his goals would help to save Arsenal
Bottom row, middle: Bill Morris – he 'took the sugar from his own tea'
Bottom row, right: Walter 'Rocket' Ricketts – who would score the season's last, decisive goal

WILF MANNION
Middlesbrough and England

Wilf Mannion, golden-haired, angel-faced soccer craftsman picked up his artistry in the back streets of South Bank, grimy Middlesbrough industrial suburb. From school football he graduated to St. Peter's "nursery" where he unnerved many a junior full-back. Middlesbrough, as a professional, was the obvious move. Just as inevitable was his selection for England. After four war-time caps he served with the Green Howards at Salerno, and in Palestine. Back at Ayresome Park there were misunderstandings. Wilf wanted to move, talked of a Dutch coaching offer. But he's there—and to stay, says manager David Jack.

3

The Home Front

'No one can tell what lies before us, but whatever it is we will meet it as sportsmen' (President, Derby County, 28 August 1939).

Jimmy Guthrie was helpless, lying in hospital with serious head injuries – a victim even before the war started. At 2am on 14 July 1939 Guthrie's car, with Everton's captain Jock Thomson one of the passengers, was travelling back from an FA summer school in Leeds. The north of England was blacked out by an Air Raid Precautions practice. The car crashed into a small traffic island and hit an unlit streetlight. Only three months before, the tough Scot had captained Portsmouth in the Cup final, doing his bit to undermine hot favourites Wolves. Jimmy had floored his winger early on, helped him up, gave a winning smile and muttered: 'Next time you'll finish in the Queen's lap.' Portsmouth won 4-1.

Soon Jimmy felt helpless and angry, but not at the world war which overwhelmed the nascent 1939-40 football season. Guthrie's anger burnt bright throughout, expressed – 'pouring out his anger and frustration at the conditions under which footballers laboured' – in constant letters to veteran Players' Union Secretary Jimmy Fay. It was an anger that, as union Chairman, challenged the Football League through the historic 1945-47 dispute, and convinced football journalists and new Labour MPs of his righteous cause. An anger that sustained him through conflict and controversy until the union threw him out. Not that Guthrie's anger had burnt out: by 1957 he was a dinosaur, his heroic attitude now out of time: 'the trouble with Jimmy was he was still living in the immediate postwar period when the big spectacular issues were being fought' (Harding, 1991, pp.210-49).

From his convalescent bed, through football's cold war, Guthrie fought football clubs. Directors banned him from their grounds, called him a communist and threatened to 'run him out of the game' (Guthrie, 1976, p.38). Jimmy was already his own man: the car crash itself – injuring the captains of 1939's Cup winners (Portsmouth) and League champions (Everton) – defied Portsmouth's ban on players using cars. But the catalyst in making him the postwar union champion was clubs' wartime behaviour, taking prewar injustices on to a 'fantastic' new level.

These feelings coloured a generation. They were recorded by players famous enough to write biographies. But in 1939 the star and journeyman were treated alike. Raich Carter was 26, 'inside-forward of the century,'

League Champion and Cup-winning captain: 'my contract with Sunderland had been terminated without notice or any money in lieu ... we were given half a week's wages (£4) and told we were finished ... I was not entitled to unemployment benefit' (Carter, 1950, pp.147-48).

Another prewar champion, Peter Doherty, generalised the same experience: 'the cleavage was a harsh one; contracts were automatically torn up, and for those players who had families to support and no savings to fall back on, the immediate prospect was grave. It was a grim lesson, and one that some of us took to heart very seriously. Without a scrap of consideration or sentiment, our means of livelihood were simply jettisoned' (Doherty, 1948, p.51).

First Division clubs were cutting their losses – an aggregate loss of £141,512 in 1939-40 – and complaining about the waste: 'just paid summer wages – a dead loss.' They were also avoiding the coruscating criticism of the First World War. Then football had completed its 1914-15 season, and got blamed for the Army's failure to 'break through' – by distracting munitions workers! This 'shells scandal' helped to bring down Asquith's Government, subjected pubs to draconian licensing laws and suspended the real football of League and Cup, its reputation already damaged: 'soccer ... remains the exercise of the munitions workers who suffer so much from varicose veins, weak knees, cod-eyed toes, fowl's livers and a general dislike for a man's duty.'

Professional footballers were scapegoated: wages were stopped, but the clubs played on, out of political scrutiny, in regional leagues. Like Jimmy Guthrie later, footballers seethed: 'players should receive pay for playing. If a player is ineligible for the Army ... The hypocrisy of the whole thing stinks in the nostrils' (Harding, 1991, p.120).

So in 1939 the League stopped abruptly, but clubs added their own thoroughgoing pettiness. The League initially advised waiting until things were clearer, and later clarified that players 'standing by' that week were entitled to extra money. Many clubs, including Guthrie's – even though the Cup win fuelled Portsmouth's 1939 profits of over £15,000 – did not comply. Guthrie would not forget.

The war gave him a chance to fight back: 'it is a long time since the Club had a captain whose presence on the field had such an inspiring effect.' Jimmy could inspire anywhere, and when Portsmouth reached a wartime Cup final the players gave an ultimatum – give us 'the week's wages the club had docked on the outbreak of war' – and something from today's takings, or they would not play. Directors made their threats, but eight minutes before kick-off and Wembley 75,000 full of servicemen, they 'ungracefully surrendered' (Guthrie, 1976, p.33).

By this time it was clear that football's role would be different. Now everyone was a 'munitions worker' and everyone a bombing target, so public morale was vital. Football as an entertainment rewarded the workforce and symbolised resistance. Football's continuance reflected the value of maintaining a traditional, if truncated way of life. The 1945 War Cup final – attended by the King, Queen and Princess Elizabeth – confirmed football's 'good' war. It had triumphed over adversity, become embedded into service life and deepened its hold on the national consciousness. Attracting increasingly large crowds as the bombing threat declined, it generated enormous tax revenue and raised good money for good causes. By attending important matches Crown and Government figures stood 'alongside the people'. Internationals especially symbolised everyday life and expressed common national purpose.

But players had to contain the contradiction of attracting £25,000 gates to Wembley and yet receive only 'one green pound note and one ten-shilling note'. Even establishment-friendly players like Stan Cullis recalled ruefully that 'I brought my wife down to one of these games and I was considerably out of pocket'. Another protested about his meagre reward, and suffered: 'one famous member of the team [reputedly Tommy Lawton] was so upset that he stood on the pavement outside Wembley Stadium waving his two Treasury notes and telling passers by, 'That's what we get for playing at Wembley.' He was not picked for England for quite a while after' (Cullis, 1960, p.183).

Players were also frustrated by discrepant rewards on grand club occasions. The 1945 War final, Chelsea v Millwall, grossed £26,000: £12,000 went in Entertainment Tax: £4,000 each to the competing clubs and the FA, and £2,000 in expenses. The players got just £2 each, plus £5 worth of National Savings Certificates for the winners and £3 worth for the losers. At the postmatch celebrations a guest Scottish player, 'having taken on a few drams, tore up his offering and threw the pieces in the Millwall chairman's face' (Guthrie, 1976, p.37).

These wartime conflicts reflected a fight that had not been had. Standing firmly on costs enabled clubs to survive the Depression, but the players fought back as crowds and profitability returned. When their Management Committee, the League's negotiators, finally met the union in 1938 it was the first time in a decade. But nothing was conceded, and in 1939 an all-out strike seemed an inevitable consequence of clubs' 'continuous, almost logic-defying, refusal of each and every request' (Harding, 1991, p.201).

Peter Doherty lost his illusions before the war, when troubled Blackpool sold him for £10,000: 'the club steered clear of the rocks ... I couldn't help thinking that my personal feelings counted for next to nothing in the transaction. I might as well have been a bale of merchandise' (Doherty, 1948, p.33).

The treatment of his 15-year-old brother, Kevin, further convinced Peter of this 'vicious, competitive world'. Kevin was brought from Ireland along with his brother-chaperone (already a one-legged victim of a football injury), but 'dropped unceremoniously' within weeks. Kevin Doherty was one of many Wolves discards: 'in one month registrations of no less than 34 players were cancelled.'

In 1939 all the footballers suddenly made unemployed had an urgent need to rethink their lives. Newcastle's Archie Livingston followed his other trade of slater, but also worked in an aircraft factory, a stone quarry, a paper mill and as a clerk. Many were at their wits' end. Raich Carter 'needed a job badly

... The Fire Service was crying out for men ... once again there would be money, if only £3 a week, coming in to pay the rent and buy some food ... It had been brought home very forcibly to me how precarious football could be ... I decided to take the big decision of packing up the football that I loved and make the Fire Service my career' (Carter, 1950, pp.148-49).

Footballers dug Civil Defence trenches. Bill Shankly shifted 'a Sahara's worth of sand' until found a job by a Preston director, as a riveter on Hampden bombers. Players needed such patronage, either to keep them with their own club, or as an inducement to join others: 'First Division players in big cities where work is scarce will have jobs found for them in Third Division towns. They will then play for the local club ... an offer of a well-paid job in a reserved occupation will accomplish more than four figure transfer offers used to do this time last year.'

Sometimes, no football, no job. Wallace Poulton, a young Stoke winger, went home to be offered a job with the local electrical works, as long as he got City's permission to play with their team in the Birmingham League. Even Stan Matthews had difficulty combining football and work in a local brass-foundry making shells. His Saturday shift prevented him playing in Stoke's away matches, so he sought permission to earn his 30 shillings match fee playing for rivals Port Vale on alternate weekends. Footballers without a trade, even internationals like Preston's Andrew Beattie, found it hardest: 'I tried for many jobs, but when I was asked what experience I had, my chances were nil. I went straight into football from school and had never learned any trade' (Rollin, 1985, p.67).

The League unilaterally suspended footballers' contracts for the war. What did 'suspend' mean? The union only tested this in April 1946, when they represented Jimmy Wynn. Jimmy had been Rochdale's leading scorer, with 50 goals in 60 games in 1937-39, but now he was 31 the club would not offer him a contract. Legislation existed to protect servicemen but Wynn's case failed, on the technicality that the Act only concerned employment in the four weeks before enlistment. Jimmy had joined the Forces in July 1940, and League contracts had been suspended in September 1939. Nevertheless secretary Fay took the opportunity to air footballers' fundamental complaints: 'if the player has no claim on his club why should the club have claim on the player?' Fay's critique of the registration power drew this exchange: 'Chairman: Rather a one-sided agreement, isn't it? Fay: I have said this is the most one-sided agreement in the world. In addition plenty of players have still not been paid the week's wage due to them on the outbreak of the war.'

There were however minor successes. Norman Wilkinson was that rare footballer: preceding George Eastham and Bosman, he took football authorities to court and won. Following his six years military service, Wilkinson obtained remedy from the local Reinstatement Board when League regulations clashed with employment law: 'Why did you stop his pay on May 4th, when the Act says you should employ him for 52 weeks?' Stoke did not pay Norman until he re-signed on 23 May, because it was against League rules.

The amount was small, £12, but the legal condemnation was potentially alarming: 'The Football League cannot govern an Act of Parliament.'

Soon after the suspension, a series of regional leagues began. Payment had such a 'ring of meanness' – 30 shillings (£1.50) a match and no travelling expenses – that it 'must have come as a bit of a shock' to football professionals. Some refused to play for a 'measly thirty bob'. Peter Doherty wanted to accept a job in Scotland, so Manchester City tried blackmail: 'I don't want you under any misapprehension, but you won't play any football in Scotland' (Doherty, 1948, p.51). City threatened Peter with jeopardising his benefit. The £650 benefit – payable after five years – was the only official way a player could build up a lump sum to provide for his future. But a benefit was discretionary, and clubs often denied payment, either pleading poverty or using it for disciplinary purposes.

Other clubs were more far-seeing, and protective. Some had tried to anticipate the war. Twenty-two players followed Liverpool manager George Kay into the Territorial Army and Brentford joined the war police *en masse*. Club motives could be selfish: West Ham's chairman proposed that 'the first team join the reserve police and the second team get into the Territorials ... anything to keep the footballers home' (Korr, 1986, p.150).

Before long, Doherty, Carter, Shankly and many more were in the Forces. Regular fireman Carter went a year without playing and when he resumed crowds 'cast slurs and smears, and made my ears burn with jibes about the fire brigade'. The taunts got 'under my skin', and Raich found refuge in RAF football: 'terrific difference ... no tension. It didn't really matter whether you won or lost ... no inquests [or] your livelihood hanging on the outcome' (Carter, 1950, pp.148-53). Bill Shankly found his competitive instincts harder to lay aside. Whether playing for a Balloon Barrage Depot, with the kids on his RAF station or as a guest player 'he had to give 100 per cent. He couldn't do anything else. When he saw some of the Arsenal players weren't trying he used to go crazy' (Bowler, 1996, p.105).

This wartime dispersal changed the balance of power. Normally players played only for the club that held their registration, but now no club could be sure of any player for any match. Many were called upon – Notts County's record was 139 in one wartime season – and their presence locally usually determined availability. The guest system was football's answer. In practice clubs had little choice and in principle, had they enforced registration, the civic authorities might have broken the power. But clubs feared the real danger: players 'could establish themselves as virtual free agents', and deterred borrowing clubs by, for example, requirement to insure 'their' player. Preston wanted Bill Shankly insured for £2,000. Ironically it was whilst playing for his own club that Bill picked up a serious knee injury, so bad that his RAF doctor told him he wouldn't play again.

Typically Shankly played on and it was only years later, through the generosity of guest club Partick Thistle, that his knee was properly treated. At another level of irony the injury ended Shankly's international career when

Scotland would not play him against England – for fear of the insurance risk of worsening the injury.

When the Army took over Preston's ground it did not worry Shankly: 'People found me ... it soon got around. I played for many teams and had a game every Saturday' (Rollin, 1985, p.56). There were means of avoiding any hindrance authorities might pose. When Bill had no permission to leave base he played anyway, famously as the Rod 'Newman' who helped Norwich score eight against the Army. Watford even acknowledged their Newman was a pseudonym, claiming 'security purposes': the security was the risk to the freedom of Fred Kurz, who had no weekend pass. A prize pseudonym went to Fulham's S.O. Else. Someone else, actually Spur George Ludford.

Players had licence. One Christmas Day Tommy Lawton played for Everton in the morning and Tranmere in the afternoon. When Len Shackleton signed as a professional with Bradford Park Avenue, 'by way of celebration' he played immediately at Leeds on Christmas morning, had a cup of tea, then travelled to Huddersfield as a Bradford City guest player. James Mills captained Rotherham and two colliery teams on the same day. George Murphy played for eight different clubs in nine weeks. Peter Doherty's experience varied, sometimes making 'five or six appearances for different league clubs in the space of little over a week'. At others, 'it wasn't always easy to get a game at all ... the insurance was fairly high, and many clubs were reluctant to pay it. The choice was therefore limited, and offers of games were sometimes very scarce indeed' (Doherty, 1948, pp.54-55).

The League payment of flat match fees encouraged playing as much as possible. Non-Football League clubs could pay more: Chelmsford's £4 a match attracted major footballers like Villa's Frank Broome and George Edwards, and Dennis Westcott of Wolves. There was also a widespread belief that players were 'selling their services to the highest bidder'. In 1944 Liverpool's captain, South African Berry Nieuwenhuys, was banned for life – later rescinded – when his extra demands became known. Newspapers railed against this belated exposure of an evil which 'everybody backstage knows to have flourished through the war years'. Players needed to play a lot or be paid 'over the odds'. It persuaded Raich Carter back from the Fire Service to brave football's jeering crowds: 'I was financially worse off than I had been for a very long time' (Carter, 1950, p.151)

When expenses became allowable, the culture of the 'scrounge' flowered. Bob Paisley, finally home after a Desert Rat war, resumed playing: 'a leave pass took me from Woolwich to Liverpool, on home to Durham and back up to Bradford for another game. All highly illegal of course, but then I was only breaking my journey, wasn't I?' (Paisley, 1983, p.7). Others were scrupulous. Before infantryman Alf Ramsey's debut, Southampton's secretary had a word: 'Oh, Ramsey, I should like to settle up with you concerning your expenses. How much are they?' I guess my answer must have staggered him. 'Just the twopenny halfpenny tram fare from my billet,' I replied. 'Are you quite sure that is all,' said the kindly Mr Sergantson, 'for I do not want you to be out of pocket.' 'No sir' I replied 'that's the only expense'. So Mr Sergantson put his notecase back into his pocket, dived into his right trouser pocket, and handed me the two pennies and one halfpenny tram fare' (Ramsey, 1952, p.19).

For the prewar pro too much water had passed under the bridge. Friction and mutual suspicion were commonplace and long-lasting. Clubs reached Wembley finals with 'guests', then recalled their registered players. Bill Shankly never forgave Arsenal: Joe Mercer remembered he 'was most indignant and his language was dreadful' (Kelly, 1996, p.41). 'So many squabbles about [guest] players are going on behind the scenes.' Peter Doherty had his fair share. Once travelling overnight to find Manchester City did not need him, he was annoyed not to be paid expenses: 'It was a thoughtless omission that remained in my mind for a long time' (Rollin, 1985, p.55).

Although Peter helped City to wartime cup wins, his nearly 200 wartime goals were spread around ten clubs. Once Peter played for Liverpool at the expense of another guest, George Ainsley. The trouble was, Ainsley had got special RAF leave. Liverpool had to apologise to the League and RAF before they could get further co-operation. Doherty fumed against registration: City had suspended their contract, so he 'objected to being ordered to play for certain clubs' (Doherty, 1948, p.55).

It came to a head when Doherty arranged to play for one club, whilst City had contracted him to another which paid insurance. Peter's further clear-the-air meeting ended with their directors' usual promise to pay his benefit. Peace did not reign long. With the war ending, the authorities renewed efforts to restrict the guest. For example the Cup enforced the original 1872 rule that a player could appear for only one club. Peter hitchhiked across country to play against Crewe but did not make kick-off. City suspected he had deliberately avoided becoming cup-tied, and withdrew permission for him to play as a guest for Derby County. Doherty demanded a transfer.

Wartime football stayed second to wartime work. Leon Leuty, England's centre-half in August 1946, was an engineer who often played for Derby on two hours sleep. Jack Nicholas, County's Cup final captain, only finished his police shift an hour before kick-off. No-show players gave unexpected opportunities to members of the crowd, or ground-staff boys like 15-year-olds Billy Wright and Nat Lofthouse. Thus in 1940, 16-year-old George Griffiths went to Bury's ground to say that older brother Bill could not play that afternoon. 'Can you?' George was asked, Bury being five players short. He played, and both brothers were still playing in the 1946-47 Second Division. Another Bury man on short notice was Leslie Hart, who got a telegram in his pit one Saturday morning asking him to play at Anfield that afternoon.

These handicaps were seen as rites of passage: 'It cost me 9s fare to go to one match, I lost half a day's pay and we lost the game by six goals to nil. I wrote to Norman Bullock [Bury's manager and an England international] to say it was not worth it, but he wrote back: "Keep it up. I had to go through the same thing".'

Some big clubs like Wolves carried on almost regardless, seeking even younger boys than Billy Wright. They attracted censure in 1942 when they brought 13-year-old Cameron Buchanan from his Lanarkshire mining village. This smacked of too little account of wartime values. An FA inquiry concluded no rules had been broken but that it was not in the best interests of football to take so young a boy so far from his home. By 1946, Cameron had returned to his mining heritage, the sixth Wolf to be conscripted into the pits. He was also entrusted as Wolves' delegate to the Players' Union meetings that spent 1945-47 challenging the distribution of football's new wealth.

The first spasm of more than two years of intense industrial conflict arrived in July 1945, within days of Labour's General Election victory: the League's AGM was to decide the immediate structure of postwar football and payment to players. One context was clubs' wealth. As the bombing threat lessened, crowds and profitability returned: Port Vale went from virtual bankruptcy in 1942 to ambitious plans to build a 80,000 capacity ground. Spurs made a record profit in 1944 and paid £9,000 in Entertainment Tax (at 33 per cent). Villa reported a profit of £5,838 in 1943 and paid £18,437 tax in 1944. Small clubs benefited from visits by top teams and star players, and even those outside the Football League paid more in tax than the total gate receipts for a prewar season. Clubs like Coventry City – £11,684 in the black – wanted continued prosperity, whereas indebted clubs were anxious to pay the past cost of building grounds: their debt was likened to the apocryphal school lesson in which the present generation are still paying the cost of the Napoleonic Wars. In London, Arsenal had debts over, and Charlton approaching, £100,000.

At the League's 1945 AGM, Wolves, her youth structure intact, albeit in local mines, sought an immediate return to prewar competition. Arsenal, in debt, with neither players nor pits, advocated continuing localised arrangements. The majority decided upon a transitional season, with senior clubs divided into Football League (South) and (North). The problem remained players. Players far-flung throughout the world, unlikely to return; players serving in Europe, only able to play on leave; players stationed at home, usually playing, not for their own club, but as a guest for one nearby; and players in restricted occupations, restricted by Essential Work Orders. This seemed a recipe for a generous settlement, especially as in 1944 union secretary Jimmy Fay had anticipated this moment: 'unless the players make a definite stand as soon as hostilities cease, the position will be little better than prewar days, when many players had only a bare minimum' (Harding, 1991, pp.210-12).

Club directors were targeted as symbolising a 'dictatorial' leadership still in a 'Victorian sleep'. Jimmy Guthrie calculated that veteran Portsmouth director Sydney Leverett, a former 'deep sea diver', gained £10,000 out of the matches he had watched free (with attendant hospitality) from his £200 outlay on shares 40 years previously. It was Leverett who, after four years of postwar boom, recalled the penny-pinching ways that kept clubs afloat through the Depression with nostalgia: 'We were happier in football when clubs were scraping around to try to find the cost of a postage stamp.'

These small businessmen were mocked: the director who pocketed advertisement money; the director-printer who benefited from programme sales; the director-builder paid for running repairs. Small, but local, they were part of the community. There were class differences between the directors and the working class fan base, but they were united in commitment to the traditions and identities of local clubs. Players, however, represented another interest. Many would share that identification, in upbringing and personal commitment, but in principle they were itinerant workers. They needed a wider horizon and the boom provided an opportunity to put the game on a different footing. The existing club directors obstructed that vision. Jimmy Fay asked: 'why no effort to bring the game up to date with the changed times.' He looked at the 'state of chaos and bewilderment' at the League's 1945 AGM, and located one part of the answer: '[Football] is big business and should be in the hands of big businessmen.'

The clubs preferred the old ways and pay-per-match: after all, the players were only available on match days. But the union could see ahead: players would be demobbed and munitions jobs would end. Without contracts, players would have little to live on, and only if they played, whilst clubs made big profits. The AGM failed to give a clear ruling: £4 a match was reaffirmed but individual clubs seemed free to enter into a new weekly contract. All too briefly the union had a glimpse of a different strategy: break the cartel, and negotiate with individual clubs. It was only a moment.

George Tadman, who had scored 26 First Division goals for Charlton in 1939, provided a first test. After a war spent working in an airplane factory Tadman came back to digs in London. Charlton wanted to offer him a contract but the League said they could only pay £4 a match, which meant if injured George had no income to pay for his own accommodation and for his family, still in Bristol. The club soon advertised in their match programme: 'Wanted, comfortable board and lodgings for Charlton players returning from the Forces. Near the ground preferred.'

The League's attitude met with anger at the union's AGM: 'it is an insult to offer such terms and will meet with great opposition from the players' (Harding, 1991, p.211). They rehearsed all the old grievances. The poverty of prewar wages: 'have you ever tried to keep a wife and kiddies on £2 or £2 5s a week. That was what I was reduced to before the war.' The sacrifices during the war for scant reward, travelling 'twelve hours to play in a match for five shillings and expenses'. The absurd discrepancy between transfer values and player payment: 'How does it feel to know an organisation is willing to pay £10,000 for your abilities, but only offer £4 for each demonstration … ridiculous.'

The players seemed ready to challenge basic employment conditions as much as next season's wages, and their independence provided a uniquely powerful opportunity: 'not one professional footballer was solely dependent on the game for his livelihood just now, and urged the strike proposers, there would never be a better chance to reveal the strength of the union.'

This was a position of tactical strength, but underlying weakness. It was not only Forces footballers who benefited from wider experiences. Those in wartime occupations had also moved on. They had had enough of football's restrictions. There was an alternative to fighting the clubs and that was the independence of work. Football would be part-time. Their champion was England's Jack Pickering: 'I urge all players to have some other job.' Pickering, an accountant, had been a pro for over twenty years and had seen it all: 'the player with another job that fits in is a far fitter player mentally on a Saturday afternoon.'

No less a figure than football's greatest star provided another model. In the first postwar season, Stan Matthews' primary interest seemed elsewhere. At 31 years, his footballing days seemed numbered. During wartime he settled in Blackpool – rarely playing for his registered club, Stoke – and now owned a hotel on the promenade. Stan rejoined Stoke but steadfastly insisted on living and training in Blackpool. His football had to fit in with his hotel.

Similarly, England's newest international, Manchester United's Henry Cockburn, could express a life view that would be incomprehensible to the millionaires of the 21st century: 'I have not made professional football a full-time career. I am still working as a fitter at a firm in Oldham.'

Whether veterans tired of the struggle, or younger men wanted to avoid it, the popularity of football as a part-time job raised questions. Not just of the union's tactics, not just for the clubs' attempts to recover their prewar controls, but for the nature of football as work. The war had brought 'the influx of a new generation' with a different attitude: 'True they are professionals, but they have another calling ... I am constantly hearing young footballers say "I enjoy my football on Saturdays because I have to work hard during the week".'

The union's 1945 AGM duly demanded that all players should be placed under contract whatever their outside employment, but that they should not strike. Instead they played 'under protest'. The League was therefore able to perform a well-practised dance of dragging the business so long that 'everybody will get fed up and call it a day.' 'This meeting-after-meeting stunt the League is now putting on can last for months.' Their Management Committee would claim it lacked authority for an agreement. Sympathetic papers warned against a recognisable strategy: 'I say, here and now to the Players' Union: don't fall for this long-distance stuff. Insist on early decision. You have been pushed around for far too much.'

The players finally lost patience and called a strike. In the extremis of a fourteen-day ultimatum, the Management Committee was 'given all necessary powers' to negotiate and an agreement was reached: after over twenty years the maximum wage was increased to £9 per week; bonuses were reintroduced; and the match fee was increased to £5.' More importantly, the League had recognised the 'principle of consultation': 'a new era for the professional footballer ... the fulfilment of 22 years struggle.' Others were more sanguine, if not disillusioned: a great opportunity had been lost.

Certainly the clear winners of 1945-46, along with the Exchequer, were the clubs. Everton boasted the highest profit, a record £21,000, and Aston Villa paid the most Entertainment Tax, £41,701. Two London clubs paid £32,787 and £21,783, whilst the best supported club, Newcastle United – averaging 38,832 – paid £33,000 in Entertainment Tax and made £7,567. Even small clubs in areas of little football heritage did well: Ipswich Town, which hardly operated during the war itself and only joined the Football League in 1938-39, reported profits of £5,546 and paid £10,000 in tax.

For the clubs, at least, the boom was well and truly on.

4

What People Wanted

'The people who don't play it take it much too seriously; and the people who do don't take it seriously enough.' (Billy Murray, Sunderland manager)

Florence, 20 May 1945: a fierce heat bounced off the concrete stadium as the British Army played football. Against itself. All-stars against the locals.

This was a special circus. All household names. Tom Lawton, Joe Mercer and Frank Swift: all captains of England. As they gathered in London on 5 May, the war ended. VE day began a month-long victory tour of Italy and Greece, although some players flew back to play in England's first postwar international, against France on 26 May.

The all-stars were there to entertain, not humiliate local troops. So they started with pretty stuff, without pressing home their advantages. Not that opponents for touring circuses were beginners. Often cosmopolitan (this Fifth Army side even included Brazilians), they mainly comprised young or would-be pros, such as Swansea's Royal Marine Roy Paul. Manchester United's Stan Pearson 'ran me silly' for Tommy Walker's Circus in India. Roy did not mind: 'it sharpened up my game' (Paul, 1956, p.18).

Exhibition football showed the flag admirably. The tourists needed to pace themselves through a punishing schedule. In a little over two weeks they travelled 2,000 miles on war-damaged mosquito-infested Italian roads in bone-shaking army trucks. They washed the dust off in mountain streams of the Apennines; they saw the old burial ground of Pompeii and the recent killing field of Cassino; and revived their spirits with a Papal audience.

But the army crowd was not best pleased. They wanted more competition, more edge. So it started. Naturally the veterans cheered the underdogs and jeered the odd all-star mistake. But this was different. Mercer remembered: 'the Tommies turned nasty.' The call went up: 'Up the real soldiers.' The stars were the D-Day Dodgers, the PT Commandos. Cowards. The stars looked at one another. This was personal: this was too much. Exhibition over.

The man in charge was Matt Busby. That spring he had decided to become Manchester United's manager, turning down Liverpool's offer to be their coach. The board retaliated by denying Matt a testimonial. So instead of Anfield, this was Busby's swansong, six days short of his 36th birthday: 'In a tacit and telling response to the incivility, Matt brought the house down in one stunning moment, dribbling past player after player on a mazy 50-yard run to leave Archie Macaulay with an open goal' (Glanville, 1994, p.39). The tourists now meant business and business meant 'scoring goals – lots of them.' 10-0. Just to show 'em.

Their figurehead was Tommy Lawton, a great hero ever since the 17-year-old replaced the great Dixie Dean. In 1939, the teenager led Everton to the championship and played eight internationals in seven months for England. All these interrupted careers have a poignancy, but the loss to this young giant, whose promise knew no bounds, has a rare resonance. But Tom's career did not stop. It just took on a new meaning. A powerful, athletic figure, the consummate centre-forward, he attracted crowds wherever he played, and he played a lot. In recorded games alone – for England, Everton, various 'guest' clubs, the Army and others besides – Tom, goalscorer par excellence, totalled 337 goals.

Tom Lawton personified the contradictions. For all their popularity, footballers were vulnerable to a special charge. If wartime evoked an unprecedented sense of solidarity – 'we are all in it together' – it also produced a powerful sensitivity towards anyone getting favoured treatment. Tom was not immune from charges that he stretched the rules. A guest appearance for Morton whilst on his Scottish honeymoon tightened the proximity required between a player's military station and eligible 'guest' clubs, and 'it is a fairly safe bet that there was something in it for Tommy each time he moved' (Guthrie, 1976, p.51). But the ambivalence towards Lawton and his profession was more profound: 'hostility from many people who thought it wrong that fit, able-bodied young fellows like myself should be playing football in England while their husbands, sons and sweethearts were fighting' (Lawton, 1946, p.95).

Lawton defended himself: he 'had not asked to stay in England', that was the 'war job' the 'War Moguls' gave him; his matches for charity had raised vast sums. Lawton confronted the ambivalence and animosity head on. When his autobiography was published there been no 'real football' for over six years. Officially his business during those years was soldiering, but pointedly Tom called his book *Football is My Business*.

For all football's magnetism, antagonism bubbled below the surface. It was there in the Channel, in seamen affronted by football on the radio as they pulled dead soldiers from the sea: there in Parliament; in the taunting of Raich Carter, fireman; and on those dusty Italian pitches. This ambivalence carried into the peace. Footballers were lauded as public figures but expected to live as other working people. Their overflowing popularity never translated into support for players' unequal struggle to improve their conditions of employment. On the contrary, crowds were aggressive, critical and parochial. In this sense, for fans as much as for paternalistic club directors, the heroic footballer was a spectral representation of the club.

The fundamental struggle of the immediate postwar period hinged around two questions: what was 'real' football, and what sort of work was it? Tom Lawton, spokesman, considered its return: 'Frankly I don't think football at the moment is good enough to return to normality.'

Lawton favoured the regional leagues continuing, to help players recover. The war had traumatised some and sapped everyone's physical resources. He was 'sold out' from too many games with insufficient food, and had aching feelings midway through matches. Tom also wanted footballers' 'stewpot of grievances' remedied first. But players hesitated to carry the blame for delay, because they already symbolised the obstacles to normality: 'ersatz football and the guest player farce have been swept into unlamented oblivion.'

The guest player was not only unpopular with clubs because it symbolised players' freedoms from their controls. It was in principle an antithesis of what 'real' football had come to mean. Guests affronted the traditional order. Thus Aldershot, usually a struggling Third Division club, could boast 30 internationals at England's military centre. Similarly, a 10-0 win by little Northampton – fielding an entirely guest eleven – against First Division Stoke exemplified the falseness of wartime competition.

More profoundly, guest players contradicted an essential value of British football – belonging. The narrow way in which footballers 'belonged' to clubs was at the heart of the 1946-47 conflict. But, in a wider sense, football's 'belonging' was about emotion and identification. Supporters needed players as committed as they. In real football a player belonged to a team: he, the club, supporters, everyone knew it. A club's strength, its success or failure, depended on its current players. Yet as late as April 1946 Luton Town had to report: 'it is impossible to make any accurate forecast of the team that will play on Saturday.'

'Normality' was also what the game meant and how it felt. This had become clear through absence. Straightaway in September 1939 it was reported that football's peace-time spark had gone, not to be rekindled until the FA Cup competition of 1945-46 and the Football League of 1946-47. Already too the secret of football's grip on the British public – 'competitive spirit and local partisanship' – was revealed. 'Partisanship is football's bread and butter' and wartime football could not tap that. Its most common description was 'ersatz' – acceptable, but not authentic. Real football in the British tradition was about allegiance to clubs who represented localities and competed with each other. Professional clubs were almost without exception named after localities – after a city, town or district. Localities in competition.

Wartime competition failed the reality test because it was not national. The normal football map reaffirmed the integrity of the nation, and its 1946 return was widely welcomed with relief: 'football without tiresome zoning and regional arrangements. Clubs who have not met for seven years will renew old rivalries.'

Wartime football lacked promotion and relegation. Normally these gave drama to each season and continuity across the seasons. Championships and promotion meant glory; the tragedy of relegation meant being 'tarred and feathered'. A club was measured by the league structure, and promotion and relegation determined movement within the league. If these motivators 'must come for survival', then 'guests', uncommitted to a club's fate, must go.

Disadvantaged London clubs wanted delay: 'several northern clubs have an embarrassment of players.' For most, however, delay was unthinkable: promotion and relegation was the life blood of English soccer, and without this competitive test football was 'aimless kicking, leading nowhere'. This then, above all, was what made the 1946-47 season the real thing.

Reconstruction in all parts of society was a struggle between a return to the past, with its safety and reassurance, and a desire for change, for a resolution of past grievances. Football was no different. Each of the major forces, the union, the FA, and the League, knew what they wanted but saw an uphill task: 'the only people who receive anything from football except a headache are the pools, the banks and the transport companies' (Sharpe, 1952, p.51). However, others saw opportunities to rethink many facets of the game: 'there is much enthusiasm for reforms inside football at the moment.'

They all came to nothing. Should matches be reduced, temporarily, to 80 minutes until players regained strength? What about four-up, four-down in promotion and relegation? Perhaps kick-ins should replace throw-ins? In September 1946 there was a half-hearted if closely observed experiment played behind closed doors. The 38 kick-ins meant more playing time – only thirteen of 70 minutes were lost, compared to 35 minutes lost in November's England v Holland international. And should referees 'take time off for stoppages?' How about 'a rule change that would cut down the fast growing (and irritating) habit of passing back to goalkeepers?' Then a controversy about whether a ball crossed the line: 'What next? I'm waiting for someone to weigh with the suggestion that clubs should install photo-finish cameras flags.' Fifty years on, heavy irony gave way to perfect seriousness as Premier League referees presented this idea as the cutting edge of technology.

But the issues that really counted in the reconstruction were: was the government interested in football; what sort of work was professional football in the postwar world; and would war break out between the FA and Football League? The League carried football's anxieties. From today's perspective its resumption looks inevitable, but even amidst the 'overwhelming boom' of May 1946, an insecure sport felt a dread fear: 'football is dying. The war has dealt it a death blow. The public will never come back to it like they used to.'

The League had advantages. It had kept going throughout, yet kept its powder dry: real football could now usurp the ersatz impostor. But it could not wait too long: 'if by some strange twist the clubs did decide to delay the return to normal, it would be the time I suggest for somebody else to step in and form a new league.'

The FA provided the only option. Was the FA interested in asserting a real rather than nominal authority? 'Twelve months ago I offered a League Management Committee man generous odds that within three years the Football League would lose its separate identity ... it would be part and parcel of the Football Association.'

The war gave the FA new momentum in this 'age-old rivalry'. First it caught up with past miscreants: players, managers and directors of Leicester and Derby were suspended or received life bans for illegal payments in the interwar years. Then it adopted a populist stance: contributing balls, equipment and other assistance to make football the soldiers' game, and thus allying itself to the common effort. So, backed by government and army, the FA humiliated the League Champions, Everton, when it took a stand against the multitudinous demands upon their players. As Denis Compton remembered: 'Cup finals, League South matches, and army representative games followed on top of each other in seemingly endless stream' (Walvin, 1994, p.148). In April 1940, Everton defied an FA selection, and an order of the War Emergency Committee, for Joe Mercer to play for England, instead requiring him to play against Liverpool in the Lancashire Cup. It was the wrong battleground to assert proprietorial rights: two directors were suspended.

The FA also provided a reminder of its power to sanction competitions, a power that eventually created the Premier League, but not until 1992. In 1941 the FA had recognised a London League after southern clubs objected to their proposed fixtures. The Minister of War approved of avoiding unnecessary travel, and the League was reduced to empty gestures, such as informing FA Cup holders Portsmouth that it ceased to be a member of the Football League.

The League, wary of this precedent, moved quickly to resume its competition in 1946, before the FA could produce a viable, smaller alternative, one that gave the England team 'two to three weeks special preparation under a team-manager for every international'. This tapped into the widely held view that the League had expanded too far: 'it is obvious that sooner or later some curtailment of the prewar League programme will be necessary.'

The FA had incentive, but no takers for radical change. There was talk of a Premier League of ten English and five Scottish clubs, backed up by further national and regional divisions. Only in July 1946 did the home Football Associations give up hope of a British League as a new way forward.

However, it was the source of the FA's prestige and original power, the Cup, which proved its Achilles heel. For 1945-46 each round was determined by aggregate home and away scores. The public were hooked and clubs loved the extra income, but traditionalists accused the money-grabbing FA of sacrificing 'the glorious uncertainty of "Cup Luck" for the greed of gold'. The Government was unimpressed, as the serious problem of footballing absenteeism challenged their priority upon industrial production. Employers knew when they were beaten, and put on their best, ironic face: to 'have notice of the numbers intending to be absent on Wednesday, will those whose relatives are to be buried on that day please apply by Tuesday for permission to attend' (Rollin, 1985, p.118).

The attendances and excitement of Cup-ties far exceeded the transitional leagues – ultimately too much so. The crowds rose to a crescendo: over 65,000 for two successive rounds at Stamford Bridge; then 135,000 for the semi-finals at Maine Road and Villa Park. The FA relented and killed midweek second legs as an 'irresistible inducement to people to desert their work' and 'disorganise local industry'. Instead the determination to play cup-ties to a finish produced the longest match on record: in sweltering heat, Stockport and Doncaster drew 4-4 – then played in vain for a 'golden goal' – 203 minutes! But the change came too late: on 9 March the second-leg crowd at Bolton was too big and too uncontrolled. Thirty-three people were killed in Britain's worst sporting disaster. It ended thoughts of an expanded FA competition replacing the League.

In truth the FA was more interested in the international than domestic stage. It rejoined FIFA in April 1946 and promoted new ways of playing football by sponsoring the hugely successful Moscow Dynamos tour in November 1945. The FA could not have hoped for a bigger impact on British life: 'Russians ... snap up a moving ball without attempting to trap it first: switch defence to attack and vice versa in split seconds and generally waste less time than a hungry schoolboy diving into a bag of buns.' '[Dynamos'] superlative soccer skill, allied to a pace which makes much of our present-day league football look like an Oxford Street traffic block.'

Tours by three further continental sides in the autumn of 1946 – Sweden's Norrkopping, Sparta Prague and Copenhagen – were almost as influential. As these teams cantered to too many easy wins, the defeated clubs complained that these blows to English sporting prestige were self-inflicted: that players were not freed from other work, or had not recovered from 'hurly-burly' League football. The FA also overruled complaints about English professionals coaching abroad during the summer of 1946, and even freed Frank Swift from playing in internationals. Clubs complained: 'many footballers can get fed up with their job ... [they] fear that key men may return in August in a punk condition.'

In practice the opposite was truer: Sheffield United goalkeeper Jack Smith was one of only two players to play in all 42 league games of 1938-39 and 1946-47, after returning from three months in Norway, 'brown as a berry and full of vim'. These senior professionals lived the message in the FA's blueprint for the future: coaching, coaching, coaching. The FA backed the continentals' 'all out policy of making the ball do the work' but England's great individuals, Matthews, Mannion and Carter, responded defensively when the first national coach, Walter Winterbottom, exerted his influence: 'you just cannot tell star players how they must play. You must let them play their natural game' (Greaves, 1994, p.21).

It was an attitude that drove coaches abroad. Sam Wadsworth, who had only just escaped the Nazis in 1939, returned to Eindhoven to find 'willing and eager' youngsters rather than the 'know it all' English. Jimmy Hogan remained at home, but jobless. Jimmy embodied the itinerant English coach. He coached Austria in the 1912 Olympic Games, had been interned during the Great War, and then roamed the continent: Germany, France, Czechoslovakia, Holland, Switzerland, Italy, Spain, Portugal and Sweden. When Hungary traumatically ended England's unbeaten home record against continental opposition in 1953, their director commented: 'Jimmy Hogan taught us everything we know' (Shackleton, 1955, p.114).

In his only English managerial experience, Hogan won Aston Villa promotion: otherwise he was pooh-poohed by those who viewed coaching as an interference with natural sporting expression. In the summer of 1946 Hogan advised a French FA course in Rheims, paying close attention to catering arrangements. Each day 80 would-be coaches began their 'battle course' at 5am with breakfast of black coffee – 'I never saw milk ... reserved for children' – and a piece of bread. Theoretical sessions started at 6am, then practice. After a 'good lunch', afternoons were spent studying and preparing for the examinations, which produced 46 graduates. The tabloids of course made jokes at the expense of this Gallic extremism: 'Oui Monsieur! You are now a real footballer.'

That autumn this 'unsung prophet' was sponsored on a 6,000-mile tour of demonstration evenings: teaching 30,000 boys (and watching pros) who commonly had no idea of the importance of playing football 'on the ground'. Hogan preached nine-tenths possession, whereas what he saw was war reminders: 'ack-ack – up in the air football.'

Nevertheless this champion of continental enlightenment was as committed as any Colonel Blimp to 'the island myth of British superiority at football' (Glanville, 1986, p.139). Coaching was the path back to righteousness: 'the foreigner is not a natural football player ... but with intense and thorough coaching he is beginning to get on top. I say: 'Wake up, England.' Let us have more coaching ... and get back to the constructive and intelligent game which was once ours alone.'

The FA's gaze on a future Camelot freed the League to reassert their Depression-era powers over players. But would the Government intervene?

Again the clubs had reason to fear. They had long behaved in a manner that symbolically the Labour Government was elected to change. Clubs maintained rigid wage restrictions on top players whilst keeping the rank and file barely above poverty levels. They either ignored or shamelessly exploited football's private rules with little regard to the law of the land. At their 1943 AGM, the anticipated brave new world persuaded union secretary Jimmy Fay to 'visualise a great opportunity for the player to demand a thorough overhauling of the out-of-date rules ... There is something to work upon, such as the Beveridge Report.' However he ended on an uncertain note: 'these appear to cover everybody except the professional footballer' (Harding, 1991, p.209).

He was right to have doubts. Essentially the Government's interest was of a different order. July 1945 saw Labour elected by a landslide. Their Government was future oriented, to make a better world by continuing the successful wartime economic planning, and past oriented, to avoid return to the deprivations of the Depression. But the range of its interventions was unclear, and the idea that sport could become part of a planned society threatened deep meanings: 'do we want nationalised sport in Great Britain? State subsidy for youth, yes. Sports ministry, no, no, a thousand times, no. Any attempt to set one up, even under the guise of a British Sporting Corporation, on BBC lines, must be strenuously opposed.'

The Government balanced its radical programme of economic planning and social security, of nationalisations and the Welfare State, with an attachment to what has been called Deep England (Hewison, 1995, pp.23-24). Deep England, notably the imagery of the English landscape, expressed continuity. Deep England enabled the Government to hold the country together, and assert essential traditions in the midst of structural change. Football was the urban and working class equivalent of the British romantic tradition, now reaffirmed by the war as the national game. So at a deep level, Labour was happier to see tradition than change in football. In any event, outside nationalisations, government either restricted industries, in the interests of planning the economy, or exhorted them to produce and export. It did not otherwise promote radical change. So if footballers, like other workers, were going to change their industrial conditions, they would have to do it for themselves.

Tommy Lawton's hopes were dashed when he learnt that real football would resume on 31 August 1946. The League had thrown out the union's proposals and many players fled the country, glad to be out of it, if only briefly. As usual, in 1946 feelings were expressed in terms of food. Thus the 'bread and butter problem back home' not being settled, tours abroad are 'as popular at the moment as iced drinks in a heat wave'. Reflecting on his coaching experience in Norway, Lawton's envy at freedom from old ways and structures was palpable: 'they are beginning from the beginning, which is just about the best thing that could happen.'

1946-47's imagery was just the opposite. The season was a series of reunions to the 'background music of "Auld Lang Syne".' Newspaper after newspaper ran stories to explain 'who began it all': how we had got here. The message was continuity, symbolised by the clubs and their representation of local communities. This tradition was not just symbolic: there was still a generation that had lived through the 60 years of professional football and could testify to the continuity between its origins and the revival. Joe Reader had been with West Brom for 62 years: continuous service since the foundation of the Football League – from Cup-winning England goalkeeper to ground steward. There were also belated celebrations. When Villa visited Goodison Park, Fred Geary, Everton's 1890s centre-forward, presented the winners with the 1897 Cup final match ball: 'there was an intense cut on its leather – where the Everton player who collared it at Crystal Palace knifed it and hid it underneath his jersey.'

The game was criss crossed by figures from its long past. Fred Everiss, West Brom's secretary-manager, celebrated 50 years in the job in October 1946. Derby's trainer Dave Willis had spent 51 years in football: their cobbler, 84-year-old Jack Beswick, started in 1890. There were those who long ago switched from playing to watching. 'Old Jim' Laverick, 73, saw all Newcastle's games, still working at Haggies' Rope Works, as he was in 1893 when he was United's right-back, and had joined a previous football strike: 'Aye, we got three and a tanner a match, thought we should have more, had a secret chin-wag and demanded five bob. I never got it – never the chance of playing again for canny Newcastle. Why man, I walked thirty miles a day up and down the ropes at my job ... used to knock off at 12 on a Saturday, dash home, have a steak and kidney pudding and a couple of pints and away to play soccer.'

Authority figures also testified to continuity. Sunderland's start was watched by Eric Foster: as the ten-year-old son of the Mayor of Sunderland, he had seen their first ever League game. William Gregor McGregor, son of the League's founder, attended his 46th Cup final in 1947: after his first, 'I slept with the original FA Cup tucked away under my bed.' George Wagstaffe Simmons, a leading FA official and sometime England selector, recalled as a teenager paying one shilling for the 1887 Cup final, another for his meal that evening and a third for the West End play to complete his day.

If reconstruction is a moment between innovation and tradition, football had little choice but to go back, to reassert England itself in time and place. To Pioneerland. To Deep England. Football had to restore a fractured country by recreating a national competition. August 31st would see clubs return to their 1939-40 division and, symbolically, that season's fixture list. The traditional professional game, established in the nineteenth and developed in the twentieth century, was back. There was an end to guests, the return of promotion and relegation. These delicious flavours carried a Victorian ring of the survival of the fittest: 'rich championship and promotion rewards for the fortunate and the spectre of relegation to haunt the laggards.'

A return to normality was what the Government sought. People now had money, but could buy little. Spectator sports met an increasing need as the collective spirit that elected the Government 'dissolved as perils faded'. Inevitably Labour's large legislative programme took time to have visible effect. Meanwhile there were delays in demobilisation and housebuilding, continuing food shortages, unofficial strikes, and a rise in the Black Market. Austerity, like poverty, heightens the appreciation of a treat. Football was that treat. The run up to the Budget of April 1946 saw energetic lobbying that provided an opportunity for government to get onside. The big crowds of 1945-46 had produced a windfall. Even record profits were dwarfed by returns to the Exchequer. For example, eight of the 88 League clubs (Birmingham, Derby, Villa, Manchester City, Grimsby, Liverpool, Stoke, West Brom) averaged £8,000 profit and £21,000 in tax. Similarly the 1946 Cup final made £14,000 more than prewar: it all went in Entertainment Tax. The competing clubs, Derby and Charlton, each received £4,000; the players shared less than £500.

The outcome was a Mephistophelian bargain that for 40 years kept football within the constraints of cheap entertainment. During 1945-46 the admission charge for the 'popular' side was one shilling and sixpence, of which 7½d. went in tax. The Chancellor reduced that by 5d, but expected an admission reduction of 3d. Clubs complained that spectators were not demanding a reduction, and the massive crowds spoke for themselves. The Chancellor's was a populist gesture, rewarding the 'bobsider' spectator and placing the

Government behind the urgency to restore real football: 'the public stood gal-
lantly by us during the war and they shall be repaid for that loyalty as soon as
possible.'

But the Government's requirement to pass on the tax savings also reflected understandable caution: an unrestricted market would mean clubs making
extraordinary profits. At a time of widespread deprivation, of government
indebtedness and of a search for egalitarian social relations, such 'windfall
profits' were unwelcome. The concern reflected a plausible insight into what
the clubs would want to do – keep the money. The Football League had
already reasserted its 'all for one, one for all' motto: the principle that what
was decided for the richest clubs was affordable by the poorest. This fortress
kept out all potentially divisive forces – players, fans, the Press, the FA, the
Government and the law.

At the League's AGM in April 1946, after their profitable season, clubs
welcomed the change: for every '£600 gate we handed £280 to the treasury:
now just over £100.' So would they meet the Players' Union's demands for
1946-47, or would they join the Chancellor in his populist gesture? They did
neither: they went for broke. No to the Chancellor, and no to the players. They
reaffirmed the wage scale they wanted and voted 32-16 against reducing the
ground admission charge. Only when the Chancellor threatened more taxes
did they give in, or appear to. Their reputation remained 'behaving so badly,
with such disregard for public opinion. At times their flouting of agreements
– even political directives – bordered on the breathtaking' (Harding, 1991,
p.223).

Experienced commentators knew that the clubs would 'smart-alec' the
Government: 'clubs will find a way out.' So when turnstiles were unobtainable, and police criticised slow admittance, Third Division Cardiff adopted a
policy of no change; and promptly attracted 50,000! Another method was to
invite fans to donate the extra threepence for a transfer fund. But the most
popular and enterprising way was to create artificial enclosures, and charge
more. It was the 'battle of the threepenny bit'. Fans became aggrieved:
Barnsley spectators directed rude remarks at the 'little bit of muck' on the
'knob' limiting the 1s 3d supporter and dividing their Spion Kop. Labour MPs
hounded clubs in Parliament for 'defeating the Chancellor's object'. Thus
Charlton (capacity 80,000) made only 25,000 available at 1s 3d; and Luton
had 10,000 at 1s 3d and 8,000 at two shillings.

After Christmas the Chancellor complained about 'football clubs who
have not done what I had reason to expect they would do'. He threatened them
with the upcoming Budget. However the clubs had supporters in the House of
Commons, even from surprising quarters. Thus radical left winger Michael
Foot (then a Plymouth MP), albeit light-heartedly, supported their freedom:
'while he appreciated the Chancellor's desire that this concession should be
passed on to the public, if clubs were not able to build up their funds could
the Chancellor give any advice as to how Plymouth Argyle were going to get
hold of a really good inside left.'

Government policy in effect encouraged conservatism. Clubs were run by the same people who had struggled through the Depression when penny pinching on player costs was a way to survive. They feared the attendance boom would not last. They wanted none of government interference and resented restrictions on spending their money by developing their grounds (rather than housebuilding). Usually far too old to have served themselves, they ignored the players' wartime experiences and aimed to reassert their control by trusted old methods.

A greater freedom to increase charges could have had interesting consequences. The League myth of equivalence between inherently prosperous big city clubs and the struggling small town, mainly northern clubs, may have become unsustainable, ever more an affront to common sense. Crowds in 1946-47 regularly and dangerously exceeded ground capacities. There were the usual suspects: 'Newcastle United could probably fill their ground whatever price they cared to charge now for admission;' and Liverpool too if 'they were playing the Blind School at water polo'. Increases reducing crowds to manageable proportions would have produced astronomical profits. This in turn would have made the restrictions on top players' wages even more untenable. Yet general increases would jeopardise Third Division support. The League might therefore have had to adopt a more realistic structure and rationale. This boom of 1945 to the early 1950s proved to be a lost opportunity when it might have established a healthier basis for following decades.

However, higher ground admission charges did not feature in the reconstruction debates. Working people could afford an increase but it was unthinkable: perhaps a consequence of football's wartime role as cheap entertainment for working people; perhaps an intuition that crowds would already unleash much of their anger upon players, without this further excuse. Whatever, 'football as an entertainment is dirt cheap.' This may have benefited supporters and hardly harmed clubs, but it held back generations of footballers.

By contrast, American baseball admission charges were the equivalent of six shillings. An increased sensitivity to overseas sports earnings gave players' longstanding dissatisfactions a new poignancy. The revival of crowds in the late 1930s highlighted old discrepancies. When, in 1938, baseball legend Babe Ruth attended an Arsenal match, he admired the 60,000 crowd: 'Gee, how much are the players on?' When told £8 a week he was as disparaging as he had earlier been impressed: 'Jeez, are they bloody idiots or something' (Varley, 1997, p.199). In 1947, pitcher Bob Feller, baseball's top earner, got £20,000, plus attendance bonuses. Football's emblematic star Stan Matthews earned £10 a week. By 1949 baseball's Joe Di Maggio made $100,000, whilst Stan got £12 a week.

Such comparisons presented footballer-as-entertainer, in which box-office was king. The paradigm was highly-paid Hollywood stars. Or comedians. Tommy Lawton recalled his earnings during his great year of 1938-39, the glamour player of England and its Champions: '£531 10s which is about £31 10s more than Tommy Trinder gets in one week.' There were other models.

Real Madrid increased players' wages to £88 a month and extraordinarily each Moscow Dynamo communist was paid £460 for four matches: 'Yes, sir, more than our top-notch players earn in twelve months.'

So footballers were 'the most poorly paid entertainers'. The FA recognised this when they increased their England fee from its prewar £8, equivalent to one week's maximum wage, to £20 for 1946-47 and promised £50 for 1947-48.

At its heart the postwar campaign for better conditions had to address the question, what sort of work was professional football? The imagery of footballers as entertainers had usurped an earlier identification with craftsmen, skilled workers. Stockport manager and former Scotland international Bob Marshall spoke of his 17-year-old son: 'I do not think he will take up football as a career. He is an electrical engineer. That's a trade. Football, if you're frank about it, isn't.'

In the century's big clash between authorities and players, in 1909, the Players' Union embraced the protection both of other trade unions and the law relating to compensation for industrial injuries. Instead the authorities asserted footballers' primary identity as sportsman, subject to the rules of the game, who happened to get paid. The war then weakened the occupation. Ex-pros played regularly alongside fellow servicemen and many matches used volunteers from the crowd. After a wartime of occasional players, who needed full-time professionals?

Furthermore, the public perceived the Dynamos as the Red Army team, Russian soldiers providing vibrant, innovative football. In vain did English pros claim they were effectively the Soviet national side, well trained, well drilled and opposed by scratch sides of half-fit Brits. But then other foreign sides – Norrkopping, Sparta Prague and Copenhagen – did much the same thing when the English professionals were nominally back to normal. The message seemed clear: controlled and athletic football could be played by amateurs and part-timers.

1946-47 saw a resurgence of amateur players. In October, Arsenal played the First Division's hottest team. Six successive wins, 22 goals, Stoke were so good Stan Matthews could not get into the side. Yet Arsenal won, with a goal scored by one of their three amateurs. Dr Kevin O'Flanagan was the ultimate sportsman: in January 1946 he could have played internationals for Ireland on three successive Saturdays – rugby, soccer, rugby – had he not missed the connection across the Irish Sea for the final match.

Another amateur was Burnley's left-winger Peter Kippax, son of a local cotton mill owner, and wartime bomber escort fighter pilot. Peter ended a stirring season by becoming the first amateur selected for the full England team since 1927. But if real amateurs could make it to the very top, what price football's pretensions to full-time status?

Fundamental damage was done by football continuing its wartime secondary role, providing diversionary entertainment. Footballers' other work remained the more important. From the League President to those advocating amateur Third Divisions, authorities agreed 'it was not in the national interest ... to employ a lot of fit young men in a highly paid, but blind-alley occupation.' The postwar economic crisis prompted a more caustic view: 'footballers should work as well as play for a living. This card-playing and picture-going in their spare time is no life for a fit young man and no way to build a new world.'

The profession's counter – to demonstrate how full-time preparation increased quality – proved very elusive. Everything conspired against it, and anyway quality was not essential. The clubs saw this early, in September 1945: 'we're in for a boom. The crowds will turn up whatever football they see.' It still felt true to Chelsea's John Harris a year later: 'we've got this starved public eating out of our hands.'

John Harris's metaphor had a double meaning. Food shortages meant people brought hunger and intensity to their football watching. They also brought a growing moral emptiness: 'our young people were unsettled after roaming the world during the war ... Pockets were full of money, but the shop windows were empty ... We had won the war, but not the peace.' Wartime football had lacked edge, what Raich Carter had experienced as relief and Bill Shankly as frustrating. By Christmas 1946, it was clear what people had wanted: 'experience now tells us plainly that the public, anyhow, was ready for a return to severely competitive football ... The standard of play is not their first consideration.'

Even as Tommy Lawton argued for more time, he was swimming against the current: 'I know the public are clamouring for competitive stuff.' The structure of real football ensured this. It was more important than money as an incentive, because win bonuses had returned in December 1945, and yet still players were more concerned with personal style than effort: 'restoration of win-draw bonuses have pulled up austerity socks but more "kick" wouldn't disturb the creases in well oiled hair.' John Harris indicated to any naïve players a darker meaning: 'war-time discoveries know precious little about the grimness, the tension of the "life and death" struggles.'

Football in 1946-47 was fast and furious: a joint production by players and crowds. Released from wartime insecurity yet burdened by longstanding austerity, they joined to create din and crush, colour and movement.

Players were ill-equipped to provide a technical game. Their diet did not compensate for the rigours of war. Their lives were disturbed: living apart either from their families or their club. Instinctive teamwork was impossible because no club could get all its players together. If spectators hungered for competitive-aggressive football, so did they. Footballers returned from the war with contradictory emotions: an intense need for security and a restless search for freedom. The postwar world proved to be a profound disappointment. Football's immense popularity, which by rights should have produced welcome changes, in practice meant little. Footballers' disaffection was both public knowledge, through the long-standing union dispute and the newspaper columns of stars like Lawton and Harris, and privately known to journalists who mixed with players and saw 'how far the rather disappointing standard of football is traceable to the "browned off" feeling of many players'.

There were three groups for whom aggressive play exorcised some demons. Firstly, those who maintained their 'other job'. This was little sacrifice because football was not significantly better paid and there were other jobs. Football was inherently insecure – at any moment an injury might end your career. For these players, spending their week doing other work, either through compulsion (conscription or Essential Work Orders) or choice, football served as relaxation. Physical commitment rather than technical expertise provided this relief, disguised a war-damaged technique and might protect players from a crowd's wrath.

Secondly, if part-timers were cutting their losses, career men had a greater urge to challenge the status quo and its anachronisms. For example, wartime experience gave influential players a greater appreciation of the science of bodies, and awareness of how inadequately this had penetrated their profession. Being Physical Instructors opened their eyes into psychological dimensions of performance. Stars like Carter and Doherty worked directly in rehabilitation centres where disabled servicemen strove towards recovery. It was hard to return to haphazard preparation under the supervision of trainers who could date back to Edwardian times and whose views were as much magical as scientific. Newcomers like Roy Bentley, Newcastle's record signing, were amazed at being 'left very much to their own devices'. Frank Swift, an FA coaching ambassador, was frustrated: 'the monotonous grind of out-of-date training is getting them down.' Players complained they never saw a football from 'shooting day' – Tuesday – until Saturday.

Above all, for stars playing in front of overflowing crowds, the economics of reward must have been literally unbelievable. They were further burdened by the weight of time, the loss of seven years from a notoriously short-lived career. Peter Doherty said, 'of course, our time is done.' Those who survived knew that there was never a time when so many players finished without 'practical sympathy' or financial 'wherewithal'. The sense of urgency was palpable. An England international commented on the wages controversy: 'well, £10 is a very good wage for a player … if he can keep going until he's 65.'

The cave-in on the 1945 dispute (which Tommy Lawton, recalling the humiliations of the country's discredited prewar diplomacy, called 'an appeasement policy') was followed by clubs riding roughshod over their union for 1946-47. Players were left fuming – 'small wonder [they] are kicking at something other than a football.'

Thirdly, for every experienced pro willing to make a stand for status and reward, there were many only too anxious to 'make it' at all. They would play hard and fast. Needs must. Roy Paul came from that well-known breeding ground, the Rhondda coalfields: 'my pals the miners had seen it all before. They kidded me about it. They had seen the lads leave the pits, and then come crawling back to the coal face football failures.' His manager reinforced the message in pre-season training: 'yards too slow Roy. You must quicken up, or you might as well go back to the pits' (Paul, 1956, pp.14-19).

Barnsley manager Angus Seed knew this link only too well from his County Durham upbringing, and put it to good use when he went north in search of footballer-miners like Jimmy Baxter. Negotiations were primarily with Jim's mother: 'We can offer him a job, Mrs Baxter. There are a lot of pits in Barnsley' (Alston and Ward, 1981, p.1).

Other footballers spoke for themselves. Alf Ramsey had been a Co-op assistant prewar, but knew his value. His negotiations read like a scene out of the era's definitive film, 'Brief Encounter'. Like those would-be lovers, Alf met Southampton manager Bill Dodgin over 'a sandwich in the buffet' of Waterloo station. Dodgin offered £6 a week winter, £4 summer, and £7 in the first team: 'I've never been a fellow to rush a decision, but that afternoon I did not need second thought before telling Mr Dodgin his offer just would not do.'

They parted. Alf's football career might have ended there and then. No manager of England in 1966. No Sir Alf. He was no star, had not even thought of his international position of right-back: just another wartime utility player. But Southampton could not afford to be choosy. They had no coal mines on their doorstep. So they made a better offer: £7 winter, £6 summer, and £8 in the first team. Ramsey was no radical on materialist matters: even by 1952, 'this is the first and only time I have ever discussed wages – or money come to that – with anyone since I entered first-class football.' Nor was he selfish, as the increase provided 'something for Mother' (Ramsey, 1952, pp.23-58).

It was an endlessly repeated process. Desperate clubs found players in strange places. There were often intermediaries: Alf's Commanding Officer encouraged him to join Southampton. The experience of servicemen playing alongside established pros lessened the distance to the professional game. Members of the crowd could still make up the numbers. Twenty-two-year-old Tony Waddington's start owed much to luck. The soldier went to see a friend play for Crewe reserves. A man short, Waddington was asked to play, and played well. He had embarked on a career that culminated in the early 1960s, when, as Stoke's manager, Tony Waddington re-signed Stan Matthews for City, thus reviving the fortunes of all concerned.

Victor Cromack volunteered to play goal in a PoW camp game and impressed enough for an ex-England captain to sign him for Mansfield. Best entree was contacts. Tom Cheadle's legendary Port Vale career began after their trainer, working in a rehab centre, saw him kickabout whilst recovering from a D-Day wound. Brentford's captain Tom Manley got Roddy Munro a trial after watching him in the Middle East. His coach and manager quickly agreed: 'As soon as he kicked a ball, Mr Curtis and I looked at each other. That one kick told us that Munro was a first-class player and the guv'nor signed him.'

Similarly, Sheffield United were recommended a goalie from a Dundee junior club. Manager Teddy Davison replied: 'Sorry, we have several, but do you know of a good centre-forward.' A fortnight later teenage Alex Forbes arrived on a week's holiday with his 'boots wrapped in brown paper underneath his arm'. As an all-action wing-half Forbes became a Scottish international in April 1947, battling from the first to the very last match of a 42-week season. If the player officially only got the regulation £10 signing on fee, his discoverer could get more imaginative reward: Derby gave a box of cigars for the Scot who spotted centre-forward Angus Morrison.

Trust in informants led clubs to send registration forms 'to Germany, France, the Middle East and the Far East. Many a club got men on their books they had never seen.' Club rank was decisive. Jock Sharp was an Everton director young enough to serve as a major in the Royal Ordnance Corps. There he saw Londoner Wally Fielding's 'cool approach, confident swagger on the ball and natural swerve' (Rollin, 1985, p.174). However Wally's swagger got him into trouble. He had been a Charlton amateur and they complained. Wally, an ex-PoW who had made his football name in the Eighth Army, was suspended: 'experienced clubmen in the Army abroad ... urged him to "get a bit under the table" before signing. He tried ... and parachuted into the Football League inquiry.'

Sometimes what the pro could see in his fellow soldier was not immediately apparent. Whilst in the Guards, Stockport's captain undertook a parachute course. He was impressed not only by his instructor's parajumping abilities but also his footballing potential, and indeed Billy McCulloch proved a rare bird in the tough world of 1946-47: an ever-present. Mysterious intuition was at play in another meteoric rise. A local dentist came to Brentford's ground to announce 'I have got a good player for you. He is a patient of mine.' Maurice Roberts was demobbed in August 1946; got married; played in a private trial the Saturday before opening day; trained the following Tuesday; played half of a public trial Wednesday; signed as a professional Thursday and 'played a blinder' in front of 55,338 at Goodison on Saturday.

Even top clubs advertised: 'Liverpool Football Club invite applications from Amateur Players. Particulars of age, height, weight and clubs played for (mark envelope "Trial") to be sent to George Kay, Anfield Road, Liverpool 4.' Grimsby tried 478 local youngsters. Among innumerable anonymous 'young men with boots' during August 1946 'a young West Indian seaman marched in. He was hard up and had walked from his ship. He lost his way several times and ended up hot and dusty. Given a ball, he dribbled and shot happily for a spell. But destiny could not always be planned. And the unknown remains unknown, gratefully returning to his ship on a number 52 bus. The fare was paid by a Millwall management which never did condemn anyone for trying.'

This search could be a talisman of hope, against all reality. England's Frank Swift took the FA Cup to a military hospital. Asked by a patient to get him a trial when he got out, Frank said 'certainly, I'll see you get it', only to learn later that 'the fellow had lost both legs below the knee'. Similarly Tommy Lawton visited Roehampton Hospital, where he met Jock Mason, a prewar Scottish player with Queen of the South. Mason's arm was permanently raised, his shoulder shot away at Caen: 'an 88 scored a direct hit on my bulldozer.'

Some succeeded. George Dick earned a letter of recommendation from his Army football, and whilst working in a hotel on Blackpool's promenade ... 'One afternoon the hotel was quiet. The bushy haired young waiter idly wondered how to pass the time. The local League club, he had heard, were holding a trial. Dick decided to ask for a game.' He impressed and signed on, giving up his job (stimulating stories of the 'where's-George-with-my-beer'-'he's-left-to-play-football' variety). In October 1946 Dick's prodigious leap and spectacular winning goal on his debut kept Blackpool on top of Division One.

Clubs went to unusual lengths. Liverpool had made a prewar speciality of signing South Africans. Wingman Priday was the latest, but when Chairman Bill McConnell heard Nottingham Forest were also on the trail, McConnell hotfooted it to Southampton. There, meeting the 'Capetown Castle' as she docked, he marooned Priday in his cabin and enlisted him.

Notts County spent their record profit on the summer's most adventurous signing – 'even a First Division team had not thought of'. Manager Arthur Stollery, recently an RAF Commanding Officer, read in a Canadian paper that 'Dynamite' Fred Whittaker, centre-forward of North Shore Reds, could run 100 yards in 10.2 seconds. On this evidence Stollery spent 60 hours flying to Vancouver. Whitaker, a linoleum salesman struck a hard bargain – he required housing. He and his bride of five days took nine days to get to Nottingham, by train and ocean liner, and he was still wearing his overcoat when he joined his teammates (in football kit) for the official 1946 team photo. Whitaker did not remain County's centre-forward for long, but later in the season, when the regular keeper could not get to a match, played a mean game in goal.

Others were not interested. Back home, football often could not compete against other careers: Murray Carlin turned down Cup holders Derby County 'for business reasons' – he had also been offered the job of assistant manager of a Nottingham store. The reasons could be even simpler, and more heartfelt. The alliteratively named Bobbie Bennie, of charmingly named junior club Irvine Meadow, turned down football because he could not leave home again after six years away. Some soldiers did not return. Norman Adcock stayed in Italy on demobilisation, joining Padua for a 650,000 lira signing-on fee and became Serie B's leading scorer.

1946-47 was only Ipswich's second Football League season. Like established clubs, they had to pick up the pieces. No Town player had been killed but two had received career-ending wartime injuries. And not all wanted to come back, like their three Jacks. Jack Hick would not leave his tenancy of a hotel in the shires. Jack Wardlow would not be enticed back after leaving the RAF and was required to 'kick his heels in Greenock' until Town agreed to sell him to a Scottish club. And Jack Smith, who was happy to sign when demobbed, found his widowed mother, who lived 'almost on top of Everton's ground … did not like the idea of coming south, so Jack decided he wouldn't come either – and didn't.'

Finally, young Swinnerton had been a promising Torquay forward before the war. Now 26, he had as good a life as possible in postwar Britain, and did not need football: married and 'settled down with a civilian job and a house and furniture, as I am told. Lucky chap.'

5

The Legacy of a
Railway Embankment

Fred Battersby was evacuated from Dunkirk, served as Sergeant, Royal Artillery, in the Middle East, and had begun operating the crane at Gin Pit Colliery. He died in a football ground. In Bolton.

As Europe returned to life after the war, public entertainment provided catharsis. People needed to go somewhere, do something, break the everyday reality of having nothing. They needed it badly, and it produced crowds that became unstable and dangerous. For England's visit in May 1946 'all France has gone football crazy'. In the heart of Paris, 'gendarmes, with batons drawn, were mixed up scrum fashion in a whirling mass of people' seeking tickets: 'Nothing like it has ever been known in the history of French football … Passers-by asked me what it was all about, and immediately joined the queue when I enlightened them.' The half a million 'disappointed' had to pay 'phenomenal black market values'.

Throughout 1946 and 1947 crowds were on the edge of control. In September, 63,000 were inside war-torn Highbury for the Cup holders' visit: another 5,000 were clinging to the shells of nearby bombed buildings, whilst police foiled 'an attempt to force one of the gates'. Officially, over 70,000 at 'fever pitch' watched Nottingham's Second and Third Division clubs: police on overlooking roofs followed 'irresponsibles climbing over the top of the covered enclosure'. Miners who finished their shift at 2.30am were first in a 61,000 crowd for Newcastle's game against an 'ordinary Second Division side': 'many thousands more were besieging the entrances and converging on the ground from all the neighbouring thoroughfares.'

First Division clubs averaged 40,000 per game. League Saturdays frequently exceeded one million and even reserves could average 24,000. Three million attended over Christmas when, officially, 63,000 watched the big game at Highbury, but mounted police fought a running battle with another 20,000: 'when one enclosure was closed, 10,000 rushed to another and got in free before the police regained control.'

Even at the season's dead-end, an already relegated Second Division side attracted an all-ticket capacity crowd, plus 'an uncounted number who got in for nothing when the gates were rushed'. In match after match, 'over and over again the spectators were on the pitch … forced over the wall by pressure coming down the terraces above them.' Many times it 'looked as though the Bolton tragedy would be repeated'. The season lay under the looming shadow of March 1946, the worst crowd disaster in football history.

1946-47 began with Bolton visiting Chelsea. Commentators criticised closing the gates on 61,464, with thousands still outside, as an over reaction – the Bridge could hold 80,000! Those with shorter memories felt differently: 'I would have given anything to get out of that jam,' said a Bolton man who survived it. Burnden Park, before the tragic cup-tie of 9 March, 'provided nothing as frightening as this, and yet nothing whatsoever was done … One wondered if the willing Londoners, many in a frenzy of excitement, had read the story of that disaster … admission by ticket only will have to come, for only by guaranteeing entry can anxiety be allayed, and it is anxiety on that score, rising to frenzy, that constitutes the great menace to safety.'

It was a combustible mix. Chelsea's manager acknowledged 'supporters were pushed around more than was strictly necessary': 'war has made everyone more aggressive … The temper of soccer crowds has changed radically since the war … The former Commando, for instance, when he comes along here and secures a good vantage point, refuses to move up, down, or along for anyone.'

Where demand for admission was especially high there was ambivalence. At Anfield 'half Liverpool were at the match and the other half were outside listening'. Commentators criticised admitting only 49,995, but, with many illegal entrants, those inside felt only the crush: 'only time you can move is when you breathe out, when you breathe in you are wedged like a sardine.'

The postwar boom was about attendances: the crowds were the biggest the game would ever know. Second Division Newcastle's average was highest at 49,400. Remarkably Norwich attracted 23,000 at Christmas and 30,000 at Easter when bottom of Third Division (South), and Swindon's average represented a quarter of the town's population. Despite awful weather, 35,604,606 people watched league matches, and over 41 million would do so in 1947-48 and 1948-49, and 39 to 40 million between 1949 and 1952.

Before Bolton, the chaotic potential in football's big crowds had never been fully realised. The disaster took the innocence out of watching big football matches but, unlike those of the 1980s, that changed the physical shape and the social nature of football crowds, the wonder is how little difference it made.

1946's Cup matches were a countdown to disaster. Over half a million watched sixteen ties in January, and 310,000 saw just eight in February. March's quarter-final first legs included 76,500 at Villa Park, and officially 185,000 attended the second legs – officially 65,419 at Burnden Park. The casualties at Bolton, 33 people killed – crushed or asphyxiated – and over 500 injured, occurred in just twenty to thirty feet square. Events resembled the later Heysel and Hillsborough disasters, but contemporary accounts also provide a picture of crowd behaviour equally true for many other matches.

Bolton had won 2-0 in Stoke in the first leg and left the Potteries mocking: 'Pull t'blinds deahn, yoan lost.' But City still had the great Stan Matthews. The fine spring weather persuaded Thomas Smith, 65, a well-known cotton manufacturer and freemason, to go to the match with his grown-up daughter. For others it was prearranged. John Flinders, 32, went with Fothergill and Harvey's Mill coach party: and John Blackshaw with the Gasworks and Dane Street Social Club. Six Leigh lads went straight from work. Only two survived, and Joe Harrison remembered being trampled on for half an hour.

Fifty thousand were expected: ninety thousand arrived. The ground record was 69,912, established in 1933, when 28,000 had inhabited the giant railway embankment. However a stand for 4,000 was currently closed, storing chemicals, food, something. Sixty police were inside the ground and 43 outside: fourteen on the railway embankment. There it became 'pretty strained' soon after 2pm: small boys 'were continually squirming their way between the solid ranks of the crowd in an endeavour to find a spot': 'the crowd began surging backwards and forwards, like corn being swayed first in one direction and then the other by a changing wind.'

Soon there was the 'remarkable, and to a certain extent humorous, sight of boys being propelled by hand over the heads of the crowd from the upper portions of the embankment to the rails at the bottom'. From 2.20pm this 'continuous procession' included adults overcome by the crush: 'sometimes roughly – it being no happy matter for those doing the handing down. Their sagging heads jerked perilously, and frequently they disappeared entirely as though they had been allowed to drop to the ground.' Already people were 'being made a carpet of'.

The sole route onto the embankment was a solid 18,000 throng: 'for the next hour I swayed and struggled and swore, amid a cursing, laughing, roaring, mauling crowd.' Old men fainted, but could not fall. Boys were passed over, including one who 'kept up a staccato solo on a rattle', and wore the 'biggest pair of boot clogs … my head is still sore'. No chance of reaching the turnstiles: 'I'd be awreet if when I moved mi feet came wi' mi'.' A roar as the players came out: 'by magic it was possible to breathe;' then 'T'ref's stopped t'match', yelled a voice up high.

A police inspector's portable loud speaker was drowned by a fanfare of rattles. When the ground was closed, some pleaded to be allowed in to escape the crush outside, and hundreds threatened gatemen before climbing over the turnstiles. More went into adjacent railway property. Police pulled many off the fencing but were overwhelmed. Some climbed onto a stationary locomotive and extraordinarily were borne away when it steamed off, but the majority swarmed over a palisade of sleepers. The sudden incursion at the top of the embankment caused a surging forward and two tubular steel crash barriers gave way. Witnesses told their stories: 'When the crowd began to surge forward I was lifted off my feet and flung on the heads of those in front. I saw people on the ground and others sweeping over them, but nothing could be done to keep the crowd back.' 'I could see men being crushed to death against the barriers before they gave way. It was horrible.'

On the pitch the players had an eerie sight: 'It seemed strange to see one side of the ground – the Burnden Stand – completely empty, and the rest of the ground completely packed. But queer things happened during the war and just after it.' After five minutes, the casualties on the sunken running track obstructed the linesman, and then spilt from the track onto the pitch. Only then did the crash barriers give way and the Bolton Crowd Disaster occurred. Everything up to this point was unexceptional during 1946 and 1947.

The 'completely baffled' crowd loudly booed the players' departure, and then eased their overcrowding: 'our walk-off was the signal for a mass invasion of the playing pitch. Some people invaded the closed part of the stand and paddock' (Franklin, 1956, pp.61-62).

How aware were players? It was said Stan Matthews only found out when he read his Sunday paper. In his autobiography Stan recalled rumours: Stoke's reserves talked of two or three dead. When the Chief Constable insisted on completing the match, Matthews remembered walking back along a 'tunnel packed with spectators who had obviously not been able to see the game', and recalled one grabbing a teammate saying: 'It's a crime to carry on.' Stan however felt the volatility of a 'blissfully unaware' crowd: 'It would have been the case of an excited mob believing they had been denied their rights.' Neil Franklin had a more graphic memory: 'you walk along a corridor, past the home team's dressing room … Usually the corridor is clear, but on this occasion it was full of bodies. We saw the victims laid out there and suddenly realised they were dead' (Franklin, 1956, p.62).

It was a day which still haunted Neil Franklin ten years later and depressed Stan Matthews as the reality dawned. Driving back to Blackpool a 'shadow descended', and when he opened his Sunday paper with his breakfast next morning and 'read the tragic facts I pushed the food before me aside. I felt quite sick' (Matthews, 1948, pp.51-52).

Survivors told sad stories. Peter Campbell went home for tea before finding his ex-Marine son and daughter had been killed: 'Frederick had only been married five weeks and his wife should have been at the match with him but they missed each other in town.' His other son Albert, an ex-Grenadier Guard, managed to lift his ten-year-old nephew 'over the rail and onto the perimeter track' before being swept aside. He just kept his feet. Thomas Smith was another victim. He and his daughter got separated in the turnstile queues and, finding the crowds so dense, she took refuge under the stand. She heard of the disaster on the train home to Rochdale.

Mrs Flinders and her seven-year-old son were leaving the cinema Saturday evening when they met another member of John's coach party. She hurried home, to find the police waiting. Wilfred Allison, nineteen, went straight from work as a spinner and grinder 'with his clogs on'. His mother had said 'what would he look like if anything happened to him'. A little boy hanging about 'would not leave without his father, Winston Finch, seen on the field with a mac over his face'. He knew his father was dead. Frank Judd, 30, had survived being a Royal Artillery gunner and three years as a PoW. Just demobbed, on Monday he was to start work again. Stan Matthews captured the poignancy of such deaths: 'To survive a war, only to die at a football match sent a shiver running down the spine of nearly every one of us' (Matthews, 1948, p.50).

The FA admitted that these events 'might easily happen on twenty or thirty other grounds in their present state of structure'. Warnings had come only weeks before, following a 'near miss' gate-crashing at Leeds: 'For a couple of years I've been on about the boom which is coming and pleading for improved arrangements to handle large crowds ... I fear that some day there may be a tragedy.'

The Bolton Disaster Fund culminated in August's England v Scotland match: its £10,853 gate enabled the FA to donate £14,259. Stan Matthews contributed £50, the Mayor of Bolton £20: 5,000 watched the Bolton Ladies revive to beat a Welsh team 8-0 – but they were not allowed to play at Burnden Park. The fund closed at £50,936: £29,282 to widows and ten shillings weekly to each child (at least one unborn) who had lost a father. The remainder was held in trust. Among the contributors was a gatecrasher who gained illegal entry that day.

The government enquiry recommended: inspecting and licensing grounds; making unauthorised entry a punishable offence; and decisions to close a ground should be informed by a mechanical means indicating admission levels. Clubs soon complained that this last, the main innovation, was too expensive. They took a different lesson: 'you cannot cater for hooligans.'

The authorities were in no hurry to implement, and the Government indicated that early legislation was unlikely. There followed several seasons of conflict between the cash-rich clubs, eager to repair bomb damage and improve their grounds, and licensing authorities directing men and materials to housebuilding. Many grounds featured the kind of embankment that had proved fatal. Often just mounds, some boasted railway sleepers and the like. Huddersfield's 'Kop' even hosted the England v Holland international despite fans standing on broken bricks or 'tightly folded newspapers' to keep 'on an even keel' on the 'steeply sloping, unterraced top half'. Stoke's 80-foot-high embankment was 'terraced in concrete only halfway up, the top half being rough and uneven'. A safety plan to complete the terracing would cost £4,000. The Ministry approved only £200.

Sometimes licences depended on work being done by a club's existing staff, or supporters. Clubs made inventive use of war debris. Hull supporters built City's new ground at Boothferry Park from blitzed sites. Watford made an 'interesting purchase during the close season – a flame thrower to exterminate the weeds on the terracing'. QPR's fences – strengthened by air-raid shelter armour-plating – 'should last for years'. The financial promise of the boom deceived clubs into over-ambition: Doncaster Rovers wanted to build a stand at the southern end of the ground but 'are unable to do this as any building would obstruct planes landing at an adjoining airport.' Football struggled with a combination of make do in the present and high-flown ambition in the future. Wembley needed to be replaced by a stadium holding 250,000; each big city required a 100,000 stadium; Walsall planned for 55,000. At Plymouth 'rubble from the [blitzed] city is being dumped on the terraces, and there will certainly be solid foundations and the making of a really big ground.'

So when football resumed, little had changed. For Bolton's first match the ability of fans to get in free through the railway embankment was still unremarkable. The crowd for the first home match was given as 35,000, of which '31,924 paid'. Grounds remained scary and games hard to see – one self-confessed 'small chap' in the 50,000-plus opening day crowd at Molineux 'never saw the ball being kicked, let alone the seven goals. I left at half-time and bought the *Sporting Star* to see the result.' Complaints were legion: 'the letters ... would make club officials blush ... Certainly they are unprintable. Many have a ring of truth about them in their description of some of the discomforts that are experienced on the once popular, now unpopular side.'

The Disaster struck hard at the morale of British football. The game that had helped people survive the war had killed people who had survived: more died at Burnden Park than died in Bolton throughout the war. A restatement of the relationship between football and the British was needed, and came quickly. Bolton won the Disaster match, qualifying for the semi-final a fortnight later, where the programme proclaimed a defiant message: 'Of all the games men have played and witnessed, football, association football, is peculiarly British, and British it will remain.'

An important project for the reconstruction was the recreation of what was uniquely British about football. This was about more than results. Of course the continentals should be beaten. Not to do so betrayed the legacy of Pioneerland. But there were other things, to do with sport: teamwork, being brave, accepting what chance brings, a level playing field. Some of these proved tough to recreate in postwar Britain.

Another Bolton victim, 31-year-old fish and chip shop owner Walter Wilmot, had not wanted to be there: he 'preferred playing to watching'. The unruly crowds of 1946-47 were full of frustrated players, affronted by the riches available to the professionals – a pitch, boots, kit ... a ball.

There were far fewer pitches available for public football. Wartime 'Dig For Victory' and postwar austerity meant 'pitches are still under cultivation' or grazing. With only 74 out of 180 prewar pitches available, Birmingham's Parks Committee attracted controversy by preferring adults and refusing schools permission to play on Saturday mornings, ruling out most of their games. As the pitches were used mornings and afternoons at weekends, they were in a sad state, especially as the Committee relented and allowed school teams to resume playing.

There was a shortage of boots. Each sports outfitter turned away hundreds: 'if I could obtain 1,000 pairs tomorrow, I should have none left by the end of the week.' In the soccer-daft north-east, 'there are practically no football boots on the market.' Those in second-hand shops were quickly snapped up: the delivery of new ones was 'heartbreakingly slow'. Unsurprisingly a pair was among the booty of a burglary of Chesterfield FC's offices, and two Derwent Valley League players pleaded guilty to selling nine pairs from their factory team. They were retaliating at broken promises of jobs and payment for their part-time ground-keeping: one match was cancelled through lack of boots.

Even internationalists struggled. Ivor Powell returned home from India to play for Wales: 'but he has no football boots … all we can hope, as we have no coupons, is that some kind folk who have a pair of football boots size 6, 7 or 8, will send them to us. We should be grateful and so would Powell. If you have a pair of football boots you'd like an international to wear, drop them to Ivor Powell c/o QPR.'

Similarly Denis Compton played for England at Hampden 'in a pair borrowed from the young son of Arsenal's assistant manager'. He decided to 'break in' a new pair on the 1946-47 Ashes tour. Breaking-in was complicated: 'first try on new boots bare footed. See that they are a nice close fit. Covering the foot with Vaseline when first putting on will prevent sore toes and skinned heels and make them more comfortable … When used for an hour or so they will seem more comfortable, and that is the time to put on a thin sock. Later after a spell of kicking, it will be possible to get football stockings on.'

Current pros took a dimmer view: 'If you got the right size they would be swimming around you by the end of the season, so you used to get a size and a half small, and push your feet into them and try and run around the ground. It was like a torture boot. You used to take them off and there was blood and everything ' (Taylor *et al*, 1993, pp.69-70).

Players swapped and shared boots. Even England internationals were loath to bid them goodbye. Leslie Smith played in only one pair in nine years at Brentford, and quickly went through four at Aston Villa: 'he still sighs for footwear as comfortable as the old ones.' This was a common refrain: 'present-day boots compare unfavourably with pre-war quality.' The newer stars, like Liverpool's left-half – 'all energy and eagle eye' – were pragmatic: 'Bob Paisley's football boots are different sizes, and each fits perfectly.'

Some saw the need to change. On a bone hard pitch Peter Doherty wore RAF boots weighing only one and a half pounds, with rubber soles and studs: 'these light boots enable "Peerless Peter" to cover the ground at great speed and still put in those cracking shots that bring goals.' Chelsea's Swiss international Will Steffen also wore softer, pliable lightweights. Tommy Lawton applauded their grip, but would only wear his in practice because they gave no ankle support. Tom often wrote about the effect of equipment: 'what's a footballer's biggest worry? Boots … even studs.'

Manchester United's Henry Cockburn was dropped by England for playing poorly after his boots wore his heels raw, and Charlton's Bert Johnson played the last hour of the Cup final 'with a nail in each boot stabbing into his feet.' Ninety per cent of footballers' injuries were due to kicks on the boot, and the preponderance of 'ball and ankle' tackles meant that players wore 'half a pound of cotton wool' in that vulnerable area. Players who had 'a vein punctured' by a boot nail played on through agony despite damage down to the bone. There were others with an eye on footballers' footwear: at Bradford's AGM, 'one shareholder … wanted assurance that Bradford's players were correctly studded. He said he once counted Gibbons as having been "on the floor" 29 times.'

It didn't need to be that way. The British boot was a response to the British ball. The Swiss again offered alternatives: not only lighter boots – 'your footballs are bigger and harder'. The British were suspicious: the balls got so small they disappeared. The referee for the Switzerland v England international in May 1946 forgot to bring the ball out for the second half, so a spectator threw them a tennis ball. On West Ham's Swiss tour: 'everything was ready for the kick-off when it was noticed there was no ball … the official kept pointing to the sky. "I thought he must be crazy waiting for it to rain footballs, and lo and behold it did." Out of the distance came a plane which dropped the ball right in the middle of the field.'

After losing in Switzerland in 1947, England fielded a ball-playing forward-line in Lisbon: Matthews, Mortensen, Lawton, Mannion, and Finney. The ball was centre stage in what Stan Matthews called 'the most bizarre game of all time'. England team manager Walter Winterbottom delayed the kick-off until Portugal agreed to play with the traditionally British, size-five ball. Within seventeen seconds Lawton headed home, but immediately Portuguese sleight of hand produced a 'schoolboy's' size-four. The famous five showed what they could do with something manoeuvrable, beating highly rated Portugal 10-0.

Like boots, balls were precious (60 per cent were exported) and not to be treated lightly. Managers ensured they were not to be kicked in 'back lanes and spoiled'. The moral pressure could be great. For example, on the morning of a game, Stan Matthews and Stoke's Lord Mayor visited teenagers in an orthopaedic hospital: 'unable to resist the pathetic appeal, the party took it upon themselves to guarantee the provision of a ball, though not necessarily a new one.' Stoke City, who would make a record £32,207 profit, subsequently agreed to honour the commitment, when 'opportunity permits'.

November's excessive rainfall made footballs like 'so much lead'. Again, Arsenal manager George Allison put the case for reason over tradition: 'at the start the ball weighs between 14 and 16 oz … the obvious conclusion must be that it should remain more or less that weight throughout the match. But we know it doesn't in slushy, muddy days … the strongest of footballers have found the ball too heavy.' George's solution was simple – 'let's keep changing the ball'. Chelsea's John Harris weighed the ball after a match watched by 66,000 at four ounces above the maximum sixteen, far, far heavier than today. It was another opportunity to link players' lifestyles with unreasonable expectations: 'how can you expect footballers, minus steaks, to be playing good football with such an overweight implement.' Jackie Sewell, later of England and a British transfer record-holder, but in 1946 a footballing miner with Notts County, recalled another experiment. After one wet match the absorbent kit – socks, jersey and shorts – weighed eight pounds.

The heavy ball was often injurious. Many a 'solid header ... put [a player] out to the world'. A rocket-like drive sent Hull's Jack Brownsword 'reeling into the net'. City's 23,000 crowd was unsympathetic – their opponents were struck by the disgust if anything went wrong – but one fan sent a note of appreciation, 'enclosing a one pound note as a small recompense for the headache.' Coventry's Harry Barratt, a Dunkirk survivor, would have extended his run of 100 consecutive games 'but for the heavy ground and leaden ball ... Harry flopped after a header ... Got up a bit dazed, but carried on directly. With the tie over, he had his bath, got dressed and was ready for home. And he collapsed suddenly. Apparently he had made the acquaintance of a kind of delayed action concussion.'

The saddest 1947 casualty was former England captain Stan Cullis, now 30. Crowds mocked that the war 'had put whiskers on his football craft', and 'like so many returning warriors, he did not bargain for the shortness of human memory'. But it was concussion that meant he 'could not afford to risk my health in a prolonged football career'. Stan was first stretchered off in 1938, to spend seven days in hospital. Then, playing for the British Army, 'a fierce shot caught me on the chin ... five days on the danger list in a Liverpool hospital and, altogether, I was on my back for nearly a fortnight.' In Italy, Cullis organised sport and entertainment for resting troops and once again he 'spent five days in a military hospital with concussion'. Finally on 8 March 1947 First Division leaders Wolves faced second-placed Middlesbrough with a heavy ball 'covered with ice from the frozen pitch and, in the course of an exciting match, I was constantly heading it'. After Cullis withstood all that was thrown at him, he collapsed at the end and, still semi-conscious, was taken from the train on the way home ... 'the specialist advised me to retire at once' (Cullis, 1960, pp.20-21).

Cullis's caution was well-advised: these old pros proved more likely to develop Alzheimer's Disease. Bob Paisley, a notable sufferer, was rendered unconscious in the 1947 Cup quarter-final.

Free-kicks near goal posed a special hazard and discretion could get the better of valour: Sheffield Wednesday's wall 'ducked with alacrity as the cannon-like hot whistled over their heads and into the net'. Goalkeepers were more often crazy than discreet. Leeds' John Hodgson broke a hand saving a penalty, likewise Fulham's Ted Hinton when he fisted out a hard drive. Damage could be routine and cumulative. Centre-forwards, faced with heading a ball whose lace ripped across their face, demanded their winger deliver the impossible: 'hard and low and lace away' (Taylor *et al*, 1993, pp.70-71).

Referees made popular casualties: 'he went down like a log, face first in the mud,' and elicited the biggest cheer of the afternoon. When referee Sunderland was knocked out during an FA Cup-tie, Rochdale captain Tom

Barkas, 'seeing the whistle on the ground where it had fallen from the referee's hand, picked it up and blew up for a stoppage.' Normally Rochdale journalists advocated 'leave the tactics to captain Barkas' but this time questioned the timing, as Dale's centre-forward was 'just then going through on goal'.

Appeals for boots were part of a widespread request for assistance. Ironically, in terms of the vast current earnings of 'Manchester United PLC', United were among many clubs to make a 'spare a coupon' plea to supporters. These were not always very successful. Barnsley 'urgently need coupons to provide the necessary equipment for their players … [for] training gear, running pumps and sweaters. Most of the players have each given up five coupons for their boots.' Three weeks later, despite works collections, they had only 50 of the 300 needed. Barnsley players still had to share boots and tunics, and so could not all train at the same time. Luckily, this suited them: full-timers trained mornings and part-timers used the newly dried kit in the evenings. Their success determined contrasting initial turn-outs: Southport's 'sartorial elegance would have made a good Persil advertisement [whereas] Rovers' biggest handicap seemed to be the difficulty they had in keeping their shorts up.' It was not that the clubs lacked money: 'Exeter's set of familiar red and white stripes are faded and threadbare, and replacements of vertical striped jerseys are off the market: so they will be in red and white hooped shirts.'

Clubs could provide mutual assistance. When Southend played Everton in the Cup, their chairman waxed about the Essex club's new-found prosperity. Despite closing during the war, Southend had since cleared off their £8,000 overdraft. Nevertheless before coming to Merseyside they had to make good a lack that money could not buy. Their shirts clashed with Everton's but, without an alternative, United broke their journey north to borrow Aston Villa's.

Generally, at a time when access to goods and services was prescribed by regulation, clubs needed to exploit the egalitarian basis of rationing. A shabbily dressed man proved Fulham's saviour: 'I understand you're having trouble fitting your players out with kit.' From a pocket in his battered jacket he pulled out a complete book of clothing coupons. 'Have these,' he says. And with a smile he added: 'I know you're thinking I could do with them myself … But you see I'm not a particular sort of bloke with clothes.' Grimsby Town received an unusual but much needed transfer fee: 'three and a half yards of elastic to keep the Fishermen's knickers from slipping.'

The detritus of war could prove useful. Spurs temporarily deserted their traditional dark blue shorts for something even darker – shorts made from old blackout material. Unfortunately neighbours Chelsea, despite attendances regularly topping 50,000, were unable to mark the sudden death overseas, whilst still serving in the Forces, of one of their legendary inter-war stars, the original Blue Devil Alec Jackson: Chelsea could not get material for black armbands.

Supporters' generosity was sometimes only achieved at the cost of deceiving their womenfolk. Thus men who left clothing coupons at Lincoln's offices cautioned: 'You're welcome to the coupons but don't tell the wife.' Women themselves had given up getting what they really wanted. By Christmas Southampton had gone through four sets of stockings – they shrank in the wash – and the survivors did not come 'much above the ankles'. So one lady supporter gave her all to Southampton's giant 6ft 4in goalkeeper: 'these are to buy George Ephgrave some Nylons. He might as well have them. I can't get any.' Others played harder to get. QPR's 'mighty atom' Arthur Jefferson quickly got through seven or eight new shirts, two pairs of boots, and new shorts every match: 'Jeff is a regular liability … he gets stuck in and that sliding tackle of his does the rest.'

Clubs' experiences everywhere were in stark contrast with today's world of replica kits. West Brom were consigned to threadbare plain dark blue jerseys, unable to 'acquire new set of their usual blue and white vertical stripes': 'The problem of acquiring new outfits is a headache … Goalie Joe Rutherford of Aston Villa wears an old green jersey with more patches than a ten year old inner tube.' There were few spares. When Fulham hosted high-flying Newcastle, free-scoring Ronnie Rooke found his kit had gone with the reserves – 44,000 saw him in an old pair of boots, someone else's shorts and a shirt on which his number had been hurriedly sewn.

The men bringing back real football had everything going against them. Playing before crowds quick to express their envy and anger, their only defence was that they looked like professionals, which was always problematic, and played like professionals. That was tough on 1946 pitches. First Division playing surfaces 'badly needed rolling and the grass cutting'; and in the Third Division, 'the grass and weeds were very rough, the ground exceedingly bumpy, and where it was not that, it was doky.' Even the most skilful, like Peter Doherty, were helpless: 'I have now lost count of the number of times Doherty has tricked a defence with a cunning dribble only to have the ball bounce awkwardly at the finish and his shot has gone astray.'

Some pitches, like Millwall's, were devoid of grass by the end of October. Then the rains fell, overwhelming war-damaged draining systems. Four bombs had fallen on the pitch at Sheffield United, which by Christmas, 'was so bad as to beggar description.' Afterwards, the worst winter in the history of professional football made surviving the dangerously frozen pitches the greatest priority. By April, Bramall Lane was 'black and dead looking, without a hint of green'.

6

The Hold Out and the Hole in the Wall: Footballer as Outlaw

August 1946. Training began. After seven long years, real football was coming home. For the youngsters it was really new; with footballers the prize catch in the autograph-hunting craze. For others it felt timeless: back to how things were meant to be. But hunger bred anxiety. Can it be as good as it was? Will it be good enough? Doubts centred on the players. They seemed happy enough. Every local newspaper welcomed home smiley players. Running round damaged stadia, shaking hands with plump, besuited managers or ancient trainers in strange garb. Players bearing the weight of excessive expectations. Always smiling.

Appearances were deceptive. The players would not accept the romantic world of the autograph-seeking boys or the Peter Pan directors. Footballers asserted their right for a place in the adult world. The right to a home and a future. Right now, football did not give them that. Football had to change.

The papers also told this real story: 'everyone is looking forward to the new season apart from the players.' Stars said so in their weekly columns. The union said so. In their AGM only twelve days before the season started, the players vented their fury. Enough was enough: they wanted a strike.

Other stars spoke through their own actions. Jimmy Hagan, at 29, announced he was quitting – there was not enough money in football. Jock Dodds, 31, quit the Football League, whose clubs would not offer enough money. They were both outlaws: Hagan was 'holding out'; Dodds went through the 'hole in the wall'. Their actions were sensational and baffling. Grounds were overflowing with spectators. How could there not be enough money? But it was more than money. Hagan's despair and Dodds' two-fingered defiance both expressed resistance to football's control over its players. The money was a symptom. Registration – of a player with his club – was the means of control.

Jimmy Hagan and Jock Dodds, the star columnists, the union, all forced a rethink. How much did football owe to its traditional structure for its powerful hold on the people? How much did the financial viability of football depend on these controls?

The power of registration came early in football history. First, when the Football Association established the FA Cup in 1872, it restricted players to just one club in the competition. The rule constrained those pioneers who might play for Old Etonians or Royal Engineers on different occasions. This historical moment became an important principle, enshrined with the coming of professionalism. The FA's reluctant acceptance was achieved through registration enabling professionals to be 'known': so that they would not be confused with gentlemen. When the Football League was established in 1888, the clubs needed to contain those competitive elements that would increase costs. One way was to encourage a strong sense of solidarity: all for one and one for all, and to constrain the temptation for clubs to outbid each other. That way lay conflict and inflation, even annihilation, the nightmare of losing all players: 'if clubs had no security of possession and players could leave at the end of a season without let or hindrance, the game could not be carried on. It would be possible for any club to be without a team at the beginning of a new season.'

Clubs grabbed the oar of registration like drowning men. If a player rejected the conditions offered by his only potential employer, he couldn't play or earn at all. From registration flowed the other means of controlling players: signing-on fees were limited to £10 in 1891, and remained in place 55 inflationary years later; the imposition of a maximum wage; and the transfer system, the paying of compensation from one club to another – as long as they were in the League. As League clubs dominated football excellence, the FA built an alternative power base: the rules, the Cup, the England team, the amateur game and the soul of the sport. An uneasy cohabitation emerged although, perhaps because the clubs could not quite trust themselves, the FA retained ultimate authority over registration.

Wartime complicated things. At Christmas 1946 Manchester United's season-long search for a goalkeeper took them to Ireland. As their target, Hugh Kelly, wanted to continue in his father's business, United offered to fly him back and forth for games. However Chesterfield claimed him as their player: they had loaned Kelly to Glenavon only for the duration of the war. But Glenavon went out of business, and Hugh signed for Belfast Celtic who were not party to the original agreement. The English and Irish needed the Scottish FA to resolve matters.

Similarly, in 1938 Scottish international Jackie Milne joined Middlesbrough for £7,000, and struck up a productive partnership with the teenage Wilf Mannion. During the war Milne worked in the Glasgow shipyards and afterwards became Dumbarton's player-manager, until in 1946 Middlesbrough asserted their prior and ancient rights of registration. Milne was forced through a 'hole in the wall': he sailed for Mexico on a two-year contract worth £600 a year plus win bonuses.

Such contracts are now the basis for footballers' employment in the post-Bosman era. In 1946 they were 'outlaw' arrangements. Another outlaw was all-time great Dixie Dean, who fell foul of the regulation that once a professional you could not revert to amateur status until the FA approved an application. Northgate Athletic were fined for playing Dixie in a charity cup-tie.

An enduring controversy about registration throughout 1946-47 concerned amateur Arthur Turner. Turner was leading scorer of 1945-46's strongest side – Charlton Athletic. Demobbed Arthur joined his father's timber-merchant business and disdained professional terms: 'I already collect more.' Charlton regarded Turner 'as the happiest of a happy bunch ... he surprised us by saying he wanted to leave' and cried foul: Arthur was being enticed away. Deadlock. Turner had few rights, even though unpaid, and only found sanctuary at hole-in-the-wall Colchester. The Football League refused to cancel his registration and, although Turner appealed to the FA, he tired of the delay. After frequent discussions with the Colchester directors – there was no maximum wage in the Southern League – Arthur turned professional: 'the terms cannot be revealed.' So in November, without any diminution of his skills, the Cup final's centre-forward played in a 0-5 first round defeat.

The dispute continued. Relegation-threatened First Division clubs offered £10,000 for Turner, but Charlton wanted their share: 'it is the League registration which is transferred, not the player, and whichever club has it holds the interest in the transfer fee. The question whether the player is an amateur or a professional makes no difference.' As Turner was equally determined that Charlton should not benefit, he stayed out in the cold.

The 'hold out' response to registration was refusal to play. It was not a strike because the player's contract had finished. He 'held out' for what he wanted for the coming season. The odds were stacked against him. He did not play and he did not get paid.

That August Jimmy Hagan 'held out'. Even in an era replete with fine inside-forwards Hagan was one for the 'aficionado'. Inspired by a popular radio programme, he was football's 'one-man's-brains-trust'. Hagan returned from overseas to lead a vibrant Sheffield United to the Football League (North) Championship. He played in sixteen wartime internationals – only five men played in more – and featured among the mythic England forwards who beat Scotland 8-0 in 1943. As the man in possession – England's inside-left against Scotland in April 1946 – Hagan had an edge over his main rival, Wilf Mannion: and perhaps could have maintained his advantage if he had not practised this age-old form of resistance.

The hold out was a matter of time. Each close season, out of the headlines, rank-and-file professionals made their protest by refusing terms. It was generally a futile gesture because the club did not suffer for four months, but the player suffered straightaway. It was either a risky strategy designed to get the best of a limited deal, or the despairing action of a profoundly frustrated man. Jimmy Guthrie described how, for clubs, it was 'heads I win' 'tails you lose'. He recalled life with Dundee in the mid-1930s. Like other clubs, Dundee suffered during the Depression and were taken over by Watty Simpson, a millionaire made rich as a Jute Wallah by 'learning to control men with a long whip in India'. Each spring Simpson cut the players' wages. If they re-signed he saved on the following season's weekly wage bill. If they refused they would get neither summer wages nor, since footballers were classed as seasonal workers, would they qualify for unemployment benefit. One year the players refused to re-sign *en masse* and challenged Simpson to let them go. The reply was that of all clubs faced with player hold-out: 'we were Dundee players and the club would hold our registrations, if necessary, for ever.'

There was a postscript. Guthrie manipulated a transfer to Portsmouth in 1936 but first wanted to collect his benefit for five years service. Not so, said the Jute king, it was only four and a half years – remember that summer strike. Guthrie upped the ante: he wanted an illegal payment for his share of the transfer: something 'on top, or under the counter'. Watty was prepared to play hardball but Portsmouth were offering a financial lifeline so 'another Dundee director paid me the useful sum of £600' (Guthrie, 1976, pp.29-30).

Clubs could always realise their asset on the transfer market, or they might offer other, not necessarily legal inducements. Sheffield United's 1946 AGM revealed their prosperity: £20,231 paid in Entertainment Tax; £4,500 profits; and another £5,000 put into reserve against future taxation. United had wiped off earlier bank debts, had £9,150 in hand and paid backdated dividends to their shareholders. Not enough money in football, said Jimmy Hagan, surely with some irony. The AGM also learnt that their captain had turned down the maximum wage. It was, said the chairman, difficult to know what the lad wanted.

United could do without a transfer fee and maybe, as Northern champions, Hagan. Wrong. On opening day, with 'lightning flashes over a badly-blitzed ground', Sheffield United were 'the fastest thing in 22 football boots', but lacked Hagan's subtle touch. In the last few minutes, the inside-left of visiting Liverpool won the game. In August 1939 Sheffield's inside-left, Jimmy Hagan, had scored the winner. The imagery was persuasive. Hagan was known to stick to his guns. As a boy he signed for Derby and was put to work with a building firm: 'Young Jimmy didn't like the job, so manager Jobey delivered the ultimatum: "You work here, or you go back home." "All right," said Jimmy "I go back home." And he did, with Jobey chasing back after him almost on the next train.'

And Sheffield United soon chased Hagan. It was already clear that good players were scarce and Jimmy was irreplaceable. Clubs everywhere were desperately scouring the land and here United had one of the best. They gave Hagan what he wanted, security after football, another career. He would play football part-time whilst training to be a surveyor.

The tragedy in a 'hold out' is the player's. Jimmy Hagan held out for little more than a summer yet it cost him his England place. Ironically his international replacement Wilf Mannion 'held out' for eight months in 1948 and returned ignominiously without getting his transfer (Varley, 1997, pp.109-32). Doubly ironic, because Wilf's 'hold out' gave Hagan his one and only full England international. The final 'hold out', by George Eastham in 1961, proved the most effective. Despite his club caving in, Eastham continued a restraint of trade action. George would have known the history of restraint upon footballers: both his father and uncle were 'sixpenny piece dribblers' with Liverpool and Blackpool respectively, challenging for the 1947 championship. He won his case, but lost momentum in his career. Eastham was a reserve in England's 1966 World Cup winning squad. If it hadn't had been for his hold out …

If Jimmy Hagan embodied the 'hold out', Ephraim 'Jock' Dodds symbolised the 'hole in the wall': escaping the jurisdiction of the restraining football authorities. Jock and Jimmy played together, briefly, in Sheffield United's 1939 promotion team before Dodds' £10,000 transfer to Blackpool, the last big deal before the war. Jock then came into his own. His 289 wartime goals, second only to Lawton, included eight in eight internationals for Scotland. In 1941-42 he scored an all-time season-high 77 goals from 40 matches, including a hat-trick in wartime's most dramatic international, a 5-4 win over England. Dodds was 'good box office', reducing Blackpool's overdraft by £22,000 as they won more wartime matches than any other club. Their title prospects for the coming season were as good as any. Also, in an England otherwise covered in industrial smog, Dodds owned a hotel in desirable Blackpool. Nevertheless when their offer reduced the maximum by £2 if he was injured or out of the team for four weeks, Jock refused: 'I am happy enough at Blackpool but this is a business matter.'

On the pitch, whereas Jimmy Hagan showed subtlety and elegance, Dodds refined the straight-up-the-middle rush. His lack of 'half measures' earned the respect of opponents as good as England's Neil Franklin: 'when Jock Dodds came bearing down on you it made your blood run cold, because he was the fiercest-looking centre forward I have ever known. He had something of the charge of a buffalo about him … Just when you thought he would charge right through you, he would produce a dainty body-swerve or some dainty piece of footwork and you would tackle thin air' (Franklin, 1956, p.118).

In 1950 Dodds and Franklin would be linked in the most famous footballer-as-outlaw case, which prefigured England's most humiliating defeat – by USA in the World Cup. By 1950 Neil Franklin had been England's only postwar centre half – 27 consecutive internationals. But as England prepared for the finals Neil withdrew, too late for his country to find an effective replacement. England's embarrassing loss was then seen as a culmination of the registration-related disputes and a failure of football's postwar reconstruction: 'we've got to pay players what they're worth. That's the root cause of the humiliation we've suffered in America.'

Franklin did not just withdraw: he escaped the trap of football's power of registration. His hole-in-the-wall was Colombia, outside FIFA's jurisdiction. Neil's flight symbolised a disaffection that had been festering over the four postwar seasons and the failure of the 1945-47 settlement. England's premier defender still earned only £12 a week. His club Stoke enjoyed a record (for any club) profit of £32,207 in 1947, beat it with £44,000 in 1948 and made £22,000 in 1949. But City would not grant Neil a transfer, so he spent a year of misery, looking for a way out, and found it. His high-risk manoeuvre (within days, Stoke had taken the keys to the Franklin family's clubhouse and installed their new Scottish signing) carried the potential for significant change. In 1946 English football's model for how sportsmen should be rewarded was American baseball. Baseball players had once staged a mass defection to Mexico, and to get them back, the owners had to pay. Now Franklin received £5,000 for signing-on, bonuses, and £5,000 salary. And the same for next season. And, unlike in England, the deal was out in the open. Franklin highlighted football's other accumulating ills, all too often the result of the restrictive power of registration: 'the plain truth is that there is something rotten in the state of League football today.'

The game was alive with the 'illegal payment racket': money as an incentive to be transferred, club purchases on behalf of a player out of proportion to real worth but passable in the accounts. 'It's a thousand here, twelve hundred there.' Societally, the wartime acceptance of regulation had been corrupted: 'we live in an age of fiddling.'

Franklin's departure was more than dirty linen being washed in public or the harbinger of a humiliating defeat on the pitch. Here was another opportunity to destabilise the system. If Jimmy Guthrie thought Franklin had struck a blow for freedom, others thought the outlaws 'have done more for the average professional footballer in this country than the Players' Union or anyone else. Make no mistake, nearly every player hopes that the move of these players will waken up the Football Association to the fact that professionals must be better treated financially.'

Soon other Colombian clubs recruited British pros. And who should emerge as their representative? 'I'm the agent,' announced Jock Dodds. By 1950 Dodds had become the first postwar player to score 200 peacetime goals, but the authorities ensured this latest business initiative ended his football career. At his rock factory in Blackpool he received 100 applications from British professionals. There was the much sought after Scottish player – and wartime football circus tourist – Jimmy Mason, whose wife made her feelings clear: 'I don't know what my husband will do but I'm all for it.'

Trevor Ford hoped 'the League bosses would be forced to plug the leak in the only fair way possible – by offering the players better terms'. Charlie Mitten left Manchester United's tour of the USA to fly to Colombia: 'I should not turn up my nose ... there are no two ways about it – football in England today is slavery.'

Ironically when the beginning of the end of football 'slavery' arrived – with George Eastham's High Court victory in 1963 – the action was against Newcastle, whose manager, representing the 'slave owners', was ... Charlie Mitten. In fact Charlie was the only one of the 'slaves' to stick it out and 'hit the jackpot' (Ford, 1957, p.19).

The threat from Colombia's hole in the wall quickly evaporated. Neil Franklin soon came home, nursing a sick child but in many ways finding Colombia too foreign. The experience, rather than hastening change, instead served to reaffirm the British ways of doing things. Neil apologised, received a modest suspension but never recovered his former stature.

Until 1946, the British struggled for an international role. At home, the FA settled into uneasy cohabitation with the League, standing for the game itself, its spirit and soul, its rules. But on the world stage this degenerated into upholding the amateur principle. Other countries commonly fudged the distinction between professional and amateur whereas FA ideology, and the basis of their power in England, required a clear distinction. Thus the FA left FIFA in 1928, refusing to yield to the principle of 'broken time payment' i.e. recompense for earnings a footballer would otherwise have made. And with this departure went international control. English players could go anywhere within FIFA and their clubs could neither enforce their registration nor get compensation via its transfer. In the autumn of 1946 this chill wind sent a shiver through the League.

Colombia's hole-in-the-wall gang may have collapsed ignominiously but it carried the potential to disrupt the balance of power between player and club that had been restored after the war. In 1946 that balance was still in the crucible, and it was North America which presented the potent threat. This was one of those false dawns when soccer's shining rays seemed about to warm America's professional sportsworld. Eddie McIlvenny, 22 years old, was one such. He had signed from Scotland's Klondyke club to become a fringe figure with Wrexham during 1946-47, playing just four games. But Eddie found football gold when he emigrated, and captained USA to World Cup victory over England.

There were sound reasons for believing soccer might prosper in the USA. First, many American troops stationed in Britain had become familiar with soccer, and wanted it at home. Then, owners like Branch Rickey, President of Brooklyn Dodgers, were interested in a winter sport to fill stadia unused between baseball's summer seasons. Soccer fitted the bill. In June 1946 Rickey hosted Liverpool's USA matches. Their unbeaten 10-games-in-7-weeks tour was a great success: the crowds were good, Liverpool were impressed by the Americans' floodlighting facilities and their hosts offered the Brits five-year contracts at £20 a week. Liverpool returned the hospitality when Rickey was their guest at Anfield in November. By then the English clubs were anxious about the financial temptation offered by Rickey and Chewing Gum magnate Phil Wrigley, who were setting up the North American Professional Soccer League. Wrigley was prepared to pay top Brits £25 a match. Indebted clubs like Arsenal felt financially out-gunned: '[they] offer infinitely better salaries to sign British players than we could possibly pay, even if we were free to bargain.'

The Americans placed adverts, and newspapers ran headlines 'USA want our soccer pros.' It was a sensitive time. One metaphor for life in Britain was that many wanted to leave the country. The structure of real football provided few incentives to stay. Yet English football could not afford to lose their pros. Football's problem was that of the country's: 'just as in other industries today, there is an acute shortage of competent craftsmen in professional football.'

Panic set in: English professionals might decamp for the good life in the States, without hindrance of transfer fees. Then relief, as it was recalled that the British Football Associations had rejoined the USA within FIFA, producing the immediate dividend of preventing the poaching of a whole swathe of top players. Nevertheless, the Americans received 'a stack of letters from English and Scottish players following the report that they would double salaries'. Players were grabbing at the proverbial crock of gold, hoping to escape the restrictions of the football industry and the depression of English life. They were quickly disabused: an alarmed FA clarified that the advert was intended for players not currently under contract and therefore current professionals were ineligible.

Typical of the professionals tempted to uproot was Liverpool's 28-year-old Bernard Ramsden. By romantic standards he was on top of the football world, his club leading November's First Division, but Ramsden's sights were firmly set on emigrating to the New World. Publicly Bernard said he would not play football there. Instead he would marry an American girl and become a florist! In the war Ramsden had saved the life of a Greek partisan fighter. This attracted the devotion of relatives in New York, who formed a welcoming party when Liverpool arrived on tour. 'His romance is the happy sequel,' as was the prospect of an interest in the florist's business: 'all being well he hoped to leave early in December.' All was not well: a visa to enter USA proved elusive and Ramsden stayed on into the terrible winter of 1947.

Jock Dodds had deeper roots. Like his friend, Stan Matthews, he was also a Blackpool hotel proprietor. Dodds therefore found the more traditional hole-in-the-wall – Southern Ireland. It operated both ways. Eire had remained within FIFA and were frustrated that the Football League, ignoring their retained list, felt free to entice players to England. However it was double-edged. In the mid-1930s Chelsea signed a 'wonderful young inside-forward' for £2,000, 'every penny of which was handed over to the boy.' 'The boy' also got £6 a week school-teaching and £400 in football wages, but after a year refused to re-sign: the club were staggered when that lot 'went down the drain' for one season's work. Impotent Chelsea's only recourse was to put Tom Priestley on their list of players whose registrations they retained but who were open to transfer, where he remained ten years, not one penny piece and one world war later.

When Jock Dodds signed for Dublin club Shamrock Rovers on the eve of the 1946-47 season it was a sensation. 'Big fish want big bait,' and Rovers outbid the financial backers of British non-Football League clubs – £750 signing on fee, £20 per match and £500 for the following season. English clubs' worst fears were being realised: players simply walking away to play for someone else. However, the rejoining of FIFA provided the potential to enforce their regulations internationally, if interpretations could be agreed. Shamrock argued that 'Dodds' contract ended in April', so how could the FA 'refuse a clearance?' 'Once a contract is terminated he is at liberty to engage himself in any country.' The FA wanted the Irish to withhold Dodds' registration until Blackpool received an acceptable transfer fee and he got international clearance. But the Irish realised that what was good for the gander was sauce for the goose: 'registration would put into the hands of the Council a weapon whereby they could bargain with the English FA.'

The Football Association offered a carrot to foster a 'get together spirit'. Out of the blue they arranged an international match with Eire on 30 September, only two days after an existing commitment to play (Northern) Ireland. It was an explosive ploy. The Northern Irish were 'livid' and it opened a Pandora's box of disagreements. For example the FA of (Northern) Ireland claimed jurisdiction over Eire-born players, so up to six men might play against England in both internationals – in the event, two did. The northerners were pressurised by FIFA regulations favouring the primacy of birth as eligibility: 'we cannot play the men we selected and now we cannot select a team we can play.'

Meanwhile Eire's emboldened FA called the registration bluff in a 10-9 vote. The English gave in and the two FAs announced they would respect each other's retained lists. This was not good news for the players. Even if they had no serious intention to cross the Irish Sea it was a plausible negotiating manoeuvre: 'it gives them bargaining power when they want a transfer. If the clubs don't agree they go to Eire and the clubs get nothing.'

Less than a year before, Peter Doherty had used Shamrock Rovers' 'blank cheque offer, with a good job thrown in,' to persuade Manchester City to transfer him. At the end of 1946-47 the Players' Union tried, and failed, to take revenge by threatening the Great Britain v Rest of Europe match, held to celebrate and enrich FIFA – 'the body which has been closing doors all over the world against British players'.

So Dodds terminated his stay in Ireland. He spent a last weekend there with Stan Matthews, then reverted to the Football League. He had only played five games: what about the £750 signing on fee? Shamrock Rovers were sympathetic – the greatly increased membership of their Social Club more than justified the deal – and his next club Everton were 'generous'.

Jock Dodds was suitably contrite: he had been unwise but, after all, it was just 'a business matter'.

7

All was Speculative and Mysterious

When Jimmy Hagan got home from service overseas in January 1946, almost the first thing he did was to pay at the gate and see Chelsea at Stamford Bridge. Afterwards he went to the dressing rooms to meet England teammate Tommy Lawton. Hagan then travelled up to Sheffield, where United were top of the Football League (North). But championship prospects did not feature strongly in his thoughts: 'as a demobbed professional footballer I have my problems. Problem number one is to find a house or flat ... Problem number two is employment additional to football ... I have to look ahead.'

He was not alone. Demobbed servicemen everywhere struggled with the same basic needs – for a home, food, work. And families to make. There was a word for all this, and for much else besides, 'security'. Everyone wanted security and for everyone it allowed thoughts of the future, rather than the past war or the present uncertainty, to predominate, as Lawton expressed a few days after this reunion: 'looking to the future has become practically the prime preoccupation of professional footballers these days.' This private reconstruction was echoed in the public world: writ large as social security, a main project of the first majority Labour government.

Labour had it worse. They ruled a poverty-stricken country exhausted by war and 'faced problems which had to be solved, but could not be solved'. Thirteen months elapsed between their election and the 1946-47 football season: 'Britain's hour of perilous but spectacular glory was over. The inheritance was bleak.' The USA ended Britain's wartime credit, shortages of food and fuel bit hard and the country faced a standard of life well below wartime. A new US loan carried the humiliating and potentially ruinous condition that after a year holders of sterling were free to convert them to dollars. A Sword of Democles hung over Britain's currency and economy. The 'convertibility crisis' hit in July 1947, a month after a protracted football season ended, played under the shadow of 'a time bomb ticking beneath the exhausted, depleted and overstretched British economy' (Hennessy, 1993, pp.87-98).

The £937,500,000 loan enabled Britain to kickstart international trade, not ease their debilitating austerity. The loan was 'a springboard, not a sofa'. At least one small comfort was allowed: the loan bought more newsprint, and when the football season began, Saturday Specials returned.

This underlying insecurity changed the public mood: from relief and collective hope, to impatience and division. The war was won: the peace was being lost – greater shortages and new restrictions. It was harder to see why.

The Labour Government spent 1946 in an unceasing pursuit – a 24-7 effort, in modern parlance – to enact the reforms that created their election victory. But they were not here and now, and confidence in government seeped away. Time and again war and peace were contrasted: 'if the war had been conducted as has the post-war administration we would have been the bond-slaves of Hitler. As it is, we are the underfed and haghidden victims of one incompetent minister after another.'

At the heart of all this was a growing tension between the government view of what was needed and the popular view of what people could put up with. Labour believed demand management economics would provide stable employment and social reforms. The 'amazingly intrusive' wartime restraints – rationing, restriction, allocation and direction – were retained for fear of the economy going out of control. A people starved of the basics of life were to restrain their 'private interest'. But a burgeoning black market – antithesis of a fair distribution of scarce resources – indicated that 'the people of this country cannot go on living within the present austerity limits'.

Football was in the front line. If everything took second place to productivity as the means to economic recovery, football was vulnerable. Football had to know its place, otherwise it was a luxury the country could do without. The 'gate-snatching, cumbersome, ill-conceived' two-legged FA Cup-ties of early 1946 had overstepped the mark, productivity was hit and 'football was to blame'. That Cup led to the Bolton Disaster, pressure for all-ticket matches, and therefore a black market ticket tout invasion. Football's vulnerability created a climate of defensiveness, which encouraged a return to the football of tradition, and retention of its wartime role as a secondary function.

Mining was the intersection between football, industry and the promise of a planned economy. Mining was embedded in the texture of 1946-47 football. Promotion challenging sides from Barnsley, Doncaster, Rotherham and Cardiff were all 'straight from the pits'. Internationals like Scotland's captain and England's Len Shackleton were held by Essential Works Orders. Footballing miners bestrode a strange irony: mining had the highest value, but the worst reputation; footballers were an optional extra, but attracted large, passionate crowds.

It is difficult to exaggerate the importance of mining. The ubiquitous smell of smoke testified to coal's place in the fabric of economic life, providing the fuel for homes, railways and manufacture. Footballers sought transfers to avoid its worst excesses. Preston's Willie McIntosh moved south from the Glasgow shipyards on medical advice that it would benefit his child. This 'authentic bit of guid auld fitba' Scotland,' feasted on the openings provided by Tom Finney, and reached 26 goals in 1946-47. Blackpool goalkeeper and wartime miner Jock Wallace had similar thoughts. In the midst of the 1947 winter in which every journey was an endurance test, he travelled to Glasgow each weekend to visit his sick wife and hoped for better things: 'now she is improving and Wallace is anxious to settle at Blackpool, the air of which would be beneficial to his wife.'

The mines also symbolised Britain's future. They would be nationalised in the middle of the football season – on 1 January 1947 – just in time to front the biggest fuel and economic crisis the country had ever experienced. Foreign Secretary Bevin once famously told miners if they would give him a million more tons of coal he would give them a foreign policy justifying superpower pretensions. It was a rueful promise because productivity, over dependent on human effort, always disappointed and labour relations (those that translated so well into football teamwork) always frustrated. Strikes continued even when illegal under the emergency wartime legislation. When a six-day week was imposed, absenteeism doubled. Conscripts were diverted from the Armed Forces – the Bevin Boys – but to little avail.

As the war ended some causes of resentment faded – there were no longer higher wages to be had in the munitions factories – but they were held in the pits whilst the Armed Forces were being demobilised. The frustrated Emmanuel Shinwell, Minister for Mines and Fuel, threatened absentee Bevin Boys with being sent into the Army, to little effect: 'no gratuities, no demob leave, seven and a half hours underground, no release when your number comes up and Mr Shinwell thinks that the possibility of going into the army will stop absenteeism. That isn't a threat! It's a promise!' Shinwell spent 1946 denying a coming crisis. So when the coldest winter in living memory coincided with lack of coal, fuel and therefore warmth, he became government's most vilified member. That summer the lack of food and homes was the nation's preoccupation and Aneurin Bevan, the minister responsible for housing and Minister of Food John Strachey were in the firing line.

Food shortage was the defining experience of the age. Food was the vocabulary of difference – when footballers went abroad – and the vocabulary of blame: 'confidence in the ability of the Ministry of Food to solve today's problems has sunk to an all-time low level.' Strachey sparked fury during the summer of 1946 by introducing bread rationing. The nation had been 'mildly hungry for five years and now saw itself getting hungrier still'. This was too much, a last straw: something even the war had not made necessary – 'the people of Britain should revolt'. It summed up 'all the frustration and worry and fiddling fuss of life in post-war Britain' (Cooper, 1986, pp.26-29).

Amid 'uproarious scenes' in Parliament, Strachey raged against profligate bread-eaters and the evils of 'side plate nibbling': 'a scandal that men and women who eat in restaurants can take bread and either eat it or not eat it, or play with it or not play with it.' Bread rationing was fervently hated: even the British Housewives League was provoked into a 'we-are-sick-of-everything' march. Ration day itself brought chaotic queues: reluctant roundsmen were threatened with gaol. Bread went bad, being given to pigs – bread flour was already 'thirty-five per cent cattle food'. The Ministry of Food helpfully clarified that this was a privilege available to others, on condition: 'provided bread is unfit for human consumption, housewives are still quite at liberty to dispose of it in the pig bins.' The chaos worsened when bread coupons became exchangeable for 'points' to buy other goods. Grocers quickly despaired: 'what is the use of extra points' when shelves were empty. Undaunted, 'women are just rushing the shops and buying anything and everything they can see that is on points.' Where the Government gave extra rations to miners, they were 'quite swamped in the rush'. The Players' Union also asked for more. Strachey's Parliamentary Private Secretary was Bill Mallilieu, a Huddersfield fan, son-in-law of Portsmouth's manager and one of those whom Jimmy Guthrie lobbied on behalf of the footballers' cause. The Union was unsuccessful: footballers' need for extra food might be persuasive, but productivity came first.

The bread struggle mediated a declining sympathy with wartime regulation. It 'was symptomatic of a widespread weariness of restrictions, controls and forms which affects nearly every trade and nearly every individual'. Government even threatened prosecution when demobilised soldiers shared their clothing coupons: 'strictly speaking, members of families who have been freely interchanging coupons had been committing crimes.'

This resentment – 'we are being governed to death' – also underlaid 'the phenomenal increase in black market activities since the end of the war'. There was a crisis in allegiance to the collective system of allocation. Newspapers ran campaigns, asking readers to inform against black marketeers, or railing against selfishness – everyone seeking their own gain rather than the good of all. Yet the 'phenomenal increase' spoke for itself. This was a context for an age which even as instinctive a socialist as Bill Shankly lamented the realisation that 'everyone was out for themselves' (Kelly, 1996, p.47).

News from abroad that summer brought little relief. Despite its economic weakness, Britain maintained its status within a triumvirate of world superpowers, but relations were going badly: the peace conference to reshape a future Europe was becoming increasingly combative. The Soviet Union was obstructive and the US flaunted a nuclear status that Britain envied. Overseas military commitments hit trouble: a Jewish bomb aimed at the British officer class in Palestine killed over a hundred, demonstrating the fragility of Britain's role as world policeman; whilst the communal violence in India indicated Britain's impotence as an imperial power in decline.

Attitudes were exemplified by Foreign Secretary Bevin, reviewing England's footballers before an international with France: 'they all look fit enough to eat the Froggies' (Varley, 1997, p.86). Similarly, at the postmatch banquet after England beat Switzerland in May, stand-in captain Raich Carter 'accepted the gift of a cigarette lighter from the Swiss FA. Never shall I forget Raich's smile'.

Carter took that combination of suspicion at the continentals' strange ways with a determination to prove best on Derby's summer tour of Czechoslovakia. County were among many tourists, a welcome experience for those who had spent a war in Britain: 'having spent two weeks across the water, I've never felt fitter for eight years.' Cultural exchange proved difficult: hundreds of Swedish fans stoned Wolves' coach in Malmo, and afterwards the referee explained his first-ever sending off: 'I have seen many British teams play here but none like Wolves. Galley kicked the Swedish player from behind ... what he did was not gentlemanly.' When the FA punished such transgressors, the press mocked them for expecting footballers to be sporting ambassadors: 'Don't charge the goalkeeper, George. Remember, the FO [Foreign Office] are watching.'

Charging the goalkeeper was a touchstone of difference between British and continental football, redolent of old traditions: 'I want to see more slow-minded goalkeepers charged into the back of the net so long as the law is not broken ... And more players who can take legitimate knocks in the spirit of rugby.' Postwar football would resurrect tradition with wartime vigour. Football was a tough sport, for 'commandos' and 'iron men'. The FA and the coaching approach they championed became proxies for soft continentals. So the fierce Wolves thought the Swedes could not 'take a licking', and remembered their wartime neutrality: 'we fought to stop a single bomb falling on Stockholm.'

Raich Carter joined Derby's tour after England's spring matches: we were 'supposed to play in Vienna and arrangements had been made for the Army to fly us there' (Doherty, 1948, p.78). These arrangements failed, and the team refused to travel 200 miles to Graz in Army lorries. So an additional fixture was arranged in Prague, which became the 'worst game I ever played in': 'the crowd, with yells, whistles and waving arms, charged on to the pitch ... dashed past. It was not my blood they were after; it was Peter's' (Carter, 1950, p.176).

Meanwhile, hundreds of thousands of demobbed servicemen returned home to the full force of the national depression and anger: 'everywhere I go in the Midlands I find ... only despair ... disillusionment, lack of faith in a future.' It would not be easy. Relieved to have survived but remembering those who had not: yearning for a lost, past world. Returning to a depressed country often unsympathetic with their ambivalence, whilst still trying to make sense of what they had seen. Servicemen were often told pointedly that they were 'lucky to have seen the world at government expense.' Domestic conflict and divorce were common: one service husband in five had been unfaithful abroad, and a third of home war births were illegitimate.

The question of housing loomed largest. As the military camps of Britain emptied of demobbed servicemen, reunited families found nowhere to live. Government, earlier urged to demobilise more quickly, was now denounced for doing nothing to stop them being 'ripped off' in 'vicious rent ramps'. Grasping landladies added insult to injury by imposing humiliating rules: one required her tenants to avoid 'scraping chairs on the lino'. The family subsequently lost their temper at not being allowed to 'put the baby's pram at the front of the house'. Their consequent notice to quit added another family to the many homeless. Suddenly, in August, the equation was made between homeless ex-servicemen and the vacated military camps. 'The idea spread like smallpox.' When squatters filled the thousands of military camps, they besieged other institutions – appropriately, even an infectious diseases isolation hospital. Sports grounds were favoured: cricket ground huts in Balliol College, Oxford were invaded and, on the eve of the season, workmen preparing Slough United's pitch stopped dismantling Army huts and turned on the water when 'squatters began infiltrating through the hedges'.

Footballers shared these housing problems. Few were as lucky as veteran West Ham manager Charlie Paynter, who sat tight in the East End house he had lived in for 50 years as the bombs fell all around. Others were bombed out. Raich Carter moved in with his wife's family in Derby when their Sunderland house was destroyed. England's prewar full-back George Male started his eighteenth season with Arsenal training with Leeds: his London home had been blitzed and his unwell wife had moved back to Yorkshire.

Managers pondered these intractable problems: 'the vast majority of professional players have contracted war-time marriages. Most of them now have children, and when they are released from the Services they will naturally be looking for homes.' Managers had gains and losses in the immediate postwar period. Their salary differential over players increased significantly – Matt Busby's rose from £750 a year to £3,250 by 1950 – but there was a significant loss of security – the high level of public emotion and expectation created a greater need of scapegoats. During 1947, departures left less than a third of prewar managers in place.

Some things did not change. Alex Massie accepted that becoming Villa's manager 'was a reward for services rendered on the field'. The directors chose the team: 'I know the exact set up. The chairman will buy and sell the players, pick the team, and hand me a nice cheque every month' (Shackleton, 1955, pp.127-28).

Arsenal reluctantly allowed Scottish international Gordon Bremner to leave – 'a brilliant ball player, who but for the war' could have been Alex James's successor. Homeless Bremner's wife and two children were living in Chester, and Motherwell were offering a bungalow. Such solutions were a great relief: Leslie Smith, who played for England before 75,000 at Stamford Bridge, moved to Aston Villa for a bungalow: 'it has taken a weight off my shoulders.'

Housing problems limited summer transfers. Most clubs wanted to buy but few were under financial pressure to sell. None were confident about the quality of their staff and thus hung on to what they had: 'good players with whom clubs are willing to part are about as scarce as cigarettes on a Saturday night.' Even where clubs agreed it was often 'a hopeless quest ... unless they can place a house with vacant possession' at their target's disposal: 'it is a well-known fact that several intended transfers on the large scale have "flopped" because of the housing situation.'

As well as shortages in food and housing, players found it difficult to return to the old deferential social relations. Joe Mercer, England's wartime captain, explained his deteriorating relations with Everton's Secretary-Manager Theo Kelly: 'I wasn't easy to handle ... as a Sergeant-Major I had run my own show.' Mercer's career might have gone in various directions: 29

years later he became England manager, but many thought he had better credentials than the first incumbent, Walter Winterbottom, appointed in the summer of 1946.

But for his joining his father-in-law's grocery business, Liverpool would have fancied Mercer as their coach. Quarter Master Sergeant Instructor Joe had already established a renowned reputation on football tours for being able to 'cadge' supplies. Matt Busby remembered his returns from Italian villages 'with dozens of tins of all sorts of produce from bully beef to spaghetti and cheese, nobody asked any questions' (Busby, 1957, p.69). Mercer's grocer habits caused his break with Everton and continued at Arsenal, where once before kick-off, 'Smiling Jim' Wiltshire, 1947 Cup final referee, told him: 'I've got a good job with a jam preserving firm.' One thing led to another, despite the presence of 60,000 impatient fans, and Smiler's salesmanship hooked Grocer Joe: 'OK, book me for a ton.'

Even those who appeared to make the transition later bespoke their alienation. Wilf Mannion returned to challenge for the title and for his England place, but remained full of resentment: 'I had that ex-serviceman's urge to move. Middlesbrough said no and that was that. That piece of paper I signed in 1936 really put me in the slave class' (Varley, 1997, p.168).

Some players played harder to get, which in turn caused 'a bit of bother' with teammates. Jimmy McAlinden, the most expensive Irish signing and a Cup winner in 1939, spent the war playing in Ulster and Dublin before rejoining Portsmouth's team of war-scarred soldiers. Jimmy had also married, had three children, and was no keener to return than Mannion.

In May 1950 the FA spoiled the celebrations of Portsmouth's second successive League Championship by banning for life Chairman Vernon Stokes for persuading McAlinden from his 'hole in the wall' back in 1946. Jimmy received £750 (about twice the average annual wage), in one pound notes. (In 1951 the ban was lifted and Stokes was free to reach the highest positions within the Football Association, including Chair of its Disciplinary Committee.) Portsmouth were under extra pressure to produce a competitive team – it had no nearby coalmine to supply footballers and had finished near the bottom of the transitional Football League (South). But it is unlikely that McAlinden's was an isolated case: he was good but not exceptional and many other clubs had money sloshing around.

Yet favouring one player over another was risky, especially if housing was involved: 'any club finding an empty house for a genius at the expense of players in lodgings and waiting their turn in the queue will find a peck of trouble.' Not all geniuses were favoured. Newcastle bought 22-year-old Roy Bentley without seeing him play. The Newcastle money-men, flush with profits, flaunted their wealth when it came to deciding the difference between their £8,000 offer and the £8,500 Bristol City demanded. United, in macho mood, offered to toss a coin – and lost. Roy Bentley was ex-Royal Navy, and had braved the Arctic convoy missions to Russia, yet he shivered through eighteen months with Newcastle, first in digs, then a flat belonging to a sister of a United director, until he became desperate to 'go south' and get warm (Hutchinson, 1997, p.131).

Marriage could spark difficulties because it brought material improvement. Middlesbrough manager David Jack anticipated the problem in January 1947: 'the greatest of all post-war domestic problems – getting a house, which inevitably enters the question if the player is a married man.' When Wilf Mannion married, the club provided a house and a benefit which bought a bedroom suite: his teammates complained about his preferential treatment. 'In the dressing room, he was shunned by those of his colleagues consumed with envy' (Varley, 1997, pp.110-11)

Mannion was Middlesbrough's star. If ever a differential reward was to be acceptable, this was it. Elsewhere the distribution of a club's 'largesse' seemed arbitrary – 'why him rather than me'. Bradford were another to lack team 'harmony', as their discreet *Saturday Special* noted: 'I knew full well that spirit was not by any means all it needed to be. I have no intention of entering into the whys and wherefores.' Bradford bought houses for selected players: like Scotland captain Jimmy Stephen; or long-time amateurs persuaded to turn professional, like Jack Gibbons and Roy White; or captures from London like future England manager Ron Greenwood, or George (newly married and future father of Ray) Wilkins. Such clubs were smouldering embers.

Bryn Jones was more laid-back. Bryn had now been the most expensive player for eight years – since his record £14,000 transfer. Now he symbolised age – nearly 35 – and uncertainty. Jones may have served with the Royal Artillery in North Africa and elsewhere but he was football's 'mystery man': Arsenal hardly knew his whereabouts. Every so often the papers found him – in no hurry. In August Jones was househunting in London, in anticipation of marrying a girl he had met in Wolverhampton in 1934. Even four days before the season's start he was 'found perched on a tennis table in an unemployed men's club. Bryn Jones explained he was taking demob leave since he got back from Italy, before signing with Arsenal on 3 September and starting training. He then went back to his cards.'

Within a world of shortages the community of professional footballers came under mounting stress. Players had bitten their lips during the Depression years. Deference to football's paternalism was a price worth paying for '£4 or £5 a week in 1933 made me the richest man on our street' (Korr, 1986, p.155).

Their place within those back streets now took on a rosy glow. Even internationals travelled in the same trams, like Jackie Bestall (all-conquering Doncaster's manager in 1946-47) in 1935: 'I was riding on the top of a tram car in Grimsby when I noticed that several people sitting opposite were staring hard at me and smiling. I didn't know them and I began to feel embarrassed ... Then one big fellow leaned across and said "Congratulations, Jackie." It was my time to stare. "What for?" I asked. "Don't you know?" he replied. "Why you have been chosen to play for England".'

1946-47 was a world of conflict. Rough play on the field. Conflict between players and their aggressively critical crowds. Conflict between union and clubs. Conflict too within a club, sometimes arising from the full-time–part-time split. One club attributed their relegation to its demoralising effect: 'how can you expect a player to take a justifiable risk on the field if he happens to be a part timer enjoying top wages as a player, plus almost as much again in his every day work? These men had to be granted privileges that we could not extend to others.'

Players' origins caused tensions: 'local pride is not best sustained when the local team consists of men from widely separated places.' The power of real football came from competition between local communities. Clubs took their names and support from urban places, whose distinctiveness and achievements they celebrated. But success demanded a relaxed view of players' origins, and from the earliest days of professionalism the ability to recruit from far away was part of the triumph of the industrial age.

In 1946 this tension was revived. The transfer market, constantly contaminated by motives of panic and black market-type corruption, was contrasted to the innocence of a club developing its own players. Several voiced an unlikely ambition to field a wholly local side, e.g. a Hampshire eleven for Southampton. But Cardiff won Third Division (South) with just one Englishman, and in the First Division, 32 of Sheffield United's 37 professionals were local lads, as were twenty of Stoke City's regular first and second teams.

The circumstances of postwar Britain brought 'local talent into a new and powerful limelight'. Essential Work Orders, holding men to their own localities, conjured up an innocent ideal, 'for professional teams to be really representative of the districts whose names they use.' Spurs' secretary Arthur Turner expressed the same point provocatively: 'the south should never need to buy from the north. We should train our own young players down here. There are plenty of them.'

Spurs' proclaimed policy of recruiting Londoners challenged the traditional reality that pro football was an occupation primarily for men of northern origins. Football was for 'boys from big cities and remote villages', of small areas like the Byker district of Newcastle or the mining villages of Lanarkshire that produced such disproportionately high numbers of footballers that it seemed fundamental: 'They make 'em where you come from, lad.' Southern clubs experienced this rivalry most keenly. First teams, trainer and manager were largely composed of northern 'foreigners'. The majority of managers were from Newcastle, Lancashire and Scotland who returned to their roots for new players, causing further stresses. Raids led authorities to retaliate: when amateurs had trials with English professional clubs they were then prohibited from playing again in Scottish junior football.

Players were still white, British and working class. Ten of Southampton's 26 players were named either Bill or George. Over a quarter of league clubs had someone called Jones score for them: Arsenal had three players called Jones and another three called Smith. Other social identities were rarer. There were three black, or 'coloured' players; and three Jews, including ex-flight lieutenant glider pilot Abe Rosenthal who came in for special treatment from Tranmere's barrackers.

There were immigrants. A contemporary film and song culture caused Barnsley's Chilean-born centre-forward Robledo to be dubbed 'South American George', although he had spent his childhood in Yorkshire. More genuine reflections of world events were Watford's signing of Max Noirez, ex-Racing Club de Paris and ex-French Resistance, and Emilio Aldecoa, a refugee from the Spanish civil war, in Coventry's side. Two Basque refugees, Joe and Antonio Gallego, who ran a wholesale tobacconists' business, made a brief impact with league clubs: typically, train delays prevented Joe's First Division debut.

Within weeks of being spotted playing for his Polish Division, 'Eric the Lad' Kubicki, twenty, was in York's Third Division side – and his fellow veterans were in the crowd to see him. An older Pole with a more distinguished pedigree tried a comeback with Barnsley: Stanislaw Jerula had kept goal for champions Vistula before the war. Another Polish international playing in reduced circumstances was Gienga, in the Lancashire Combination with Clitheroe, while a Greek tried to recapture a promise disrupted by war: 'Spurs' search for a centre-forward ends in the Athenian Restaurant in the Edgware Road where head waiter Stellos Platones [known as Stanley] took the day off to be interviewed ... Stellos played for Panathinaikos at fifteen and was top scorer before the war. He then became a civilian serving in an RAF mess, went with them to Egypt, joined the British Merchant Navy and became a British national.'

Another major characteristic of this workforce was its family traditions. The community contained a tension between the many players brought up within football and immersed in its bread and butter realities and means of resistance as well as its glories, and newcomers without this knowledge. The football industry was like many other working occupations, one carried on from generation to generation.

Children were absorbed into a culture. 1966 World Cup hero Geoff Hurst's 'first memory was of being taken by my Dad, Charlie Hurst, to see him earn his living ... the one thing that did get through to me was the noise and feeling of excitement among the crowd ... the atmosphere made a strong impression on me. I watched Dad play once or twice more in the League, and I suppose it was around this time I became accustomed to the idea that playing football was a perfectly normal way of making a living ... the bug got me.' Geoff, born in December 1941, remembers the football ground as his dad's 'workshop' and his 'trade' as a centre-half with attitude: 'if I can't get my head to the ball, I can always get my head to the back of *his* head. So I head the centre forward, he heads the ball ... and we're both happy!' (Hurst, 1967, pp.110-11).

Charlie Hurst scored in his last Football League game against New Brighton in 1946. But as his Rochdale sank to the bottom, Charlie took his other trade, toolmaking, to Chelmsford, where the Southern League operated no maximum wage. Charlie's early games were as a 'terrier tackling ... thrustful attacking ... tenacious half back'. His team won 13-0 on his debut, and then 5-0, 8-2 and 5-1 until Chelmsford went top. The Hurst family had arrived: Geoff would play cricket for Essex and football for West Ham.

Cousins, brothers in law, nephews and uncles were legion. Manchester United's coming star, John Morris, had two brothers and an uncle, Eddie Quigley, at Bury. Uncle and nephew followed one another, breaking the British transfer record in 1949 and 1950. There were innumerable brothers (five clubs had twins) playing, often together. Stoke, Liverpool and Millwall each had three brothers on their playing staffs. Mansfield even dropped one, Harry Everett, in favour of another, Harold.

Families specialised: all three Accrington goalies had fathers who were League goalies, and Middlesbrough's Dave Cumming was one of four goalkeeping brothers. There were dynasties: the four Barkas brothers, five Shanklys, six Wallbanks. Huddersfield's Billy Knox took on all comers in fraternal relations. The Scot was England's trainer against Holland at Town's Leeds Road ground. Billy played with Rangers and Chelsea, and his father, six brothers and five uncles were professional footballers. In retrospect the most famous family network were the four Milburn brothers, whose cousins Jackie Milburn and Jack and Bobby Charlton all became household names.

Footballers were intergenerational. England internationals Frank Moss and Neil Harris, opponents in the 1924 Cup final, both had two pro footballing sons in 1946. Miner Eddie Lowe ended the season with England but like his brothers and father played for Aston Villa. Bolton's staff included three sons, a nephew and a grandson of former players. In 1919 Billy Watson, Willie Smith and Percy Tompkin were all pros at Huddersfield; in 1946 all three had at least one son on Town's staff. England's George Hardwick and George Hunt were both third generation footballers: grandfather Frank Hardwick played for the original Middlesbrough Ironopolis, and grandfather Sam Hunt, a Barnsley player in the 1890s, was 'as fit as I am and still working'. Sheffield Wednesday's Denis Woodhead, who flew over 50 missions in Lancaster bombers, was grandson to one of the club's nineteenth century legends: Billy Betts had worked at the Neepsend Gas Works on Saturday mornings and for The Wednesday on afternoons – including the 1890 Cup final.

These connections virtually spanned professional football history. In 1946 Tom Johnson was Lincoln City's captain, but he, his brother and his father had all enjoyed honours with Sheffield United lasting half a century. Tom himself played in the 1936 Cup final, and led the 1939 promotion side; brother Harry had won the Cup in 1925; and their father played in three finals between 1899-1902.

Prospects were difficult to gauge: 'the plans of 1939 have been blown to atoms.' Teams were an uncertain mix of ageing returnees and wartime players of unknown qualities. The relationship between seasons was confusing. 1945-46's outstanding team was Charlton Athletic, pipped to the post in both the Championship of the Football League (South) and the FA Cup. It would have been an unusual double: the Cup winners appear in the record books – the two League champions do not. However, Charlton had a 42-year-old and six others in their mid-30s. Otherwise manager Jimmy Seed professed not the remotest idea of the playing abilities of a dozen returning players.

Staffs were either feast or famine. Third Division Hull City had a new board of directors, an unfinished new ground, new team colours, a famous manager, Major Frank Buckley, hired on £2,500 a year (the highest salary in British football) – and just six players! On Merseyside a *coup d'état* ousted Tranmere's chairman for his wartime autocracy – 'you have been offending against company and FA law for some time' – and New Brighton's participation became conditional not only on their war-damaged ground being made ready but enough players being recruited. Neil McBain was not appointed manager until July, at which point the club had neither players, stockings, boots, jerseys, 'not even a piece of writing paper.'

Huddersfield Town had the largest playing staff, with 60 professionals and 30 amateurs. Most First Division and senior Second Division clubs averaged over 40 professionals. In general these were the largest in the Football League since its formation 58 years previously – and they were quickly added to. They were partly cheap insurance: 'if you are in the running for promotion your players are kicked up in the air and you must have capable reserves.' And partly illusory: only five of Huddersfield's pros were available for full-time training, and half West Brom's professionals were in the Forces – their 18-year-old call-ups included 'six budding internationals'. Thus, to the great frustration of managers everywhere, there was a great scarcity of new men. Reserve teams as well as first teams were often composed 'of ripe experience'. A generation had been lost.

Players in the services, in the mines, under Essential Works Orders. There was little the clubs could do about these, but they could pressurise part-timers to end their other jobs. When Alec Lockie, Sunderland's longstanding centre-half, resisted, Sunderland would only pay him if he played, then sold him. His replacement was Fred Hall from Blackburn. Hall was a man of his time and place: a big centre-half dedicated to one thing, to 'stop' the opposing centre-forward. He was going home. Both his brothers had died within a fortnight of each other, and after demob Fred would live with his sisters. Among his creature comforts Hall, like many northern players, indulged his passion for breeding homing pigeons. In fact he signed for the considerable fee of £7,000 in his own pigeon cree. Hall's best cock bird had already won £100 in prize money despite an additional hazard for a literate bird – his home was in the County Durham village of 'No Place'.

The war had also disrupted a major presumption of British football – that the best teams were in the First Division. Rather than current ability, the pre-war standard applied. Thus Football League (South) champions Birmingham resumed in the Second Division: Portsmouth finished fourth from bottom with only 28 points but started in the First. There were similar anomalies in the north. Leeds and Blackburn, both First Division clubs, finished at the bottom: third-placed Newcastle who had gained twice as many points, would play in the Second, along with Sheffield Wednesday, fifth, ahead of nine 'First Division' clubs. Understandably, a recurrent theme was that 'there is little difference between the senior divisions'.

Newcastle quickly bought players like Roy Bentley and Frank Brennan (who had tamed Tommy Lawton in Scotland's Victory International win) to ensure their rapid promotion. In contrast, there was much headshaking at a third fallen giant, Manchester City. Despite 41 professionals they moaned: 'we can't buy ready made players for love or money.' There were many fallen giants: in fact of the ten clubs who shared the twenty inter-war League Championships, half of them were in the Second Division: West Brom, Burnley, Sheffield Wednesday, Newcastle United and Manchester City.

The initial schedule was demanding because, without floodlights and without distracting industrial production, midweek matches were crammed into the first few weeks. First Division Preston faced five, and Third Division Doncaster six matches in sixteen days, and many seven in three weeks. The season would prove very hard. Coventry 'called on 22 in the first six games', and Newport, quickly bottom of the Second Division, had used 34 players and had signed a completely new team by January. In February Eddie Quigley scored five goals debuting as Bury's ninth centre-forward and Bradford City had twelve different players at inside-left. Over 1946-47 two clubs used over 40 players in league matches and First, Second and Third Division (South) clubs averaged 26 to 27: Third Division (North) – 30. Of the 567 different First Division players, only six outfield players and five goalkeepers played in every match (Charlton keeper Sam Bartram is listed in annuals as ever-present, but contemporary papers report Sid Hobbins deputising against Manchester United, then promptly returning to the Army in Palestine). In the Second Division there were only twelve ever-presents among 583.

The game was based on a rigid sense of positional discipline, each with its own stereotyped qualities and characteristics. Inside-forwards and wing-halves had most responsibility for establishing collective play, and worked so hard that it 'took four years off your career'. The successful inside-forward was praised for his artistry, an effective wing-half for his industry. A full-back needed 'a strong kick' to 'clear his lines', 'should never dribble, and under no circumstances must he allow himself to be tackled when in possession.' Understandably, 'not more than once or twice in a season does a back score from open play.'

Full-backs opposed the most romantic and perverse of positions. 'Extreme wingers' were almost parasitic, dispensable. Like Stan Matthews: one moment he could be a magician, the next he was 'doing nothing for long periods'. Wingers, and especially their dribbling, caused great frustration when things went wrong e.g. Arsenal's decorated war pilot Ian McPherson 'has everything except football sense to hand over the ball at the right time.' Another former pilot was amateur Peter Kippax who became the 'prince in waiting' for England's problem left-wing position. However like all wingers he ran a tightrope of artistry and functionality, in each and every game: 'the crowd rose to the footwork of Kippax, but the most pleasing feature of his artistry was the way in which he middled the ball without undue finesse and time wasting.'

Time wasting: the worst crime. If even legends could irritate, so much more ordinary mortals, like Grimsby's George Wardle, another candidate as England's outside-left. The local paper gave special attention to his partner's movements: 'he ran into all sorts of positions, backwards and forwards, to position himself for the return pass but all in vain. It must have been an unpleasant experience for any inside-forward to partner a brilliantly clever ball artiste like Wardle ... This hanging on to the ball by the wing men is fatal, and the sooner more direct attacking methods *à la* Finney are employed the better. Wingers ... who run straight across the field with the ball and leave the other forwards standing like clothes props wondering what is going to happen next, will never maintain a club's position in the First Division.'

Time wasting did not apply to football's most physical duel. The centre-half was a 'Frankenstein' created by the monstrous 1925 offside law, with one mission: 'I couldn't play, but I could stop those that could' (Korr, 1986, p.154). His direct opponent bore an 'onerous duty that rarely appeals to the average player'. The centre-forward symbolised his side's potency, and was therefore most vulnerable to be blamed and barracked. He was 'as closely marked as Herman Goering by his guards' (ironically a week later, on the eve of his execution, Goering eluded surveillance long enough to commit suicide) and ended matches looking like the victim of a street corner brawl. 'At Harringay, for a tenth of the punishment, he could have picked up quite a wage packet.'

Retaliation was inevitable, but irrelevant. Centre-forwards were advised to 'wander more' instead of 'battering and bruising against a long succession of centre-halves'. A centre-forward had to suffer, and foster a 'never-say-die' attitude: 'however hopeless the task may seem to be he must constantly be searching for fresh methods to outwit this "policeman".' Good centre-forwards were as 'scarce as goods off the ration, but they're not kept under the counter'. Many were small: the League's leading scorer would be Doncaster's Clarrie Jordan, only 5' 8". Twenty-six-year-old George Lowrie (Wales, Army and Coventry) weighed only 9st 6lbs. He scored four goals in his first match, five for the Army against an FA XI that included Stan Matthews, and a hat-trick for Southern against Northern Command. He started 1947 with hat-tricks in successive matches, and altogether scored three or four goals seven times – and still he was barracked and dropped! Aggression was everything: 'a real and complete footballer' who was 'too lady-like', would be replaced by the 'biff 'em, bang 'em' school.

Whatever a team's prospects, there was high demand. Season tickets were quickly gone, partly because bomb damage had often reduced seating capacity. Clubs were still repairing war damage with the first League match imminent. Plymouth, the worst-affected, had obsolete railway coaches as dressing-rooms, tramcars for grandstands and a bus to fulfil the FA regulation that a separate seating area had to be provided for visiting directors. In the blitzed docklands Millwall's 'main stand has given way to a steep, muddy slope', and West Ham lacked a grandstand roof. During 1945-46, West Ham called the match against Arsenal, then unable to use Highbury, Roofless v Homeless.

The increased concern for safety, in the wake of the Bolton Disaster, also created an immense task. Bradford City worked frantically to replace crash barriers declared unsafe only nine days before opening day, and Hull supporters helped build Boothferry Park with picks and shovels, using debris from the bombed city, until the eve of the season: 'long after 8 o'clock last night the erection of turnstiles and barriers was still proceeding; even when darkness had set in, an army of phantom-like figures kept on working in a race against time.' Nor was it just scarce workmen, or devoted supporters bending their backs. Players too were 'volunteered to work a couple of hours every afternoon. They will start next week with the job of laying sleepers and getting the covered popular side in shape.' Manchester United were the only homeless club left. They and Manchester City shared Maine Road, where over two million spectators would watch matches in 1946-47.

Maine Road was also the pre-season venue for the last 'wartime' international, England versus Scotland. The gate allowed the FA to contribute over a quarter of the Fund for victims of the Bolton Disaster. Attendance was limited symbolically to 70,000, well under the ground record. Stan Matthews gave the first demonstration that he was still Britain's premier footballer – a 'complete personal triumph' for the old maestro, his ball control 'a conjuring trick': 'a master of artifice and strategy with the soft turf ideally suiting him when others were slipping and floundering on it. His dribbling and finesse … a joy to watch.' The Scots saw him as a cross between the Sorcerer's Apprentice and the Emperor's New Clothes: 'Matthews played like a man possessed, which I honestly believe to be the case … under the spell of his own genius, ball and player an affinity … Then we saw that Matthews was practically the England team.'

It had been a wet August almost everywhere as clubs completed their preparations through the tradition of public trials. Players were still returning: Eddie Shimwell, successor to Joe Carr, football's first war death, was demobbed Friday, got back to his family's home in the early hours of Saturday morning, and played in Sheffield United's trial that afternoon – he was England's reserve within the month. Huddersfield organised four teams in two practice matches on the same afternoon: one player played in both. Among Exeter's keen hopefuls was a goalscorer called Mustard.

There was due deference to the traditional rhythms of the sporting year – both Burnley and West Brom delayed kick-offs so that spectators could also go to vital local cricket matches. Crowds were extraordinary: Newcastle's Whites versus Stripes attracted 27,783 people. There were also deeper rhythms at play: whilst Port Vale captain Arthur Cooper was playing in their trial, his wife gave birth to their daughter. Sadly a telegram awaited Swansea's Eddie Passmore: he was called home to Durham where his daughter was dying of pneumonia. Passmore, an ex-Coldstream Guard, had joined Swansea after an interesting assignation: 'one dark night as he was about to catch a train, he met manager Green outside a cinema. An umbrella and candle was borrowed and sheltering beneath the umbrella and with the flickering light of the candle to guide him, Passmore signed.'

One thing was for certain. With 'promotion and relegation the guiding stars' the general welcome and optimism of the return of real football would be shortlived, and bread rationing provided a nice image: 'You can bet the wife's surplus BUs [Bread Units] that before the end of the season many a manager's head will be demanded on a salver, and many a board will be told it's time they chucked up football and took to managing boys' marbles teams.'

The first decisions of real football were now imminent: 'all directors and managers have fixed selection meetings for tonight.' Selection was not easy. England's Billy Wright had to play Army cricket rather than for Wolves. Crewe's Chandler was one of many required to work at his factory. That Wednesday the weather worsened further as Britain was swept by a fierce storm. To these Shakespearean omens were added a 'bombshell': the 'storm clouds' of the players' dispute. The first week's matches could be the last: 'will the flying start come to a sudden full stop?'

The Players' Union promised a 'strike before it is time to play next Saturday's matches'.

8

All-Action and No Slow Motion

FIRST SATURDAY: 31 AUGUST 1946
'the players kicked six balls about before the start – austerity was visibly mocked.'

Despite often tempestuous weather, 944,000 people watched 43 Football League matches, welcoming home real football. The exception, Newport's first Second Division game, with thousands queuing outside, was postponed when torrential rain defeated even the Fire Brigade's pumps. In December, when the rains returned with a vengeance, the Brigade were again summoned – and again failed. County feared the football gods were elsewhere this season. They were.

Elsewhere, 'thunder and lightning brought a storm of extraordinary intensity. It developed almost the force of a tornado, with showers of sleet driving across the ground, which was rapidly transformed into a remarkably waterlogged state … a pace that made me wonder how in the world they would be able to keep it up in such heavy going, in which players slipped and floundered all over the place.'

Half the First Division matches attracted over 50,000 spectators: 61,484 saw Chelsea beat Bolton 4-3; Wolves scored six goals in 39 second-half minutes against prewar giants Arsenal; Brentford's 'liberal sprinkling of bald heads' (average age 31) surprised the prewar champions Everton and 55,338 supporters by winning at Goodison Park – war hero George Wilkins opened the scoring. Many thought the surge from 53,000 at Roker Park took Sunderland past Cup-holders Derby, but someone had to take the blame. Disappointment focused on ex-Arsenal winger Wilf Walsh – 'his war experience had apparently spoiled his nerve'. Walsh did not play again.

The other 50,000 crowd saw fancied Aston Villa entertain unfancied Middlesbrough, who proved 'gluttons for the loose ball'. In early skirmishes Boro 'emerged unscathed from a machine-gun-like battering'. This did not deter their inside-left, for whom a real machine gun assault was not a distant memory – Wilf Mannion described his winner two minutes from time with military understatement: 'the ball rebounded off the crossbar. There was such a backspin on the ball that it nearly flew out again. And that if it had happened, might have been awkward.'

Whilst Mannion was golden boy once again, the opposing inside-left became dross. Tommy Dodds was another north-easterner, who joined Aston

Villa in 1938-39, then served in the Fleet Air Arm, before repairing ships in the Royal Naval Dockyard. It was Tom's first and last game for Villa.

Second Division Newcastle also suffered a metaphorical rather than meteorological hurricane at Millwall. The gates were closed on 39,187 at The Den, a 'bomb scarred ground, where the stands are just memories'. The Lions began in rampant fashion, but later, losing 1-4 they showed their teeth, being 'not too particular in their methods'. 51,256 saw Ambrose Mulraney's 30-yard winner for Birmingham at Spurs. Earlier, the former Flight Sergeant had been a fan himself, at Waterloo Station, bidding farewell to the MCC cricketers, including Arsenal's Denis Compton, as they forced their way through crowds to get the boat-train to Southampton and thence to Australia for the Ashes tour. 'I'm only a footballer,' said Ambrose as he sought autographs along with everyone else.

Gates were closed everywhere as the season's themes quickly emerged. The quality may have been doubtful – 'perspiration was more pronounced than inspiration' – but the competitive edge was sharp. Disputing teams swarmed around 'lynx-eyed' referees. Swansea Town's Burns became the first to be sent off as the return of real football gripped players and crowd alike: 'angry players grasped [the referee] by his arms and shoulders and wouldn't allow him to restart the game for a minute … the disapproving crowd whistled and hooted – just like the old days.'

William Furness, veteran of England's 1933 win in Italy, scored for Norwich, and four Football League debutants – including Jesse Pye of Wolves and Barnsley's George Robledo – achieved the first postwar hat-tricks.

FIRST MIDWEEK: 2-6 SEPTEMBER

Continuing floods and gales, 'tropical in intensity,' made the harvest the worst in living memory, and delayed the end of bread rationing. It anticipated how the coming winter would disfigure these virgin days: 'it is a delight to see the new green carpet at Burnden as September dawns, but it is gradually reduced to a black quagmire as the football days pass along. These hours of rain left the pitch today soft and yielding and every tackle and every turn left a scar that will never be wholly repaired. Why oh why could we not have a dry season's opening.'

The oldies started playing again. Arsenal lost in a driving rainstorm, and with nine goals conceded already, thought about playing Bryn Jones on the basis of only two days training. Among the coaches to come out of retirement was Derby's Sammy Crooks, who faced Villa's Eric Houghton: the two had played alongside each other for England fifteen years earlier. Liverpool 'are still wondering how it all came about' that their Welsh international goalkeeper George Poland found himself in Cardiff's team. Liverpool had ended Poland's registration, his career finished by an arm broken whilst guesting for Leeds. He then got a job only two miles from Ninian Park. When Cardiff were looking for a goalkeeper someone remembered George. He was taken on trial, and became permanent when Cardiff directors watched their centre-forward put 'everything he had into shots,' thus proving the resilience of George Poland's arm.

Liverpool started their midweek match 'in whirlwind fashion, flinging the ball from wing to wing in dazzling and spectacular football', but soon become confused: 'five hard-working forwards keeping up a cracking pace in desperation – but all too haphazard and planless to get them anywhere.' Wilf inspired Middlesbrough to another martial victory: 'no commando cut through Volksturm with greater precision or calmer confidence than fair-haired Mannion.' Spectators' anger proved equally potent: 'a hurriedly called meeting of Liverpool fans, who assembled outside the club's offices after the match, apparently with the object of calling upon the directors to make quick team changes.'

Up and coming Tom Finney had made Preston's opening win 'too much a one man show'. Leeds' Jim Milburn was left 'baffled staring leg-locked and deceived by a slow and fascinating dribble reminiscent of Matthews' finesse'. So Sheffield United decided to stop him: eight of their sixteen fouls were on Finney. The Blades were well equipped: 'a hard-bitten, robust team, most of them mighty, big striding fellows quick into action ... bursting with exuberance and steam.' Similarly Stoke's star winger was soon knocked out of their line-up: 'the only blot was the rough and ready tackling of [Stan] Matthews which received scant punishment.'

SECOND SATURDAY: 7 SEPTEMBER
'bring 'em back alive football.'

Critics rushed to judgement: 'reports from grounds far and wide reflect the gruelling nature of this post-war football ... This is cut-for-cut and thrust-for-thrust, battling with a vengeance.' Over one million watched the 44 league games, a frenzied horde who craved footballers to 'sacrifice craft on the altar of speed'. Celtic newcomers provided testimony. Everton's Irishman 'was aghast at the speed of it all', and Grimsby's Scot faced Manchester United and Wolves in his first week: 'It was not quite so strange, but the speed. There's no time to hold the ball and look forward like we do in Scotland.'

Twenty-year-olds like Jimmy McGill underwent steep learning curves: 'I started doing the tricks I was used to in Scotland when I played against Derby County, but I found myself off the pitch and in the cinder track. I soon changed my tactics.'

Chelsea won the first big transfer race, signing the charismatic Scot, Tommy Walker, for the maximum wage plus extras like a house and another job – 'a nice tax-free piece of what they call "security"' – prompting an explosive re-appraisal of player rewards: 'this business may seem all right for the individual's point of view, but it may be decidedly unfair to players who are the newcomer's colleagues.'

Inducements could backfire. Wolves manager Ted Vizard refused a player's request for 'something under the counter' but someone signed him: 'Soon afterwards, the other players were remarking that the new chap had a house full of brand-new furniture. From that discovery sprang a great mushroom of discontent, and the directors knew no peace for months afterwards' (Cullis, 1960, pp.168-70).

Without Tommy Walker, Chelsea were in the dungheap: 0-6 down at Anfield, four back, then a late goal – Liverpool 7, Chelsea 4. The gates were closed on 44,000 – 'at a fever pitch of excitement' – with 8,000 more outside for Middlesbrough's first home game. The match was a personal shootout between two prewar England centre-forwards: Micky Fenton 4, Freddie Steele 3; Boro 5, Stoke 4.

The thirtysomethings of Reading went top of Third Division (South). Days after mauling Crystal Palace 10-2 they put seven goals past Southend. Magnus McPhee had now scored eight of Reading's nineteen goals, and 290 in eight seasons. Their veterans were counterbalanced by Victor Barney, in at inside-left a fortnight after being demobbed and asking for a trial: easy street, pro football!

SECOND MIDWEEK: 9-13 SEPTEMBER

Having lost his first three matches, Huddersfield manager David Steele contemplated the nature of current transfer work: 'It is not only the fees asked these days, but housing, travelling, and family affairs.'

After being outbid for the star Tommy Walker, Steele struck it lucky with a member of the supporting cast and signed Harry McShane (his son Ian played for Manchester Boys, but found lasting fame as an actor, notably as the rapscallion antique dealer 'Lovejoy'). Harry had graduated from that prolific breeding ground for footballers, the Lanarkshire mining villages around Bellshill – in company with Busby, Shankly *et al* – and played in Walker's Circus in India during the war. Now, his 'pile-driving left boot' helped Huddersfield win 5-2.

Shaky Everton dropped Wally Fielding, England's inside-forward only a fortnight earlier, and recalled their own veteran circus performer to beat Arsenal 3-2. The 5ft 4in Irishman Alec 'Mickie Mouse' Stevenson, the last survivor from Dixie Dean's forward line, showed 'a magic combination of practical go-ahead stuff with box-office tricks to set the crowd laughing and the opposition running the wrong way.'

There were as many tricks behind the scenes. Derailed goods wagons delayed Arsenal's arrival at Goodison Park by three hours: then Joe Mercer pointed to his deformed knee and said Arsenal were facing ten men. Tom 'The Healer' Whittaker was undeterred: Mercer transferred to Arsenal ten weeks later. Liverpool chairman Bill McConnell was also there, unable to get to Maine Road where '41,657 operatives called in on the way home' to see Manchester United win 5-0 with 'absurd ease'. McConnell heard that Newcastle centre-forward Albert Stubbins was available for transfer. So, stealing a march on Everton, he drove through the night 'to find the stranger who will be so welcome'.

Inevitably, 'the quicktackling careless bustlers' brought consequences – 'now the proof comes in: injuries and still more injuries'. With fifteen of his 29 professionals unfit, 'at 12.30 manager John Duncan of Leicester phoned for a taxi, put on his hat and hurried to a local building site. Three of his young forwards, Anderson, Revie and Dawson, were working there as bricklayers. Duncan arranged for them to work through their lunch hour so they could play that evening.'

This is the Don Revie who managed Leeds and England, and whose character default was regarded as a preoccupation with material security. Labouring had built the 18-year-old up onto the threshold of great things: certain to play for England. A year later Don's broken ankle would give him a one in a thousand chance of playing again.

THIRD SATURDAY: 14 SEPTEMBER

65,112 saw Manchester United defeat Middlesbrough in the clash of perfect records. Matt Busby, 'hiding behind a door to escape youthful autograph hunters after the game,' thought United had passed their sternest test by shackling Mannion: 'if Cockburn isn't picked for England before the season is out, I will eat a size nine hat!'

Foolhardiness at Wolverhampton: Brentford centre-forward Fred Durrant was 'knocked sensible' by a collision with England goalkeeper Bert Williams and spent over half an hour unconscious. Still dazed and dizzy, he returned and within minutes blocked an attempted clearance to equalise. Wolves told the referee that Durrant didn't know where he was but he knew enough to head the winner – and didn't remember a thing about it afterwards. Durrant had defied 'strict orders not to head – this might have been the first posthumous goal on record'.

Crewe's goalkeeper demonstrated similar heroics: knocked out, recovered, 'then literally collapsed. He was put on a stretcher … Amazingly, Mawson scrambled from the stretcher and resumed his place, though he was obviously "all in" for a time.' Meanwhile centre-forward, miner and pigeon fancier Clarrie Jordan spotted similar inattention: 'The County goalkeeper, apparently assuming that the referee had penalised a Doncaster player in the Stockport goalmouth, placed the ball for a free kick and was running back to take a kick when quick-witted Jordan realised the ref's whistle hadn't been heard. He dashed up and kicked the stationary ball into the net, amid much protest.'

THIRD MIDWEEK: 16-20 SEPTEMBER

'Shortage of houses held up four big transfers this week.'

'Will let to footballer: modern house, semi or det. Blt. 1946 … two minutes from football ground, bus and station.' 'Is soccer coming to this? "Yes, sir, from the biggest clubs to the smallest, there is just as big a house-hunting scramble as there is for players. Clubs see a good idea to make players happy, get rid of surplus profits, increase their own assets and pay less in super tax." Not bad.'

Arthur Ellis took his wife to watch him referee Sheffield Wednesday's Monday match. Already, without floodlights, half-time intervals were being abandoned. Kathleen Ellis judged Arthur's performance: 'not so bad, but I couldn't see you in the gloom. I'll have to do something to make you stand out and look smarter.' Her efforts were commended in Arthur's next match: 'at the bottom of his dyed RAF battledress he wore white cuffs' (Ellis, 1954, pp.50-51).

These little fashion touches continued to take the eye. Later George Appleyard refereed at Liverpool in conspicuous style: 'wearing black pit stockings covering the knees, long black shorts, a black blouse trimmed with a yellow collar and fancy frills on the sleeves.'

Footballers' domestic lives were now centre stage. Stoke City had only one point and approached Saturday's game with an air of crisis: 'Stoke stakes its future largely on what happens in the next few days.' Captain Jock Kirton lost patience after living, with two children, with his wife's parents for nine months. He gave City an ultimatum: find me a house or I quit. Initially Kirton was told to take his chances on the council housing list, along with many others, but soon local commerce and municipal interest were fighting over the credit: 'one of several houses being built by private builders ... who is a supporter, telephoned Mr McGrory [Stoke's manager] with an offer of one of them for Kirton and his wife and family.' 'Even the Lord Mayor of Stoke has given personal attention to the ultimatum ... Kirton is now happy.'

Meanwhile the official negotiations made little progress. The anticipated strike had been stopped under the War-time Emergency Powers Act. Neither side was happy. The union's Jimmy Fay was frustrated that his executive's meeting 'will not now be as exciting as it might have been', whereas League President Will Cuff 'could not see any reason why the clubs should be called together to consider the same requests'. The union took the next step under the procedures of applying for compulsory arbitration. Then, after 21 days, they were free to strike.

Bryn Jones's return saw Arsenal win in the wet at Blackburn. Sadly *Anno Domini* had caught up with Arsenal's ageing stars, especially record goalscorer Cliff Bastin. It was 'a sorry exhibition by both clubs. There was hardly a moment's football throughout the whole game.' Mr Chad, the wartime symbol of grumbling, put in an appearance: 'What! No Football! ... there was too much pulling and pushing, and the crowd of 27,000 was practically cheerless ... I frankly don't know what to state.'

The wettest September since 1918 halted Manchester United's perfect start. Initially all of Manchester had wanted to see the leaders take on Chelsea's Tommies, Lawton and Walker. But Lawton was unfit and heavy rain kept the midweek attendance down. United's captain and goalkeeper both slipped in the mud, and Lawton's replacement walked the equaliser into an empty net.

'Attendances are a cause of amazement.'

Football's boom was not elitist: 388,000 watched the First Division; over 350,000 attended the Second Division games. Stan Matthews returned, briefly, as Stoke beat the leaders: 'roars of laughter from the crowd as Manchester United's McGlen trailed Matthews like a big game hunter stalking a gazelle – and about as successfully.' But the 'vigorous tackles must have told their tale' because Stan limped out of next week's internationals and, soon, into unwanted controversy.

Wolves reached a turning point. Without Billy Wright, confined to army duties, they hit the woodwork three times, made three mistakes, and lost 0-3 to Villa. Wolves manager Ted Vizard had a reputation for tact and stoicism – he 'can be even nicer than a shop assistant shaking her head to nylon seekers' – but he was losing faith: 'I thought I had a world-beating side. Apparently I don't.' Whilst Ted joined the other managers seeking new players in Scotland, Wolves won at injury-hit Blackburn – for the first time since 1897 – to start their rise to the top.

Arsenal were haunted: 'only ghosts walk' at Highbury. Bryn Jones cannot add substance to these 'shadows of pre-war greatness'. The 'careless rapture' of Derby County, with the 'waltzing duets' of ace survivors Doherty and Carter, only intensified the sense of loss. Derby's attack was almost obsolescence incarnate: Sammy Crooks, 38; Raich Carter, 33; Frank Broome, 33; Peter Doherty, 32; and Dally Duncan, 36. Middlesbrough's new star Harry Bell was the latest youngster to be 'called up'.

In the Second Division, unbeaten Bradford's internationals Jack Gibbons and Len Shackleton were combining to devastating effect. But they devastated themselves at Manchester City. Losing 2-3, having already lost their blinded captain, Bradford's stars lost their cool when last season's Cup final referee objected to Jack's protests: '"Come here Gibbons." I whispered to Jackie, "He cannot force you to go to him. I know the law backwards, and he won't be able to do a thing if you stay put." Jackie did not move.' After a third unsuccessful come hither, an imperious gesture sent Jack off: 'he passed me and I told him, "He can't do that, Jackie." He looked up and, like a teacher addressing an immature pupil, informed me, "He's done it, Len"' (Shackleton, 1955, p.152). A fascinating struggle became a long drawn out farce as nine men Bradford lost 2-7. At his hearing Gibbons denied hearing the requests and escaped with a reprimand.

Rotherham United protested against their first Third Division defeat so strongly that the referee demanded the name of young Scottish miner Stewart McLean, later to gain a master's degree in management studies. The dense Scots reply was indecipherable, but railway fireman Walter Ardron persuaded the official not to go further: 'The fellow's a stranger to me, we picked him up on the journey here – he only speaks the Gaelic so it will be more trouble than its worth to send him off' (Watson, 1986, p.16).

In the South, Cardiff also reached a turning point. 'Nothing appears to go right for City these days:' until they got a strange winning goal against Aldershot. The referee agreed that City's Roy Clarke handled during the scoring move, but played on as he 'had been fouled previously'. This hand of God fortified Cardiff as they beat promotion-chasing Swindon 5-0. Swindon finished with only eight men: a 'groggy leg', a fractured ankle, and an 'accidental kick on the jaw'. Cardiff went undefeated, just two draws in 21 league games, for six months, and built a lead of ten points.

Week after week teams were reduced to ten, nine, even eight fit men, but the idea of substitutes hardly got a mention. Their rejection for 1946-47 was part of the return to tradition. Whilst a necessary evil in ersatz wartime football, substitutes were inconceivable in the real thing, un-British, and reflected Europe's rationalist threat to football's true values. They offended ideas of abstract equality in the face of fortune. When influential FA members floated the idea of substitutes up to the 40th minute in home internationals, the Welsh FA cited the nightmare of a fresh Stan Matthews coming on for Tom Finney. This epitomised the desire to limit the advantages of big countries, with more players to call upon, just as the League embodied a formal equality between Chelsea and Chester. In each case the vagaries which could, over 90 minutes, assail eleven men starting against eleven were thought an essential part of the sport of football as opposed to ideas of technical rationality. The number of 1946-47 teams that finished with fewer than eleven players approximates to those of today, but for different reasons. In 1946 a dominant idea was luck, and coping with injuries was one aspect. Today a dominant idea is the technical offence that requires mandatory punishment – 'the referee had no choice but to send him off.' The result is the same: unequal contests.

FOURTH MIDWEEK: 23-27 SEPTEMBER

The gates were closed for the third successive match as Blackpool won 4-3 and led the First Division. Their star Jimmy Blair demonstrated 'the genius which sends opponents running the wrong way with a turn of his hips ... he made the master moves.' But Blackpool had now lost their earlier 'beautiful pattern weaving' and were battling the passions of their watchers: 'if only the crowd will be content to watch good football instead of yelling ... heard all too frequently last night, but fortunately, Buchan, Blair and Johnston went on playing their own game and not the game of the barrackers.'

The football was a consequence of this symbiosis. Critical and intimidating supporters encouraged a 'craze for pace and fierce tackling', and afterwards they left grounds 'grumbling about poor football with the severity peculiar to football crowds'. A week later, and widespread discontent was palpable: 'a remarkable state of tension exists. Spectators in many centres are severely critical.'

Clubs were driven to extremes, to picking players so out of position it was like 'Mae West playing Lady Macbeth'. Before long Blackpool experimented with Jimmy Blair at outside-left. Blair protested, and only lined up there for the kick-off. 'Where's our outside-left' fans moaned. The reporter was unsympathetic – after all, the crowd had barracked the previous incumbent out of a table-topping team.

But how long would the 'blind man's bluff' football attract Joe Public? 'What measure of satisfaction he can obtain from such rough-and-tumble scrambles is entirely beyond my comprehension.' The beautiful game was being jeopardised: 'a generation of football followers have grown up who have never seen football played on the ground ... known no other than the high-speed, kick-and-rush game.' The future was threatened: 'by far the most serious aspect ... the stars of tomorrow are getting their baptism in this atmosphere ... The art of midfield foraging, the finding of empty spaces between defences with accurate ground passes ... are becoming things of the past.'

FIFTH SATURDAY: 28 SEPTEMBER
In Ireland
Ireland bestowed its bountiful hospitality as England took 45 to Ireland for the first postwar full internationals with (Northern) Ireland and Eire, but only fourteen were players, and no trainer. The FA might have returned to tradition by overloading the dignitaries but austerity required compromises elsewhere: 'owing to the shortage of materials, it is unlikely that the players will receive their caps this year. As for the practice of allowing players to keep their England shirts, this is out of the question.'

The team borrowed an Irish trainer, paddled in the Irish Sea, and had a motor coach trip along the coast before their tactical conference. They practised positional switches on the hotel tennis court: when the ball went into the sea, onlookers returned it.

Both Irish crowds were beyond control. In Belfast 60,000 surged, eight deep, on to the cinder track. After delay, anticlimax: England won 7-2. In Dublin the Irish responded to the enthusiasm of the sardine-tight crowd of 31,988 in Dalymount Park – one man died in the excitement – and ran the English off their feet. Full-back Gorman typified the difference. He was picked for both 'Irelands': in Belfast he had given winger Bobby Langton 'at least three yards' to control the ball: now he was 'standing on his toes'. 'Will-o'-the-wisp' Alec Stevenson was simply unbeatable. Frank Swift – who had survived 'bull-like scrupulously fair onrushes' in Belfast – remembered the contrast between the prewar veteran and the wartime discoveries: 'electric, quick moving Stevenson, darting and probing in his prancing, almost dainty fashion, and the big, blundering, enthusiastic, spare-nothing Arsenal's Dr Kevin O'Flanagan ... Every second I expected to be knocked into the back of the net' (Swift, 1948, p.112).

Michael O'Flanagan, a bar owner who had entertained English journalists until the early hours, took a twenty-yard run at a mighty free-kick. Swift did not move a muscle as it fizzed past a post: 'the two O'Flanagans chased every loose ball or big kick with a wild enthusiasm which matched the frenzy of the crowd.' Only once did the 'far too fancy' English escape the relentless tackling, and then Mannion and Lawton set up Tom Finney's winner. The sudden silence was one of the season's enduring memories.

The English stars were stunned by the available luxury, by 'the difference between austerity Britain and glorious Dublin': an eight-course Sunday lunch was outshone by a post-match bouquet of overwhelming hospitality. Sated by victories and food, they went home overloaded with goodies: 'We all managed to get a little something to bring back to our families in "starving England".' (Swift, 1948, p.112). Reserve Don Welsh was doubly blessed: first by collecting his £40 fee without playing in either match and then for collecting his 'little something': 'an 18lbs ham, for which he has a weakness.'

In England
'the Rams were like a watch with the jewels extracted. They ticked over but were off balance ... and ran down in the last minute when Blackpool scored the winning goal.'

International absentees formed the context for Saturday's full League programme. Clubs like Derby lost Doherty and Carter, and thus to unaffected leaders Blackpool. So over a million people watched a devalued product: 'absence makes the art diminish'. Poetic Lancastrians likened Preston North End v Stoke City (minus injured Stan Matthews and England's Finney) to Hamlet without the Prince and Polonius. Over 62,000 turned up at Maine Road to see Arsenal's first visit to Manchester United for eight years. Centre-forward Reg Lewis, dropped by England after the August international, kept up his goal a game record for the struggling Londoners, but United, despite Henry Cockburn's international debut, won 5-2 and stayed second. Middlesbrough were the early contenders who suffered most, losing England captain George Hardwick and Wilf Mannion. Ironically in Mannion's absence his England predecessor, Sheffield United's Jimmy Hagan, ran Middlesbrough ragged.

Third Division teams changed restlessly: work demands and injuries hindered consistency, but still crowds demanded success. The comebacks of pre-war internationals, Eric Keen at ambitious Hull and Jim Cunliffe at struggling Rochdale, failed and it was back to the mines. City signed Clifton Chadwick – during the war he had dropped saboteurs into enemy territory – but Rochdale's new hero was a 'stroke of genius'. Tom Barkas, awarded the British Empire Medal at the siege of Malta, moved when Halifax decided upon a wholly part-time staff, and became Rochdale's captain, brains, and twenty-goal scorer. He began by lifting a different siege: Rochdale's 6-0 win left at the bottom ambitious Hull City and the manager with the highest salary in football.

FIFTH MIDWEEK: 30 SEPTEMBER – 4 OCTOBER
Arsenal, getting deep in trouble, were desperate – 'we have just got to get new players'. Manager George Allison went north to watch a reportedly clever

Scot, and found cleverness sadly lacking: 'he has found out that it doesn't pay him to try his clever stuff anymore. Opponents won't let him and referees allowed them to do things to him until he gave up.'

The Gunners turned to George Paterson, a prewar international and Scotland's selection in the 1946 Victory International. Holder of a MA from Glasgow University, Paterson now worked in London with a film company. If this career revealed George's softer side, football expressed his toughness. Paterson's parting shot from Glasgow was to provoke a Celtic-Rangers riot. Similarly, when Henry Cockburn – picked for England after only six matches – reminisced on his unsuccessful debut for Manchester United, he remembered George: 'I like to forget that game. I was immediately dropped. I was up against Paterson ... he taught me a lot of things.'

Paterson's three-month Scottish ban gave London clubs time to manoeuvre. He was in the directors' box for Arsenal's prestigious Wednesday afternoon match with Sparta Prague, assuring everyone he would join. However Celtic had other ideas: they had less need of Arsenal's cash than they did for Brentford's classy McAloon, who abandoned eighteen months of searching for a London house to return to his wife and child in Glasgow. But why should George reject Arsenal? Somehow 'Celtic persuaded him to go to Brentford'.

Real football, English-style, was shocking. Thrilling, yes, but there was something missing, something worrying ... good football. Then along came players to show how football could be played. Continentals. The best of these were Sweden's Norrkopping, a 'brilliant ball team ... it goes ding-dong along the carpet from man to man as it should be played'. They gave Cup finalists Charlton a lesson in ball control; northern champions Sheffield United 'did not begin to grasp what was being done to them with the greatest of ease until they were three goals down'; and 47,126 saw them beat Newcastle, England's best supported club, in 'the best game for thirty years'. Whilst Norrkopping won at a canter, Sparta Prague's positional play baffled southern champions Birmingham. These tourists inspired a new vision: an 'all European League'. How poignant that the clairvoyant was Frank Swift, killed in one of those moments – the 1958 Munich air crash – which established that venture in the public imagination.

There were more immediate lessons for complacent Britain: 'If the success of these continental sides serves only to demonstrate that craft will nearly always beat speed and brawn their visits will have been well worthwhile.'

These European visitors provided even more of an eye opener than Moscow Dynamos' victories against scratch sides. Now, English competitiveness, the 'scramble for points' and 'fetish for speed', was blamed for the loss of football arts: 'thanks and congratulations are due to these slick-moving Swedes. The blinkers are off. They have shown us the kind of football we enjoyed before promotion and relegation hopes and fears were assessed out of all proportion in terms of l.s.d. ... Yes and may we all soon enjoy the steaks and wholesome food without which our Swedish visitors could never find the stamina to keep going at the pace they do for ninety minutes.'

Nor was Sweden's neutrality forgotten: 'these fellows were playing football when ours were winning the war – they've eaten well and kept in trim. Why shouldn't they be playing well?'

SIXTH SATURDAY: 5 OCTOBER
'Soccer may stop in ten days.'

Another million-plus attendance. 55,000 saw Len Shackleton score six goals on his debut. Newcastle 13, Newport 0: a record for the top divisions. Nevertheless, some folk are never satisfied: 'a 13-0 victory ... does not lend itself to measured words of sober criticism. But ...'

Len's transfer provoked heart-searching on the effects of crowd criticism. Newcastle had started poorly, were 'disjointed, dejected and indecisive', but 'irony and barracking never help a team having a bad time'. Ironically Len Shackleton blamed Park Avenue hostility for wanting away. As fans complained about Bradford's subsequent drift down the table, the directors had their reply ready: 'Who used to shout "Give it to Shack" and later barracked him off the park? Who but the supporters who are now squealing.'

Youngsters were not exempt. Future international Eddie Baily was jeered on his sole appearance for Spurs, and when another debutant had the courage to hold the ball to assess best advantage: 'the entire unthinking mob roared at him in unison until finally he "got it away".'

As with so much else, Tommy Lawton was the players' spokesman: 'that such a great player should be driven away speaks volumes for the lack of appreciation of skilful play ... How does a player feel in such circumstances. Pretty rough I can tell you ... if they don't appear to be going wrong to him and he gets the hammer just the same that makes the position even more annoying.'

Otherwise it was a day for centre-forwards. There were bright young things like Bolton's Nat Lofthouse and Blackpool's Stan Mortensen: 'what a player Mortensen is. When on the move he seems to flash like an electric spark.' The jury was still out on Villa's George Edwards (over 40 goals in 1945-46 and chosen in September's international trial). This Saturday he scored a winner but mostly he was an enigma. 'He can look as good as Lofthouse – which is very good – or as cumbersome as a sailor enjoying a kickabout on his first day of shore leave.'

But the oldies were not finished. Freddie Steele's Stoke hat-trick meant fourteen goals in only ten games, the League's leading goalscorer. He might even challenge for the job he had almost ten years previously, as England's teenage leader, until cruel injury provided Lawton with his chance. The centre-forwards for other form teams also contributed: Albert Stubbins, in Liverpool's 6-1 rout at Grimsby; Dennis Westcott of Wolves, and Micky Fenton's 'goal in a thousand'. But Tom Lawton remained unsurpassed and his goal at Middlesbrough set up a close finish in a switchback game: 'Boro's first half display was one of the most exhilarating in club history [but] it was a relief when the final whistle sounded.' Wilf Mannion, scoring twice, gave his attack 'sustenance … there was no rationing'. Mannion produced a wonderful display of consummate ease, deadly marksmanship, and 'masterly skill which makes him stand out head and shoulders'. Chelsea pulled back to 2-3: then Mannion was fouled in the area. Chelsea captain John Harris upped the stakes to stop England captain George Hardwick making the game safe: 'Lay you five to four you don't score, George.' He put on the sort of smile which said 'I can't help it if a mug is born every minute', and replied 'You're on.' In due course I collected my four bob, because George, for the first time in his top-class career, failed to bang the ball home.'

The crowds flocked to the Third Division. Swindon broke their ground record in successive home matches, and Northern leaders Doncaster broke records on four away grounds. Bottom club Hull took more money from their first four home games than a season's receipts a decade earlier. Crowd anger remained combustible, although sometimes slow to burn. Tranmere's fans watched a Hull centre-forward's hat-trick in 'icy silence … but at the close some of the crowd surged on to the field, and the police intervened by providing an escort for the referee.' Clubs tried to dissipate the anger by establishing a dialogue. Crystal Palace invited supporters to guess the team – the lucky winners had tea with the players. Reading used improved loudspeaker technology. Despite starting with a 10-2 win, going top, and still undefeated at home, the team were soon intimidated by their own fans: 'before his team suffered their first home defeat, Reading manager Joe Edelston broadcast to the crowd appealing for less criticism.'

Struggling Leeds introduced a new format into their match programmes, with a montage of action photos on the front cover. They broadcast an invitation to suggest future inclusions, and a wag in the crowd called back: 'Get some new names on't middle page.'

SIXTH MIDWEEK: 7-11 OCTOBER
'Soccer's craziest, biggest-ever boom. Yet while everyone clamours for more money, the standard of play everywhere has reached a new low.'

In the last early season midweek match, Middlesbrough and Liverpool drew 2-2 – a game 'the football man and his wife were at'. Chelsea manager Billy Birrell wanted to buy Mannion, whilst Liverpool's record buy Albert Stubbins had already pulled in half his £13,000 fee from extra receipts. There was considerable absenteeism in local industry as the queues started at midday and the stands were full an hour later. The huge 40,000 crowd was unprecedented for a midweek, working afternoon, and set Boro's secretary thinking ahead to the real crowd pulling matches: 'What it will be like for a cup-tie, goodness only knows.' He was destined to find out, twice, in March 1947, when disaster came mighty close.

Shortening daylight now prevented later starts and at last there was a breathing space. The seaside was a good place away from the smoky cities.

Struggling Bolton escaped to Morecambe: they denied rumours that Willie Moir – future First Division top scorer, Scottish international and 1953 Cup final captain – was dropped because of victimisation: 'Moir is so unwell that we tried giving him a run in the second team, but he has not yet recovered.' Moir's problems were not physical, he needed cheering up: 'we don't want them depressed because they have lost a few matches … we would have liked to take more players, but there are still restrictions by the seaside.'

Everyone knew the Wanderers were in town and Morecambe treated them regally, which was much appreciated: 'we've got the bloomin' freedom of the city.' Bolton left Willie Moir to continue the cure.

SEVENTH SATURDAY: 12 OCTOBER

'Will tomorrow be the last of professional football for a time?'
'It looks as if we shall have to strike.'
'The general unrest caused by the war, the increased cost of living and the housing shortage have all accentuated the men's grievances on the wages question and they feel that the time has come to put their powers to the test.'

Relations between the former Allies were deteriorating and in March 1946 Winston Churchill had coined a famous phrase, an early harbinger of the Cold War. Football journalists incorporated their awareness of current events, albeit by use of mixed metaphors. Thus the first defeat of the Second Division leaders was heralded: 'the gold medallist in this smashing of Barnsley's unbeaten record was Ditchburn, whose "iron curtain" was impenetrable.'

'By gum, we're licked all reight,' said Accrington Stanley, beaten 0-5 by all-conquering Doncaster Rovers. Miner-pigeon fancier Clarrie Jordan scored his third and fourth hat-tricks in successive four-goal wins.

427,316 people watched the eleven First Division matches. Bolton crowned their week's seaside recuperation by leading a 'nonstop pulsating struggle' until the last minute. Then Boro's attack, 'laden with dynamite … concise, grandly initiated attacking movements,' equalised.

The gates were closed on 36,000 for leaders Blackpool at Preston: 'football is at its highest peak of interest.' The match was no soccer spectacle for the 'extra-noisy crowd, big kicking, elbowing, pushing'. Harassed by their own fans to abandon their patient passing game, Blackpool had now developed the reputation for 'boot-it-and-hope-for-the-best'. But 'astute, baffling' Jim Blair – 'one of the most confident of footballers' – was still a star. The result hinged on 'the save of his life' by goalkeeper Fairbrother, from Blair's flying header. Preston then went down the other end and scored a decisive goal: 'of such is the luck … a fine dividing line.' 'The second half passed in a flurry of arms, kicks and injuries … The crowd loved it all and shouted with unabashed vigour … they even drowned the Preston North End players, who are surely the most vocal of all teams.' Just as surely this referred to the notoriously garrulous Bill Shankly, in the thick of the action: 'aggressive, strong and occasionally a little wild, with excitement getting the better of him.'

First Division top six: Blackpool 16 points; Manchester United 15; Sunderland 14; Wolves, Stoke and Liverpool 13.

The biggest crowd, 68,189, saw the season's best team performance. Lawton's two goals put Chelsea 2-1 up, but Stoke came back to win 5-2. Neil Franklin remembered: 'we went to Stamford Bridge and completely thrashed Chelsea and our star performer was George Mountford.' Stoke's run of six successive wins was remarkable for being achieved largely without the injured Stan Matthews. His teammate Mountford cut a typical figure in the 1946 landscape: he 'covers miles of ground, looking tireless as a steam engine, a tribute to his evening's training after a day's work at the colliery.' The London press corps called forth other industrial images: 'this scintillating side of eight locally produced players provided a Wedgwood pattern of football which made the home side look like a piece of clumsily produced utility china.'

Stoke wingers hit 'genius' form in sharing the goals. But Stoke already had an international genius, Stan Matthews, and he now declared himself fit. The Sunday debate was whether manager Bob McGrory would change his winning team and bring back the game's greatest player. In one context it all felt academic, because there might not be a game then, or for a while after. Neil Franklin also recalled this other context: 'This game was played under a heavy shadow, because the Players' Union had announced that it would call all its members out on strike the following Thursday ... this time it was serious. The players wanted to share in the post-war boom. They wanted some security for the future ... we were all wondering whether this would be our last game for some time. In case it was like that, we decided to celebrate, and we entertained the crowd to a scorching match' (Franklin, 1956, pp.43-66).

9

Problem of the Homeless Footballer

'If you can find me houses for the players, I can get you the best team in the world.' (Ted Fenton, Manager, non-league Colchester United)

Bill Whitaker was an England prospect. He was also one of Chesterfield's five Bevin Boy miners. When they played at Plymouth in September 1946, a 585-mile round trip began 9.15 Tuesday morning, halted overnight eleven hours later at Exeter, on to Plymouth, and the same back home. Whitaker contemplated three days lost earnings, and asked for recompense. No. Whitaker asked for a transfer. No.

In public, the return of real football had brightened the grey days of rationing: the goals, tackles, controversies and disputes; the hungry, angry crowds. Football's story was told in amazed tones by newspapers expanding as the wartime restrictions on newsprint eased. Local weeklies, national dailies, evening papers, Saturday specials. A frantic coverage even outstripped the other focus of mass interest, American cinema. In some eyes they became confused. The *Liverpool Post* described the 'all week' coverage as 'football going Hollywood'. Its rival, the *Echo*, essayed the crazy excesses and retorted not Hollywood, but follywood. Like Judy Garland in Tinseltown, Liverpool's Albert Stubbins 'has to be smuggled away from the dressing room to avoid the mobs of teenage youngsters'.

In private, footballers shared these grey days. Millions paid to see them play, but as men they struggled with their other work, without adequate housing or enough food. These struggles were written about because they were special people, but what we read are mundane stories. When they changed jobs there was, officially, nothing in it for them. And when they called a strike they faced the might of the law. The next three chapters share a common theme: what is the proper social distance between player and supporter. Footballers lived through the contradiction of being public heroes and, sometimes, private paupers. This was at the heart of their postwar distress.

Recent commentators underestimate that disadvantage. Bill Shankly's biographer recognised the profound effect of these postwar years, and its material basis: 'you had to stand on your own two feet ... nobody was going to give you something for nothing' (Kelly, 1996, pp.46-47). Yet he is positively upbeat: 'wages for players were also up, with Shankly, as an established professional, now taking home the princely sum of £10 a week. It was a welcome rise.'

Others noted that the headline wage might be augmented by 'the occasional illicit £25 win-bonus in important matches'. John Moynihan, when fourteen, hero-worshipped England's greatest centre-forward, but his reference to Tommy's wages is off-hand – 'Lawton, of course, was not a handsomely paid star; nobody was in those days,' but he did quite nicely compared to the average player (Moynihan, 1982, p.58). Wilf Mannion remained embittered 50 years on, yet his biographer considered footballers' 'earnings put them among the elite' (Varley, 1997, p.112).

Comparisons were the key to a widespread controversy. The star with the journeyman, film star, or miner? Nowadays, the controversy is denied, or limited to mavericks like Newcastle's Len Shackleton, and the comparison is with real work: 'in 1946 the vassal-footballer seemed a creature of great tradition, and few other than Shackleton thought to question his life. It was, after all, better than working at the coal face.' Further insult: the maximum wage was '£10 a week [soon to rise to £15]' (Hutchinson, 1997, pp.121-29). Soon. It would take another decade – long enough for many careers – of heartfelt struggle.

Players' discontent had deeper roots than inadequate reward or failure to right old wrongs. It took greatest sustenance from the depression of postwar reality and the consequent 'prevailing mood of escapism'. Football captured that mood, partly by providing a fantastical escape – winning the pools. They were enormous, as big as the National Lottery in its first years. When Jimmy Fay and Jimmy Guthrie were pondering a strike, this was foremost in their thoughts: 'Think, no pools! What will the man in the street think?' (Harding, 1991, p.212).

The pools had grown rapidly, from a twenty to a fifty million business between 1935 and 1939, to take a firm hold on British cultural currency. So that even a few days before the war began, a cartoonist could joke Hitler would not do 'owt' [that is, invade Poland] 'till he's checked his coupon'. After the war, eleven million 'investors' changed the British week: 'from bath night, Friday has turned into pools night' (Ledbroke and Turner, 1950, p.75).

But they also symbolised irresponsibility. Everyone talked about winning the pools. It was a sign of desperate times, and a declining moral strength. It negated productivity and the export drive, which was to fuel economic recovery and pay for the social reforms. The pools required labour, and women deserted manufacturing industry in worryingly high numbers. Their detractors never forgot that they were parasitic: if no football, then no pools. Football suffered by the association, yet did not gain. The union was tempted by pools company offers to fund insurance for players forced to retire through injury. But the football authorities would not countenance acceptance, being adamantly opposed to anything connecting football with gambling.

The pools seemed the only way out of 'that weird, harsh period of postwar austerity', although often an escape of limited horizons. A record winner (£40,747 – calculated on the rise of football admission prices it would be £9 million in modern terms) expressed his buying intentions: 'I am going to buy a house and settle down in Grimsby or Cleethorpes. I am a football fan and I think I'll buy Stubbins and Matthews and let them play in my back garden.'

The fantasy that the pools promised was what everyone sought: security. So if pools winners wanted to win footballers, footballers wanted to win the pools. But because of the gambling ban they needed proxies: 'is it any wonder that most players hope that one of the lines sent up in the name of their landlady, wife or sister will come up forty thousand strong one day.'

People also escaped everyday shortages through becoming spectators. Football and cinemas were the most popular attractions and their stars attracted passionate attachment. Autographs were the dominant motif. Championship-challenging Wolves received 200 requests a day and eventually printed copies of the players' autographs on yellow paper to match their gold jerseys. The 1947 Cup campaign escalated interest still further, and a semi-finalist spoke for many professionals: 'we are only working lads,' said one of the team, a little bewildered by the reception they met everywhere. By then their boots needed patching and mending, so club and fans reached an accommodation: the team signed 5,000 requests for autographs, and supporters gave coupons for new boots.

Stars were in constant demand. Raich Carter replied to 300 fan letters a week; Tommy Lawton was a 'knight in demob armour' to urban teenagers. Their need for heroes was deep: 'in that barren age; they were monarchs of the bomb-sites, dauphins of conscripts, sporting saints in a nation pastry-eyed from dried milk. "Tommy, sign my book, please, Tommy – Sign, Mr Lawton – Put your name here, Tom – Score a couple for Uncle Arthur, Tommy".'

John Moynihan remembers a ritual of homage and supplication, 'for schoolboys outside the gates of Stamford Bridge, a god to look up to and beg ... Lawton would come swinging through the entrance, a towering figure ... His lighthouse build was enclosed on colder days in a long overcoat, hanging down near his ankles and done up with a loose, flapping belt ... half a dozen hangers on in slouch hats and untidy pin-stripe suits ... bustled small intruders aside, as if sensing their own fragile position in the hair-creamed wake of the trudging England centre forward ... He could be short with autograph hunters: "I'm in a hurry, son"' (Moynihan, 1982, p.54).

Some railed against 'this growing menace': 'players have to fight their way to their motorcoaches, only to find it already filled with a horde of eager youthful autograph hunters ... Alex Massie [Villa's manager], anxious to meet some relatives who had travelled down from Scotland, thought he had evaded a swarm of youngsters at Arsenal. But a couple followed him, boarded the Underground at Highbury, changed carriages, and triumphantly presented their album for signature.'

The same article painted another picture: footballers' lack of morale causing poor play, appearing before 60,000 'shabbily dressed in ill-fitting shorts'. This contradiction structured their working lives, and their other lives. Footballers were valued public figures, but in real life they sometimes barely got by. The contradiction was captured by a delegate at the union AGM in

August 1946: 'a footballer is a tin god everywhere he goes … he can't be seen standing in the 3d queue for the pictures.'

Footballers shared in the disillusionment. The reward of wartime sacrifice was not a peace of prosperity. The need to escape the postwar depression was behind footballers' preoccupation with security. It was located in the future but rooted in the past. The wholesale sacking in September 1939 had reinforced their vulnerability. Security was what Jimmy Hagan mediated when he 'held out' for a second career. But this was also a message of despair. The footballers of 1946 were daily tantalised by another escape, not the fantasy of the pools or the abstract future of security. Len Shackleton was not alone in seeing madness when he and war hero Doug Wright struggled into Newcastle's ground: 'it's not right, this, you know. There's people queuing up at ten in the morning, and they're paying us a tenner' (Hutchinson, 1997, p.124).

It was obvious: be better rewarded for providing escape for others. The outcome today is a coterie of Premier League players whose lives are far removed from their working class fans and a literature that bemoans the separation between local communities and their heroes. In 1946 footballers had to fight more than the cash-rich clubs. The outcome of their struggle would also be determined by the way they were squeezed: between their image as symbols of the past, Deep England; and the official view that Britain's future would be secured by the unremitting priority of productive industry.

This contradiction, between footballers as public heroes and private paupers, was developed then, as a story of the times. *The People* described the lives of the country's 'poorest paid entertainers' – 'behind the glamour, there is fear and loneliness'. At QPR, 'you can't keep them happy when they are homeless. Seven of my boys are either separated from their wives and families or have no home at all … Ivor Powell, who played for Wales against England the other day … earns the maximum £10 a week (£12 with win bonus) yet … he cannot find a home in London. His wife lives in Blackpool with her parents, whilst Ivor lodges at a restaurant in Shepherds Bush. Of his salary, he has to send about £6 10s home, feed and clothe himself as well as pay tax with the rest, and also spend nearly £3 every other weekend on the rail fare to Blackpool. And … they are expecting a little Ivor soon.'

Almost all QPR's professionals were ex-serviceman, some decorated like Danny Boxshall, Military Medal, and living 'with his wife and child in *one* room in Harrow'. On £7 a week, ex-PoW John Barr supported himself in London digs and a growing family in Scotland: Mrs Barr 'quietly bears her enforced separation … it does not give a player a chance.'

QPR's manager recalled a prewar international trialist, who fought abroad for four years and on return was offered no summer wages. The player held out but with a wife and child to keep, finally accepted £3 a week all the year round and £5 when in the first team: 'to keep his head above water, he works all the week, sweeping out their stand and doing odd jobs and training in the evenings.'

Another homeless family footballer had more leverage. As soon as he threatened a transfer, a QPR supporter 'came along with the offer of a three-bedroomed flat'. But even big stars struggled. Chris Duffy scored *the* goal of 1946 in the FA Cup semi-final, zigzagging past five defenders – just one of ten goals taking Charlton to the final. Previews considered 'get Duffy bottled and the rest is easy'. They did. Chris was eclipsed and Derby won. However just before the match this crucial player was 'forced to send his wife and small son Jack to their former home in Belfast. He travels over to visit ... Charlton can't resolve the problem.'

Duffy had had a rounded British experience: a Scots lad, he served in the Welsh Guards, fought in France, was stationed in Belfast, married an Irish lass, and was discharged suffering from battle exhaustion. His Scottish club sold him for only £325 because they thought he was 'through', and he became an overnight star in England. That summer Charlton recognised that they needed to do something: they spent £9,000 on buying seven houses for married players, and stepped up their campaign for supporters to get digs for single players.

When Crystal Palace could not find lodgings, manager George Irwin 'put up the boys at our place'. His management team, including the Players' Union chairman, co-habited nearby. Trainer Ralph Hann was 'in comfortable lodgings with Jimmy Guthrie, our coach. Once a month, I travel to my home in Derby, but I would much prefer it if my wife were down here. Jimmy is in the same boat: his home is in Scotland.' Halifax manager Jimmy Thomson slept at The Shay 'in a camp bed in a wooden hut, while his family live in Bury.'

The capital posed special difficulties. Brentford's biggest problem 'is getting houses for our players. Captain Tom Manley's wife and family live near Northwich. For the past six years they've hardly seen him because of his Army service. Now he has been demobbed the position is no better, for Tom is in digs down south and can't get a house.'

'If a player moves to London on the same salary as in the provinces he is a certain loser. London's £10 is worth £8, so he must get work.' Players gave up and went home: Ossie Evans, displaced in Fulham's goal, 'hasn't sufficient service to earn maximum salary, and with his family in Wales, £6 a week isn't enough to live on in London.' London clubs sensed the danger, and agreed to transfer players between themselves.

Big club, small club, player, manager, it was the same: 'by the way Ted Fenton, the Secretary-Manager, is living with relatives of his wife at the Railway Tavern at Ardleigh until he can secure permanent accommodation.' Colchester United's Ted linked the club's footballing potential with the national problem all working families faced: 'Mr Fenton has had letters from players whose names are almost household words, who would be pleased to join Colchester if a house could be provided.'

Like John Paton, Glasgow Celtic and RAF. John was a photographer: in fact one week he photographed play from behind the Celtic Park goal, the next week he scored into it. When stationed in Middlesex, John defied Celtic in approaching Colchester. Nothing happened, but then Chelsea paid £6,000 and put Paton straight into their first team. First Division Chelsea, with 60,000-plus attendances, or Colchester, Southern League? It could be a close call.

Not everyone accepted the situation stoically. Richard Morris lasted two months at Watford. After six years in the Army, he returned to his wife and child in Middlesbrough. In desperation Watford bought building plots to house their married players: 'if we don't do something we shan't have a team left soon. The players' wives are getting very restive and keep writing to the men and it upsets them too.'

Some wives went further. After three years of living on 'sand and sultanas' in North Africa, Birmingham's Dave Massart 'decided to listen to wifely persuasion and start in the dog breeding business.' Villa's Frank Moss was another passionate about domesticated animals: he 'bred pigs, reared pigs, sold pigs, talked pigs and dreamed pigs.' Lieutenant Trevor Churchill became the highest-ranking Royal Navy man to turn pro, with Reading, persuaded by his wife on the strength of the house in Maidenhead that went with the £6 wage. Two Bolton Wanderers had businesses with their wives, although another – hairdresser Gwilym Roberts – fell foul of union fraternity. Gwilym cut the hair of five teammates for no payment. The hairdressers' union objected – Bolton players 'at first thought the complaint was a joke' – but union secretary Jimmy Fay ensured the offence was not repeated.

English wages sabotaged overseas recruitment. Clubs could not legally register Europeans as professionals until they had completed a two-year qualification period. But they could revive a prewar fashion for signing South Africans. However the wage regulations imposed another pitfall: a £6 a week ceiling for a first-year professional, insufficient for service veterans with families to support. This restriction did not feature in the union campaign or the eventual settlement, and it served effectively to keep foreign players out. Manchester City spent £250 on flying over Viv Marais and Roy Davies, but after three weeks, and one reserve match, they returned home. They were unlucky to arrive in the great freeze-up, but the conditions of employment proved more decisive. City had promised to find them civilian posts and summer jobs as cricket pros, in addition to £6 as footballers. It was not enough. They had already left jobs paying £10 a week. Marais explained: 'I married last November and have my wife in South Africa to think about. I expected to keep myself on football alone, and study in my spare time to complete my training as an engineering draughtsman. It is impossible to remain here.'

Middlesbrough's George Hardwick was ambivalent about asserting his housing needs. In April Hardwick had no home of his own. As he had risen to stardom guesting for Chelsea, he was asked about the prospects of moving to London: 'Yes, and what about a house.' By September Hardwick had to bring his two-year-old Michael to training. England's football captain emphasised: 'I want a home.' By now Chelsea was known for finding houses. But

Hardwick hesitated, as 'he hopes to follow [his outside football] career in Middlesbrough.'

When not travelling over a thousand miles a week seeking players, Southampton manager Bill Dodgin searched ceaselessly for accommodation for 'the lads'. His reward was no vote of confidence: 'I've got to get out of my home, but where I shall go, I just do not know.' Yet when a club director – also Mayor of Southampton – had houses for rent he preferred married players like Jack Bradley. Jack had been tempted by the summer's protest movement, squatting, which involved taking along some article of household possession, usually on a pram: 'Mrs Bradley did take a bed to a hut at Netley – and then came away again.' Southampton players then demonstrated the renowned facility of British sportsmen to bestow bitter-sweet nicknames: Bradley was thereafter known as 'Squatter'.

At one point 50,000 people were squatting, and September 1946 marked its high point. Everyone competed for the same properties. As the Army camps emptied, the demobbed servicemen found no homes, and returned as squatters. The Government responded by claiming some other imminent use – usually accommodation for the young mining conscripts, to combat the growing fuel crisis. Nevertheless, squatters occupied a dormitory in a Yorkshire miners' hostel whilst the miners were out at work. The competition reached into the Cabinet. Aneurin Bevan was the minister responsible for building new homes, and he raged at delays in demobilising skilled building workers: 'where are all the people I need for my programme?' Prime Minister Attlee's reply would have found an echo in every football manager's soul: 'looking for houses, Nye!' (Hennessy, 1993, p.173).

Far-flung outposts fared no better. Torquay United suffered amid 'the postwar dearth of talent', once lining up a 24-year-old prewar First Division youngster: 'he's well built, has a good idea of the game and has the necessary speed. At present he's on demob leave. But being a married man with a family he would want a home in Torquay. Who is going to work the oracle?' Torquay ran the gamut of strategies. They sought 'rent within professional footballers' income', then lambasted the response of 1946's Basil Fawltys: 'some Torquay landladies are just about the most grasping I've ever met. One offered to let accommodation to a United player at £7 per week – or £5 10s if he provided his own coal, light and gas.'

When Torquay 'wiped out a loss of £6,000 and have a credit of £1,600', they bought their own. Similarly Nottingham Forest and Blackburn each purchased four houses, for £6,000 and £1,500 respectively, and Preston ten. Houses within a bus trip, as when Liverpool bought six in a newly built street. Correspondents satirised the practice: 'does it mean bigger and better homes for bigger and better houses for bigger and better stars until eventually we find our "stars" installed in country mansions? Or am I letting my imagination run riot?'

In fact this is what distinguishes the housing-challenged players of 1946-47 from today's privileged Premiership stars: 'He is a good but not a great player. He is a member of an unfashionable Midlands side and there are many Premiership footballers who earn much more. Yet he lives in the shires in a style beyond most people's dreams. His house is surrounded by 14 acres of parkland, lake and woods. There are seven bedrooms, five reception rooms and since he works fully three hours a week (well, not every week and not in the summer) he employs a full-time gardener and a full-time housekeeper.'

Houses and flats were for married players: the unmarried got communal settings. Wolves caused a stir when they bought a 'mansion'; Norwich a nursing home; Brentford were interested in Richmond Palace. What next, Buckingham Palace, the press queried? However, finding accommodation was only the start of an uncertain project: Chesterfield 'have now brought a big house ... A headache for the club is where to get the necessary furniture, and can a permit for food be obtained. A host and hostess are to be appointed. If that is not possible it will be sold to the colliery company who are anxious to acquire it.'

It was thought prudent to protect against the possibility of squatters by use of curtains in the windows to pretend the house was occupied, a precaution rather undermined by the local paper printing the address!

Nothing could be taken for granted. Especially not food. Once the union failed to get relief from bread rationing, luckless Newport complained their 'footballers are only getting half as much to eat as they really need'. 'Pre-war footballers ate twice as much' and, in gruelling conditions on heavy grounds, current ones lacked stamina and energy. Newcastle's Frank Brennan posed a formidable challenge to rationing limits. He worked as a Colliery Engineer 'from 7 to 4.30, then trained with the club after tea'. When United went into post-Christmas Cup purdah, captain Joe Harvey noted: 'Many's the time on the morning of matches, I have seen him demolish grapefruit, cornflakes, three or four eggs (team-mate Jackie Milburn counted twelve) bacon, sausage, tomatoes, fried bread, toast and marmalade – then polish off the mixed grills the other players left' (Hutchinson, 1997, p.118).

Others ate their hotel breakfast, then 'went out into the city and had another one'. Senior pros had access to food off-the-ration: Bill Shankly invited two Preston players new from Ireland to a welcome meal: 'Eat up, boys. Don't ever go short of grub just because it's rationed. Just come and see me' (Kelly, 1996, p.32).

West Ham provided lunch daily for twenty players so that 'no man goes without the food he needs'. Bolton decided the only guarantee was to take your own food, especially to culinary wastelands: 'on weekend trips the club always takes its own breakfasts these austere rationing days. Hotel breakfasts are still very poor, especially in London's hotels ... Wanderers had their usual kidney, liver and eggs, brought from Bolton for the purpose. This is now standard procedure.'

Food was the main talking point of British visits. Thus whilst Wolves' Swedish hosts doubted their tales of deprivation, the English ate in wonderment: 'there was as much meat in one meal as in a week in England.'

Newcastle's Albert Stubbins was wide-eyed: 'the sight of counters groaning under unrationed chocolates, sweets and fruit of every description.'

For the visiting English coaches, there were three incentives: 'a change of scenery, good pay and rich food in return for coaching the young.' Spurs' Vic Buckingham took his wife and children to Norway. The Norwegians painted a nameplate on the family chalet: Buckingham Palace.

There was always the danger of overdoing it. Liverpool players each put on half a stone on their hectic American tour, and when Clyde toured South Africa, there were 'tremendous feats of eating' – 'Billy Bunter' Cameron put on a stone. Similarly Henry Cockburn took away one memory from his first England trip, in Ireland: 'What food we had in Dublin! Chicken, eggs and lashings of wonderful ice cream.'

Notwithstanding Cockburn's pre-match diet, Jimmy Fay complained his members were at a disadvantage facing European teams. The continentals themselves took the hint. The Swedes may have doubted English summer tales of shortages but, by the autumn, tourists Norrkopping brought their own food. Conservative MPs teased the Government about what it said about the country, especially as English footballers were sent to Ireland to 'fatten up'. When competing amateur international teams breakfasted together at adjoining hotel tables, the Irish feasted on home farm eggs and bacon, the English made do with a kipper. The Dutch international team arrived on Monday for Wednesday's match with England with 23 dozen eggs, six hams, a chocolate cake three-foot-long, and a basket of fruit. Likewise, Sparta Prague and the French international squad felt 'sure we shall get enough to eat, but as our men have a sweet tooth we felt it would be wise to bring the jam and sugar.'

English footballers travelled constantly during 1946-47. National competition was fundamental to the return of real football, but its resurrection depended upon the players being available enough, and the national transport system reliable enough, to support a daunting fixture list. Both conditions proved endlessly problematic. The players struggled to free themselves, and, when they did, bore the brunt of the system's profound inadequacies. And at the end of each cold, crowded and delayed journey they had to be physically and psychologically prepared to face ferociously critical watchers.

They travelled mainly by rail. A reporter of the English social scene described a railway journey from London to Lancashire in the autumn of 1946: 'I travelled on Sunday, which is a foolish thing to do in England; on Sundays trains too often take all the time there is. Nor had it any food on board, nor was there opportunity to get any. On this train, which must surely have held a thousand seats, only twenty-seven were first class, so having paid first class I journeyed third. Not much hardship this, except one feels defrauded. We were seventy-five minutes late, so that I had no food or drink for eight hours. Again nothing much, but we are at peace – in theory, anyhow' (Hennessy, 1993, pp.114-16).

Alec Lockie was a regular traveller, in worse weather and with greater delays. Notts County's centre-half was still living in Sunderland, unable to find a house locally. Later, during the great freeze up, Lockie would get to Ipswich in deepest Suffolk, to find Town could not borrow a snowplough to clear the pitch. Match off, back to the north-east. Nottingham's *Football Post* sympathised with Lockie's thousand-mile series of exhausting journeys over Christmas: 'in these days of late running trains it is not conducive to complete fitness.'

But that afternoon Lockie's direct opponent scored five goals to knock County out of the Cup. Exit the understanding columnist: 'poor play by the centre-half caused the rot. It is no use crying over spilt milk. The damage is done ... plain speaking is for the better ... a search for a person to blame. Everyone who saw the match knows where the weakness was.'

The railways had been run into the ground, 'overloaded ... to the point of breakdown.' The terrible winter of 1947 would only exacerbate an already dire situation. Bradford quickly tired of their 'prevailing chaotic state' when two successive journeys from the Midlands returned them home in the 'stilly watches' of the early hours. But the League invoked a prewar ban to stop them flying to distant Plymouth, a ban initially provoked when Argyle took up a 16-year-old 'to see how a player stood up to air travel'. Plymouth had most reason to experiment, contributing 16,000 of a total half a million miles fulfilling League fixtures.

Journeys on the neglected, bottleneck-ridden roads were equally exhausting: 'Cramped and tired, we almost fell out of the bus Saturday night.' Third Division (South) clubs complained especially about their three-day journeys to Torquay and Exeter. It took Northampton eight hours on a Friday: to meet the costs of travel and two-nights stay they received £35 from a 5,000 gate. Worse, shortages meant Torquay were finding it difficult to get soap for the teams' post-match baths.

Overall, 'in any discussion of British transport, the starting assumption is one of chaos and overstrain – of clogged roads, crowded trains, the whole overlain by delay and squalor and stress on the part of the traveller.' However there could be secondary gains. With players scattered far and wide, Chesterfield's purchase of a coach 'helped the players to get to know each other'. Or nurse their wounds. When Coventry complimented them on a clean game, Chesterfield marvelled at the bumps and bruises in others, because 'Saturday's tussle was robust enough to make most of the Chesterfield team candidates for massage'.

Usually Chesterfield were 'vehemently hooted' on their travels – they 'stamped themselves as the most excessively robust company seen here'. But bonding could go too far. Chesterfield arrived at Spurs only twenty minutes before kick-off, their coach having collided with a dairyman's van outside Grantham. Plenty of spilt milk, most of it for Spurs, beaten 3-4. Travelling could be hazardous. Portsmouth's manager and trainer were hurt when their coach collided with an American Services vehicle, and Ipswich crashed into a bus at Brighton: when their journey was resumed they left behind their captain – 'he had got out to get a paper'.

In the best of circumstances heavy dependence on transport was part of the footballer's lot, but 1946-47 was the worst. Nor did they receive preferential treatment; in fact any hint that footballers be favoured, like sitting down, needed justification: 'before you start holding indignation meetings, ask your-selves, if you would rather see a sprightly, well-travelled team doing its stuff, than a side suffering from acute corridor cramp, ambling round the field. After all, you're paying.'

When West Ham, faced with a journey to Plymouth on a foodless train with packed compartments and corridors, asked at Paddington for permission 'to be allowed on the platform without queuing, this was turned down'. Even stars were given scant consideration: after an England win in Scotland that generated gate receipts of almost £32,000, Wilf Mannion had to stand on the slow train back to Darlington: 'carrying a painful knock on his knee from the match, he managed to squat on his suitcase and stayed there for the entire journey' (Varley, 1997, p.135).

The season abounded with incidents out of the ordinary grind. Coventry's trip to Newport was a chapter of accidents. Manager Dick Bayliss had to take his captain George Mason home by taxi after he collapsed at Birmingham. Dick then caught the next train, to find his right-back was 'marooned some-where between Bristol and Newport'. Two players were injured in the match, and a third was taken ill. Perhaps it was the food, as City carried a curse from the waiter at the Newport hotel where they took lunch. His parting shot was: 'don't come back here if you lose today.'

As they were playing the already friendless Newport County, the disloyal waiter had chosen City as one of his away wins on the pools. The result? Newport 4, Coventry 2.

When the van failed to collect their kit from a Bristol station, Torquay players had to 'trundle' it to Eastville: 'on their way a local tailor allowed them to use his premises as a temporary cloakroom whilst they had lunch.' The tight schedule meant that players could always go astray. During one London connection three Bury men could not retrieve their bags from under-neath 'some golfing equipment' until the carriage doors were closed: 'they had to run nearly a mile down the Edgware Road and board the boat train to Southampton as the guard was ready to wave it off.'

Southampton had an eventful early season mini-tour: 'Saints will travel to South Wales on Wednesday, play Swansea on Thursday, take a train to Birmingham on Friday, play WBA on Saturday, back to Southampton for 1.30 Sunday morning after 470 miles train journey.' The first match saw giant Saints goalie George Ephgrave kicked on the head and unconscious for half an hour. On their subsequent journey railway porters enquired: 'is it right your goalie died during the night?' George played less than two full days later.

Swansea themselves lost goalkeeper Jack Parry in a crucial relegation fix-ture in November. The omens had not been propitious. Their first train stopped at 27 stations before they changed at Gloucester, only to find that compartments they had engaged were occupied. They therefore stood in corridors until Sheffield. Within five minutes of the game starting, a collision with Wednesday's centre-forward took Parry to hospital. Swansea lost 0-3.

Even when players arrived safely, the noise, smoke and discomfort of their surroundings could make relaxation difficult: 'two Rovers players didn't sleep a wink at Sunderland on Friday night because of clanging trams, hooting ships and chiming clocks. One spent the night sat up in an armchair.'

Each match of 1946-47 was an achievement. Each was a disruption to family and personal life, each an uncomfortable and stressful journey, each the occasion of aggressive crowd displeasure, and some the cause of public humiliation. Was it worth it? Stars like Wilf Mannion had little alternative. Players like Alec Lockie were more typical – either through choice or compulsion they had another job: playing football was the difficult bit.

The many conscripts were always uncertain about getting permission. Thus, a capacity crowd eagerly awaited the clash of prewar giants Wolves and Arsenal on opening day. Yet England star Billy Wright was out – the Army required him for an inter-unit cricket game. Within hours of kick-off his Commanding Officer relented – allowing Wright to leave Aldershot at 6am. The Army's brinkmanship was most graphically demonstrated that May when Cyril Sidlow became The Vanishing Footballer. Sidlow's selected appearance for Wales coincided with his club sailing across the Atlantic: he rather hoped the Army would give him the seven weeks off! As kick-off approached Wales desperately sought contact with Cyril, his unit or club. An hour out of Southampton, Liverpool confirmed that Sidlow was in their party for their American tour, explaining that he was only released on condition secrecy was maintained until the Queen Mary sailed.

Newcastle winger Walker cut it fine. Stationed at Bristol, he was due to play in a services match the day United were visiting Spurs. At the last moment his release was obtained and after a dash by jeep through the night, he finished preparations by sleeping in a London hotel until just before kick-off. An even more 'spectacular dash by air and fast car' by Torquay's leading scorer from an Army course in Gloucester was the 'talk of the soccer world'. Supporters ferried Ralph Conley to the airport in 'a bit of a rush because the plane left Gloucester at 12.30, arriving at Exeter in just over an hour. There it was met by ... directors, who rushed Conley to the ground.'

Understandably a serviceman's availability 'depends on what camp he is posted to'. Bobby Davidson's frustrations were typical. He was not a young footballer: Arsenal had signed him from Scotland back in 1935. Bobby was stationed in North Yorkshire, which posed such problems in the transitional 1945-46 season that Coventry's manager Dick Bayliss would set off at 3am on a 400 mile drive to collect him, arriving back just in time for the 3pm kick-off. Bobby was just as desperate to play in the new season; his manager perhaps less keen to reproduce such heroics. Bobby turned up in nearby Newcastle in September in a vain hope that injury-hit Coventry needed him against United. However there were exceptions. Cecil McCormack was fortunately able to travel 300 miles from his RAF base down south to play for

Gateshead. Welsh international Trevor Ford was lucky to establish his fame during a twelve-month period of compassionate leave.

Soldiers played on leave. Denis Thompson, a prewar schoolboy international, went straight into Sheffield United's First Division team from duty in Germany. George Fisher played for Millwall at Manchester City and went back to Greece that night. Also on leave, Alan Ball, father of the inexhaustible 1966 England World Cup hero, demonstrated the heart and lung power his son would inherit: 'so enthusiastic that even when his side was five goals down … he roved about in defence in an effort to try to turn the tide.'

Clubs tried to influence where a serviceman was based. Availability could make the difference between success and failure. For example the magic duet of Carter and Doherty could not prevent Derby County's season from lurching into crisis: 'there's trouble in the dressing room, board room, and every other room.' Salvation came from an unlikely quarter. Derby had already persuaded the RAF to change Angus Morrison's posting from Scotland to Lichfield. Despite only just getting back from a fortnight's RAF tour of Germany, his six goals in three matches changed Derby's season. Now, in place of the Carter/Doherty 'intricacies', the modernity of their style – 'longer and with more fighting spirit' – was captured by the imagery of Morrison's impact: 'he took the pass like a super-charged vacuum cleaner.'

Huddersfield had similar need of cavalry. Town were soon bottom of Division One after a series of terrible defeats: 0-5, 1-6, 1-4, and 1-4 again. They persuaded the Army to release 20-year-old Arnold Rodgers. Rodgers scored three goals in fourteen minutes and Town won 5-0. A fortnight later he scored twice when Town defeated in-form Preston; and two more when they won a relegation battle. However Army service meant Rodgers' availability remained problematical: in his next match he fractured his skull – but did not find out for three weeks. In all Rodgers played only thirteen eventful games, scoring nine goals.

Soldiers could not train. Training arrangements were the biggest obstacle to clubs resuming their prewar control over players and proved particularly irksome when a large transfer fee failed to change availability. When England's Len Shackleton 'moved' from Bradford to Newcastle for £13,000 he was still 'held' as a miner. He, along with Scotland's current captain and five other players, 'leave home each working day at 6am and don't get back to Bradford until 9.00 in the evenings.' Newcastle's Stan Seymour raged: 'Take Shackleton. He cost us £13,000 yet I never see him during the week.'

Many players negotiated training: Vic Woodley, England's regular prewar goalkeeper, joined Derby from Chelsea on condition that he was allowed to continue his engineering job in Slough. Others had little choice: goalkeeper Jim Sanders moved to West Brom but could not find a home there and commuted from Kent: 'The travelling does get me down. I can almost hear hundreds of footballers echoing "and so say all of us".' Clubs tried to reassert their authority, compelling players to train at home. But this caused trouble: one 'well-known player' who transferred on the understanding that he could train away reacted with 'disturbed spirit' to this compulsion, especially as it cost him £3 a week.

Third Division managers constantly 'bemoaned the fact that work calls made it necessary to rearrange his team' right up to kick-off. Bradford City were typical in their efforts to regain control once players were demobbed, or cajoling them into giving up their other work, by providing housing. When City lost their manager because he couldn't get a house locally, Jack Barker, England's great prewar centre-half, took over, travelling thousands of miles in search of new players. Only five professionals then trained at Valley Parade, the rest scattered throughout the north: 'six are in the pits, three in the Forces and others in essential work in an Iron Foundry, Sunderland shipyards and as a tinsmith.' His men were thrown into competition when Barker bought City a house, 'to be occupied by two players and their wives.' Rate collector Ken Harper promptly demonstrated his need: 'the taxi rushing Harper from his work in Barnsley to the York match broke down outside Tadcaster. A passing supporter seeing the City player at the roadside, gave him a hitch and he reached the ground a few minutes before the start.'

At Christmas Barker gave up an unequal struggle, resigning to concentrate on a grocery business that his wife could not manage without him. His successor, the veteran player-coach Jack Milburn, proved more radical. Within a month he had persuaded almost all his first-team to become full-timers. Players like ex-foundry worker Jimmy Isaac regained previously elusive form: 'in the early games he was rarely a 90-minute player and always seemed to fall off in the second half.' Jack Milburn [whilst admitting he remained a "part-timer himself"] took the credit: 'I talked them into it ... Footballers doing a heavy job during the week cannot last the full ninety minutes.'

Second Division Bradford Park Avenue experienced similar change: 'in 1939 Bradford had no professional who regularly followed any other vocation: today sixteen, well over half the staff do: six Bevin boys, insurance, accountancy, shipyard worker, mechanic, apprentice joiner, textile designer and wool warehouseman.'

Other clubs exhibited less variety. At least fourteen of Mansfield's players 'work in the pit and train in their "off" time. Some work a night shift in order to be free on match days.' When their form faltered, this got the blame: 'as the mud has got deeper and deeper, so Mansfield's part-timers have struggled.' All clubs hosted players from other clubs and had their players training away. Jones of table-topping Bristol City was 'the only first-team man training at Ashton Gate on a full-time basis.' Several played without. Schoolteacher Jack Towers, a twelve-year veteran, was Darlington's amateur captain until in November he retired: 'League football is much too strenuous for a man who cannot train.'

Sergeant Major Fred Durrant's war ended with an anti-aircraft unit outside Dover, and compassionate leave to nurse his seriously ill wife. The centre-forward spent such a long vigil at her bedside that playing in a 1946 FA Cup quarter-final was a mental relief. Before the second leg, on the Bolton

Disaster Saturday, Brentford's 35,000 crowd, 'hushed in sympathy,' received the news of her death that morning. Fred was then demobbed early to assist the housebuilding programme, and travelled to London for First Division matches. His training regime? – 'playing each evening with his four brothers in a Dover park.'

The excessive demands were often noted, but rarely excused critical judgement. After losing one match 'hard as nails and fast as fury', Coventry's Simpson 'seemed slow; completely devoid of pep, although this might be an accumulation of the effect of night work as a miner and little opportunity to train properly.' He was dropped.

There was considerable ambivalence about mining. It represented every current obstacle, yet it symbolised the game's origins and raw material. Thus Arsenal manager George Allison, despairing of the advantage northern clubs enjoyed, bemoaned his full-back 'working full-time on the coal face. There are no mines in London, and it is physically impossible to travel on a Saturday morning to London and maintain the necessary physical fitness. If he leaves the mines, he will be called up immediately for service in the Forces, and that would put him out of top class football for the conscription period.'

Undoubtedly true: yet within weeks 19-year-old miner Don Mills was starring up the road. QPR manager Dave Mangnall came from Yorkshire mining stock himself, and signed young Don on the surface of his old colliery. QPR recruited another Bevin Boy due for release and with hopes of moving his family to London. On his debut Alex Lennon finished his night shift at 6am and caught the 9am train to London. For the past two years, working night shifts, his 'only training ... consists of a kick-about on a pitch near the colliery before he goes to bed for the day.' A more experienced footballer-miner who managed this endurance feat regularly was Harold Wallbanks, who played for Fulham but worked in a Durham pit. On home match days, Harold had to dash to Newcastle after his shift, travel to London, and dash back afterwards for his next shift: '600 miles and most of it standing in train corridors.'

Extraordinarily, such arrangements deterred few. Thus Cardiff's runaway success with a team 'straight out of the pits' alerted others to the potential in the Rhondda: 'with the mines working five days a week and finishing on a Friday it is a simple matter for a player, if he can be attracted.'

However, miners, the last line of defence against the coming fuel crisis, needed permission to miss shifts. John Hodgson had to appear before an absentee board to get time off to play in Leeds' goal. Hodgson soon missed more when, reporting back, found he had broken his forearm saving a Liverpool penalty. The 'other job' was equally hazardous. In 1946-47 the three leading English goalkeepers were all in the Second Division – Frank Swift at Manchester City; Ted Ditchburn of Spurs; and another miner, Chesterfield's Ray Middleton. His valuable hands were at risk when he was 'given the job of hooking wagons', so he insured them for £2,000. His caution was justified: another goalkeeper suffered from the drive for productivity. George Rymer injured his hand as a colliery haulage hand when Barnsley led the Second Division. He made the team only once more, when his handling errors cost three goals in a 1-6 defeat. More prosaically, Ipswich's goalkeeper, 38-year-old Mick Burns (Preston's 1937 Cup final goalie) 'fell down the stairs of a trolley bus'. These were the days before tractors: an Ipswich defender 'burnt his back in the sun bringing in the pea harvest.'

There remained many who jumped at the chance of pro football: David Davidson 'is a transport driver's mate, and while in Hull with a load of building material he got into conversation with a supporter. He remarked on his football career in Scotland, and this led to a trial in front of City officials. They were impressed and signed him.'

Football could be a means to an end. One of the Scots assembled at short notice for New Brighton was Alastair McLellen, whose Glasgow University studies were interrupted by the war, but now could be completed through football money. Graduate George Edwards, BSc., ex-RAF, Birmingham and Wales, was one of many teachers who were pro footballers. Another was John Galloway, formerly a major in the Royal Armoured Corps, who featured in Chelsea's conspicuous pre-season spending spree. But their £4,500 investment was immediately jeopardised by his real career: 'he got the post of schoolmaster at Tonbridge, Kent and feared he might have to give up soccer but the school governors encouraged him to continue playing.'

Chelsea's crowd certainly punished any lack of commitment: 'the "vultures" on the Stamford Bridge terraces, [took] time off from bread queues on Wednesday afternoons to watch the "Stiffs". Galloway ['Go home, Golloway'] must have been one of the most barracked players ever to appear in a Chelsea shirt, which was odd because he was an elegant player' (Moynihan, 1982, p.64). Galloway played through back pain, caused by shrapnel left in his body.

Maurice Owen had similar priorities. Although only 22, Maurice's war was spent in the Burmese jungle as one of Wingate's Chindits. His non-league goals attracted the big clubs but he joined homely Swindon, agreeing to turn professional on condition that he retain his electrician's job with the MG Sports Car Company in Abingdon and train locally. During a hat-trick debut, in ankle deep January mud, the crowd was soon calling 'Give it to Maurice'. Owen continued to 'go gay as a Third Division goal getter', scoring sixteen in as many games, and still saying no to Arsenal, Wolves, Derby, and Villa. Established players also said no to full-time football, like two of the five wingers most likely to succeed Stan Matthews in the postwar period (Tom Finney was another). Self-employed Eddie Chapman thought it better 'to be assured of £10 plus, say £6 part-time football wages, than full-time wage and neglect of business'. Similarly teenage winger Fred Basnett made his name scoring a debutant hat-trick for Stoke in 1941. With Matthews back, Stoke proposed to transfer Basnett to Portsmouth. No. Fred had a 'bungalow, a job with his father in law, a nursery gardener, and he wants a part-time engagement'. Third Division Crewe also required too many long journeys, so Basnett joined non-league Northwich Victoria.

The conflict became too great for Dick Threlfall of Bolton, whose players bravely supported the independence of another job. Dick starred in a match whose football became unimportant – the Bolton Disaster. He soon sought a move nearer work. Wanderers were ambivalent: 'now he has received promotion he will be less than ever free to play midweek games, a point likely to concern interested clubs as much as it weighed with us.' Not exactly a hard sell, and Bolton placed 'a price on his head which may stand in the way' of Dick's ambition to play Saturday afternoons only. The impasse was broken, and the spring's Cup quarter-finalist played in the autumn's Cheshire League. The conflict had historical resonance: Dick's father had starred in the Edwardian era, when footballers similarly fought to assert themselves.

Many players were only demobbed so that they could join 570,000 house-building tradesmen. Tom Finney, ex-Eighth Army tankman, was released to be a plumber, and followed another, Manchester United's Joe Walton, into the England team. An older international, Charlton's Cup final inside-left Albert 'Sailor' Brown, was ambivalent about future security. He transferred to Nottingham on the basis of Forest procuring a house and 'showing him the ropes' of football management. As an apprentice, Sailor accompanied manager Billy Walker on his exhausting scouting trips, and was taught to include in his suitcase a 'bacon and egg' breakfast! This lifestyle prompted second thoughts as Tommy Lawton soon revealed in his weekly Sunday column that Sailor was preparing for a career as a bootmaker. He had 'already got two lasts and sixteen nails towards it'.

Some of football's biggest stars, such as Matthews, Dodds and Swift, followed tradition in running licensed premises. Some clubs tolerated these ventures, others did not. Leicester manager John Duncan still ran the Turk's Head in the shadow of Leicester Gaol, but as a player he had been forced to 'quit from the club's finest-ever side'. Derby County's similar policy caused them to fall out with a 'football great' and miss signing a current international. Only a beer shortage prevented Ireland's captain Peter Doherty from becoming a publican that summer: 'I would go in now, but what's the good when there's so little to sell. People would think I'm Irish.'

But when a tenancy became available, Derby refused permission. Doherty felt betrayed – his agreement anticipated this development – and further affronted about 'this embargo on his right to make provision for his after-football future'. Doherty was on the transfer trail again.

Eddie Shimwell experienced similar difficulties: good enough to be England's reserve in Ireland, he changed clubs when Sheffield United invoked 'a rule which says a player cannot continue as a licensee whilst on the club's books. Shimwell has been searching for a house for some time and recently took over The Plough Inn because it provided him with suitable accommodation. This is the first home of his own, and he has now stated he would rather quit football than give up his inn.'

Football writers celebrated a successful freedom bid. Eddie Shimwell favoured a move to nearby Derby, but County had just fallen out with Peter

Doherty over the same issue. So Shimwell transferred to distant Blackpool, and trained with … Chesterfield.

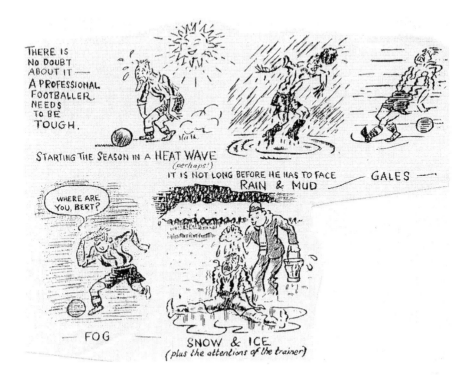

Army service cost the war deaths of two internationals – Leeds' Eric Stephenson and Liverpool's Tom Cooper

Kiddy's Favourites 'Popular Footballers' cards

Here are two Liverpool stars, Billy Liddell and
Cyril Sidlow — the Vanishing Footballer

TOM FINNEY
Preston North End and England

Meet the man who took Stan Matthews' place in the England team, lost it to the maestro—and came back on the other wing. Tom Finney won a war-time Cup Final for Preston against Arsenal (in 1941). In Egypt, serving as a Tank Corps trooper, he played with the Wanderers (British Services XI). Discovered during a Deepdale trial match in 1938, 16-year-old Finney was an inside-left. Under trainer Billy Scott and Scottish international George Mutch, he was modelled into an outside-right, good enough by 1946-47 to displace Matthews in the England XI. His left-wing chance came during the Swiss tour of June, 1947.

Tom Finney and Stan Matthews were constantly compared. Tom – 'curly from top to toe' – was the good guy, but Stan's ability to avoid both tackles and conflicts provided an example to the World Powers descending into Cold War

The frustrations over the relatively few postponements during the Great Freeze expressed the 'fiddling fuss of life in postwar Britain'

Rotherham lost their 100 per cent home record in their last home game, a 3-3 draw with Rochdale

Notice the date, June 7th. The First Division championship was not decided until a week later

The coin was lost in snow before the Bolton v Manchester City Cup-tie

10

Footballers are in Short Supply: Like Houses ... Unobtainable

'Footballers are in Short Supply: Like houses, they are almost unobtainable.'
(Exeter City programme)
'Along with food rationing, the exports drive, the jokes of Abbott and Costello, atomic energy and the modern song lyric, [football transfers] seems to be one of those things which are depressing but inevitable.'

The transfer market of 1946 was crazy. In every sense. Crazy for its time: vast sums being paid during an era of debt, make do and mend, and austerity. And crazy for football time. Tommy Lawton's transfer to Chelsea in November 1945 attracted the same judgement as the first £1,000 transfer in 1905: 'height of absurdity to imagine that a £1,000 player is only worth £4 a week for his services. The whole position is illogical' (Sharpe, 1952, p.148).

Stars like Lawton and Doherty characterised transfers as crazy for its deviations from normal employment practice. Transfers made footballers commodity – even when they exploited the system it was inherently humiliating. After all, a man was simply changing his job. Like anyone else: for negative reasons or positive ones. That is how Peter saw it: 'purely a business arrangement' (Doherty, 1948, p.60).

It was an unequal business. Formally, the fee compensated the club giving up a player's registration. The player merely assented: otherwise the 'stability of all clubs is undermined'. Within the wider world, transfers excited wide public interest. They had extraordinary power. Transfers captured a club's ambition within football's pantheon. For supporters they offered immediate hope – at a stroke, and at a price. Transfers promised exorcism: 'buy a new player' was a stick with which to beat club officials and make change tangible. They symbolised that the club is bigger than its transient members. Displaced players fed further moves on an endless merry-go-round. For officials, transfers represented renewal – an essential freedom from reliance on current players – and legitimacy – a step nearer success or salvation. They indicated competence: management was reinvesting the capital represented by the team's support; or that earned by selling a player whose value was itself a vindication of their footballing prowess. A good buy was good public relations. Inactivity, particularly if accompanied by bad results, made for trouble.

In 1946 football's business had become a 'new lunacy': 'we've got the cash and we're willing to spend *tens* of thousands on houses and players to get what we want.' Note the new order. *Houses*, then players.'

It was confusing. How could clubs spend their windfall? Shortages of labour and materials, and the constraints of government licences, obstructed ground improvements. Their 'Scrooge-like' attitude towards wages ruled out an obvious investment. Others carried their contradictions. Investing in training regimes and facilities was bedevilled by ambivalence about football as a full-time occupation and about the value of coaching. In any event, senior players were rarely available, and younger ones were soon called up.

Nor was a developmental approach acceptable. Clubs and supporters combined in wanting change now. Spending money on transfers gave the appearance of action and the hope of improvement, and also carried the resonance of tradition: big clubs had always demonstrated their status and ambition by buying. But if more clubs had money to burn, none wanted to lose their own good players, and few were under financial pressure to sell. In some senses the transfer market of 1946-47 approximated the ideal of the Football League: all clubs seemed equal. And it was a nightmare.

Initially clubs were seen to do their best in difficult circumstances: by March 1947 Portsmouth had watched 500 prospective signings. Papers followed managers as they abandoned their teams and roamed the country. Exeter's George Roughton's trip north was typical: Liverpool's Shepherd brothers declined to move; Manchester United directors were short of men themselves, and Roughton was not impressed by excess Huddersfield players. Finally soccer's 'black market' required a 'staggering' £5,000 for a 30-year-old reserve, and pay something 'under-the-counter'. Roughton concluded: 'buying footballers is very much like trying to find houses. There are very few about, but at prices very much over the odds.'

Clubs followed their old instincts and went further north, but no bargains were to be had. The war hit Scottish junior leagues hard and senior clubs would only release reserves. Only royal patronage would tempt a top Scottish international: 'we should like to approach Rangers for Willie Waddell, but our manager can't get an option on Buckingham Palace.' Manager after manager returned empty-handed, then went straight out again. It was both a wild goose chase and a sellers' market: 'never in the history of the game has there been such a shortage ... never so impossible to solve the problems in the transfer market.' It was a profound and scary lesson: 'It just amounts to this – a generation has been lost.'

The ancient breeding grounds of footballing dynasties, mining footballers, were producing a lower yield. Chelsea's Billy Birrell thought the standard in Scotland very low; Charlton's Jimmy Seed found his native north-east now barren soil: 'their happy pre-war hunting grounds strangely devoid of talent nowadays.' Confidence in a natural British talent was eroding. It was the beginning of the end of a closed shop. For replacements were to hand. Or almost. Any foreign player had to overcome a serious obstacle. In 1931

Arsenal's interest in signing Rapid Vienna's goalkeeper provoked the Home Office and FA to impose a two-year residence requirement for professionals. Nonetheless four clubs had invited Moscow Dynamos' inside-forward Bobrov to stay in England. He would, ostensibly, have been an amateur, or 'language' student, like Switzerland's Willi Steffen, who joined Chelsea.

The latent hypocrisy of the amateur requirement was glimpsed when Arne Sorensen joined Huddersfield. He didn't play, because he was already suspended at home, and therefore by FIFA, for allegedly breaking Danish amateur rules. Some were judged not ready for the hurly burly of real football: Albert Gudmundson, an Icelander studying shipbuilding, who played centre-forward for Glasgow Rangers and then Arsenal; Edwin Hansen, Grimsby's Dane; and Robert Weil, Leicester's Swiss winger. On the other hand, Norrkopping featured 'the best centre forward in Europe', and they idly wondered how Gudmundson could play for Arsenal without the two-year qualification period. Charlton's manager enlightened them: 'Let me put like this. I could take your crack centre-forward Gunnar Nordahl, find him a good job and play him in my league side. But he would get nothing for his football.' 'Could you find him a job?' they asked. 'I could,' said Jimmy with a broad smile. It was an offer Gunnar Nordahl could refuse, wait for Milan's large signing-on fee and score 210 goals in eight calcio seasons.

Increasingly a player's personal requirements mattered most, which was problematic for public relations because the rules provided virtually no motivation to move. The £10 registration fee to a player had been unchanged since 1891, when it was seven times average weekly earnings. Otherwise a player benefited from something mysteriously called 'accrued share of benefit'. This approximated the material rewards of moving with staying: through service a player would 'accrue' entitlement to a benefit. If that entitlement was disturbed by his club's willingness to transfer him he should be compensated (but only 80 per cent). Benefits were discretionary, but they were calculated at £130 a year over five years. This, officially, was what made transfers a big payday. Otherwise transfers might increase wages, but only to the maximum. For example Fred Durrant's move from the First to Third Division was unproblematic because 'QPR pay the top rate'. Nevertheless, negotiations lasted all day, so what were they talking about? This was the difficulty about reports of transfer negotiations. Where it was straightforward, why did it take so long? Where clubs competed, how could it be lawful? In reporting these essentially private matters, papers were torn between explaining what probably had happened, or describing the drama and colour.

The season's three biggest transfers occurred early, and chimed with fundamental beliefs about the state of football: its popularity was even greater than expected; and the players were not good enough. This panic was focused first on Tommy Walker, then Albert Stubbins and Len Shackleton and the 'colossal sums paid nowadays'.

Walker, a great prewar and wartime star, was a gentlemen of the game, the Ace of Hearts. He scored Scotland's winning goal against England aged twenty and turned down a record £17,000 move to Arsenal because he thought he might join the ministry. Now nearly 32 and with the buying panic on, this was the time to move. Charlton quickly cabled an offer described as a two-year contract on the maximum wage of £10, another £10 for a newspaper article and a £10 a week job with the chairman. And a house. In fact when this proved insufficient, manager Jimmy Seed publicly apologised to the estate agent waiting with keys in hand for Tom's £1,800 house. Seed later recalled: 'I nearly signed a Scottish international ... when he informed me that if I gave him £1,000 in his left hand he would sign in his right, I was disappointed and disillusioned' (Seed, 1957, p.49).

That Walker, despite football's regulations, 'wants a substantial signing fee' was widely reported. Charlton's offer was left far behind as Chelsea manager Billy Birrell and Huddersfield's David Steele joined battle in an Edinburgh hotel, 'each allocated separate rooms adjoining the bedroom where Hearts officials were ready to talk money. Each went in and out several times. Tommy Walker was called in each time.' Eventually Steele called it a day: 'well, money talks.' The terms were not announced, although papers published detailed breakdowns. The fact that the regulations had been circumvented was obvious: 'let the player who wants to change go to the highest bidder by all means, but do not have them bidding in jobs, houses, kisses from film stars and cigarette card collections.'

The football authorities were challenged to act. The League's Management Committee was 'biting its nails over the absurdity of Walker's transfer' and the FA, 'usually so quick to protect the dignity of the game,' looked away. A challenge seemed imminent: 'one Northern club intends to lay the facts of some transfer negotiations before the Football Association.' Walker's house row chimed with the mass of disgruntled players discussing strike action: 'you mustn't pay a player more than £10 a week for his football, but you can find him another job at £20, throw in a house and generally make life worth £2,000 a year or more to him without any rules breach.' The whole question undermined the traditional basis of club-player dealings: 'I see nothing to prevent a player demanding a job for his wife as a stenographer at £10 a week ... no reason why a player should not demand that a club set him up in some kind of business.'

Sheffield papers sympathised with Wednesday's autumn impotence during a series of high profile failures. They had 'no intention of taking part in a public auction. We have had some of that.' A club of ancient lineage, Wednesday gained back-to-back championships in 1928-30, and the Cup in 1935. Relegated in 1937, almost into the Third Division in 1938, and overtaken by Sheffield United's promotion, directors wriggled uncomfortably at their 1938 AGM: 'during the past ten years Wednesday had won every honour in football,' to which a voice in the crowd intoned: "And lost them" (Young, 1964, p.149).

Wednesday were now expected to win promotion but started badly, so provoking 'a tendency to cry out for a centre forward'. Before Christmas they had tried 28 players – seven at centre-forward – as the club slumped into the relegation places. The *Green 'Un* thought their readers' many complaints 'unjust, because they do not know the truth about it.' Wednesday missed out even when they bid highest. Their failure to sign Walker, Stubbins, Shackleton, Jock Dodds or Archie Macaulay was blameless: 'any club determined to stand by the rules of the game have no chance whatever of getting any well known player.'

Sheffield Wednesday were further embarrassed when their only genuine star, international inside-right Jack Robinson – six goals in seven games in a struggling side – wanted away. Jack had achieved fame at an apparently early age: he played for England at only seventeen years nine months. Jack did not find the war easy: initially a labourer in a steel works and then a PT Instructor. He worried that the Army threatened his football, that he had lost pace because of the corns caused by endless hours wearing rubber shoes on wooden gymnasia floors. Robinson returned to Wednesday as their longest-serving player, but felt the only time he saw the others was matchday: 'I was a stranger.'

Although Wednesday paid the maximum benefit of £650 for his prewar service, Robinson, married with a daughter, was unable to find a house and lived and trained at Newcastle. Whoever could solve Robinson's housing problem would sign him. Many were interested but gave up: we 'have a big housing problem regarding our players too'. But when title-challenging Sunderland agreed to pay £8,000 the transfer hit a snag, turning the whole story into a 'puzzling, tantalising tit-bit'. It was not corns which caused second thoughts, but Robinson's age. On his record he should have been 27: however he was really 29 (the scrupulous Alf Ramsey similarly understated his age: Tom Finney considered 'that two year difference might have swayed the issue whether he got signed on or not'). Sunderland would only pay £6,000 for this reduced expectation of service, which was unacceptable. Jack had to go home, discretion itself: 'a certain matter has arisen which affects the possibility of my transfer, and this must first be cleared up.' Nothing further was heard for days as Sunderland challenged Newcastle for Len Shackleton's signature, but when that failed, Robinson's protracted deal went through.

If Walker's motivation was to take a last opportunity, Albert Stubbins' transfer appears to be equally straightforward: exchanging the Second for a First Division challenger. However it did not then seem that way. Stubbins had lost time but was still only 27. A shipyard draughtsman, Albert made his name scoring more wartime goals (235) than anyone except Lawton and Dodds, becoming England's deputy centre-forward. The city of Newcastle was devastated by Albert's transfer request, which also puzzled his journalist friends: 'all Stubbins can hope for is his accrued share of benefit and a signing on fee.'

The 'accrued share of benefit' was only 80 per cent of £260 because wartime service did not count and Stubbins was likely to get more £2 win bonuses with free-spending, promotion-seeking Newcastle than with 'ordinary' Liverpool. The implication is clear: there was nothing in the move, officially, for the country's most sought-after forward when cash-rich clubs were desperate for talent. Newcastle were inundated with offers from almost every First Division club. £8,500 was the initial estimate, in deference to Tommy Lawton's £11,500 fee a year previously. The Merseyside clubs soon outbid the others: Everton because they had not replaced Lawton; Liverpool because they had lost 0-5 to Manchester United the day before. Everton secretary-manager Theo Kelly told United 'don't part until you get our final offer'. Authorised to go to £11,000, Kelly went two thousand higher. At £13,000 the Merseysiders called a truce. They would let Albert choose, but so far, at four o'clock in the afternoon, Albert had not been involved, and now he could not be found. Taxis scoured the city, messages were flashed on cinema screens. Stubbins walked in at 7.30. Liverpool were given first and only chance in a mere 35-minute interview. Kelly took it in true-blue spirit: 'to think I've come all this way and not even had the chance to talk to you.' Then off to Scotland in another fruitless search.

By way of comparison, that autumn the Tate Gallery made a shrewd purchase for £1,500, a ninth of Stubbins' fee: they bought Van Gogh's Sunflowers. In 1989 it was sold for £18 million, about nine times greater than the then transfer fees for top British footballers. However in September 1946 other comparisons were more relevant than impressionist masterpieces. Newspapers anticipated that in this soaring transfer market 'soon a star will go ... for the price of a bomber'. In moments of greater hyperbole football transfers approached 'figures rivalling the national debt', or 'stock market proportions'.

Why did Stubbins choose Liverpool? The papers had little answer, although later reported 'the bait of a house played a big part'. Albert and his wife had been living with his uncle, and Liverpool soon allocated him one of their six new houses. In these circumstances, a jaundiced view was understandable: 'any "fiddle" over a transfer usually boils down to the size of the fistful of banknotes the buying [or the selling] club is prepared to pass to the player under the table ... What we don't know is the precise method of steering these odd "outside" payments through the clubs' accounts. Sometimes the veil is half lifted: one famous club had a mystery man in constant attendance ... [for] the actual doing of the dirty deed.'

Len Shackleton promised a similar auction. Rumours of possible moves, even back to his prewar club Arsenal, circulated throughout the summer. But Arsenal faced the considerable obstacle that Len was still tied to the mines. Nevertheless, the London papers reported Charlton's Jimmy Seed negotiating for Shackleton for a fortnight. But Newcastle coveted him as Stubbins' replacement. At 2pm they arrived to top the bids of Sunderland and perennial losers Sheffield Wednesday. 'What a fee!' By 3.15pm, Len had signed: the quickest and biggest transfer in Newcastle's history. Len soon repented this haste. For some reason he thought he would be worth far less than Stubbins, about £5-6,000. So his negotiations with United went something like this:

'Stan Seymour said, "You'll be coming to Newcastle." I said "Oh yes, and what do I get out of it?" He said, "We're prepared to give you £500," which met what I thought was my standard, about 10 per cent of the transfer fee, so I signed.'

Local papers indicated that Shackleton also 'wanted a house and as Newcastle were able to promise him one and Sunderland could not, his choice was quickly made' – 'Newcastle must have influence'. Shackleton would be doubly disappointed. The promised house proved elusive, and when he collected his bundles of £100 and announced their destination, Seymour bridled: 'you can't do that, because if you put a lump like that into a building society people are going to make two and two add up to four'.

Shackleton was persuaded to leave all but £100 with the secretary for more discreet withdrawals. But as Len took the train back to Bradford the Sunday after his sensational six-goal debut and counted his booty – 'four times before we reached Durham' – he had discovered his transfer fee had been £13,000; and on his 'ten per cent standard' he should have been paid £1,300. It rankled with Shackleton throughout his stay (Hutchinson, 1997, pp.120-22).

Wolves' Ted Vizard refused a player's request for 'something under the counter'. Angry Ted said, 'let's make a case of it,' and told the selling club's directors of the illegal demands. They thanked him for the revelation, gave a bottle of whisky for his troubles and sold the player to another club (Cullis, 1960, p.170). These 1946 transfers set a pattern for decades. Clubs were forced to present for public consumption a fiction that left the game open to ridicule: 'if anyone believes, as the League would like us to think they believe, that all these big-priced players move just for the sake of changing the colour of their jerseys – they are living in a fool's paradise.'

Earthly matters became urgent when responsibilities increased, like Wilf Mannion's: 'when I got married I thought I had to get away to get some big money, because I knew people were offering it.' A decade on, Mannion spelt out the chapter and verse of illegal payments during his hold-out. Wilf described how an unnamed club, subsequently identified as Aston Villa, offered him '£3,000 in ready cash' for signing, maximum wages 'plus a 'job' – I put it that way because it was a job in name only ... which would have brought me a cool £25 a week. And, just as an incidental, I was to be given £25, to be slipped to me on the railway station, merely for making the trip to talk the offer over' (Varley, 1997, p.169). The Football League retaliated for this offence against appearances by banning for life one of the greatest of postwar players.

Villa's £13,000-equivalent signing during 1946-47 was young centre-forward Trevor Ford. A decade later Ford was himself implicated in the Sunderland affair, a rare moment when illicit payments were revealed. Ford sort of came clean about what went on: 'found guilty and fined £100 for contravening the law relating to illicit deals. Sure I was guilty – of asking for a part-time job and security.' Ford powerfully exposed the gap between appearances and reality: football 'attracts some of the world's worst bums; it has a code of conduct designed to prevent corruption, yet it does everything to encourage it. It is a game full of soccer crooks, for it is well-nigh impossible for a player to reach the top without breaking almost every law in the book.'

For example Sunderland 'see that every player on their books is fixed up with a job outside the game'. As the subject of three big deals, Ford mocked transfers: 'can you blame me for turning a scornful eye on the £10 signing on fee ... Most clubs, willing to see you get something on the side, arrange for the cash to be paid by some anonymous donor ... an envelope containing, per-haps, £1,000 in cash.' There could be a 'rake off' from the selling club and a gift, such as a house that might later be sold. Trevor was told: 'choose your own house. Not only will the club buy it, we will also have it decorated to your own requirements ... [and a job] worth £1,000 a year' (Ford, 1957, pp.13-77).

By the 1950s then, the world of 1946-47 – of the housing crisis and the threat posed by players having a real 'other job' – had been incorporated into a mesh of myriad illicit and avoidance payments. But the mould was already made.

The season's union dispute failed to give players a legitimate share of the transfer fee, so the pattern was confirmed in Lawton's move in November 1947, to Third Division Notts County! It would be like Alan Shearer making this move after his 1996 Euro triumph or Michael Owen after 1998. The occa-sion of Lawton's split was power and money. Chelsea had contracted with their Swedish hosts that Tom would be in their summer 1947 touring party. Lawton refused: still feeling the effects of non-stop play during and after the war, he wanted a break. In retaliation Chelsea refused to sell him to First Division opposition – they had little need of a record £20,000 fee. Eventually Lawton dropped two divisions, and soon lost his England place, but the extras – a house, mythical jobs, newspaper columns – took him into an estimated £3,000 surtax bracket. Lawton's transfer was only exceptional in value. The currency was all the personal-family-domestic elements that other working people were wrestling with in the postwar reconstruction. The process – dependency upon gifts and favours from directors and patrons – reasserted football's prewar patriarchy, and withheld recognition of a player's autonomy.

Newspapers continued to follow the transfer trail, which soon reached a quarter of a million pounds. The biggest story remained the search itself: managers, trainers and directors still 'living in railway carriages', still not finding or persuading players. Negotiations created a dilemma locally: trans-fers were a source of interest, and often dissatisfaction, among readers. Explanations were necessary, primarily to give a club's affairs the appearance of coherence. The veil over illegal or avoidance payments could be lifted in general comment but remained in place for individual deals: housing was a frequent medium because everyone appreciated the problem.

Selling clubs ran into trouble. Middlesbrough, under Mannion's guiding influence, looked Championship material early on. But Boro were derailed by the latest episode in Everton's obsessive search – 'miles and money have been no deterrent to attain our objective' – for a centre-forward. Everton's gaze fell upon folk hero Micky Fenton. Before the war Fenton had been an England international – the last specialist before Lawton's reign – and leading First Division scorer. £8,000 was well short of the Stubbins standard, and Fenton had a home: 'I have virtually bought my house at Stockton and it would be a big uprooting if I had to leave Teeside.' Unable to provide sufficient incentive, Everton's Theo Kelly left, embarrassed: 'this is a most difficult problem.' The public reacted against the board: 'Teesside seethed ... wild with indignation at the transfer of such a popular figure and there is talk of a boycott.' Thereafter Middlesbrough's title challenge never seemed so convincing.

Local discretion with inside information was vulnerable when a transfer took on wider overtones and nationals demonstrated fewer inhibitions. For example, in the transitional season Trevor Ford's 40 goals made his reputation, and Swansea beat off interest from a host of covetous clubs. Local resistance was strong – 'there would be something of a riot if he were allowed to leave his native heath'. The new season started in similar vein, 'we are not selling him under any circumstances' – but when Swansea and Ford fell out, Aston Villa proved persuasive. A national paper broke the scoop and Birmingham's *Sports Argus* grumbled: 'the local press is often blamed for missing such news. Usually the reason is that while we know what is cooking we respect confidences and keep mum until a ticklish deal is clinched. This "leaking" is annoying and unfair.' This time Ford suffered the abuse: they 'pointed the finger of scorn and reviled me for being a rat and leaving a sinking ship' (Ford, 1957, p.35).

Reporters sometimes found it difficult not to hint. The information that Ipswich were watching a right winger 'with the kick of a mule and a straight for goal habit' understandably created great interest in the agricultural hinterland. However the following week brought the discreetly reported disappointment that the deal was off, 'for unusual reasons, which unfortunately cannot be mentioned.' Soon afterwards Frank Neary left QPR for West Ham, an operation of the cartel keeping transfers within the capital. Frank was the 'hard shooting winger' and Ipswich's failure was because 'Neary wanted a move from Shepherds Bush but not away from London. You see he's just got a house, even if it is a prefab.'

With homelessness and squatting widespread, sensitivity was especially necessary if special treatment was a possible context for a transfer. The theme of greedy footballers was common, such as the player who said 'an empty house wasn't much use to him unless the club furnished it'. Similarly, 'Tom's house row' provoked the thought: 'thousands of bombed-out Londoners should be delighted to know houses are so easily obtainable.'

In handling such stories local newspapers were aware 'buying houses for footballers is not likely to be popular with the general public because of the clubs' deep purses'. Thus squatters occupied the many Army camps around Swindon, where injuries had struck down Town's promising start. Their transfer target, Liverpool's George Paterson 'was adamant that he would not come south until the club was able to offer him a house to replace the one he has. Manager Louis Page offered him the opportunity to travel back and forwards temporarily. But the player feels he has an obligation to his wife and child who have had their share of living in lodgings.' Town's need was great, and soon 'a house has been found' and their record signing helped the team resume winning ways.

Local papers needed to strike a balance. Criticism of player demands was either dealt with in a general way – 'it is now common knowledge that some players have made extraordinary demands when their transfers have been sought' – or as a retrospective comment on an unsuccessful negotiation. If a transfer went through, then a positive slant encouraged supporters' sympathies. Footballers' negotiations – housing, a second job or tolerance of training elsewhere – concerned the very issues of reconstruction with which readers were grappling. Supporters could empathise with Paterson's dilemma. On the other hand if George was favoured over local people with exactly the same needs then ...

The sense that footballers' dilemmas were much like anyone else's was captured by a footballer's big chance during the hysterical transfer scramble: 'Lewis, Kidderminster centre forward, was keen to come – he had an ambition to join a First Division club – but he had been waiting for a house for five years. Just as he was about to try his luck with Blackburn, he got his house. Well, what would you do?'

Blackburn's experience in 1946-47 was typical. The side had had a poor transitional season, conceding 111 goals, and finishing next to bottom. The summer initially saw no new signings, with only winger Bobby Langton a major returnee from the Forces. The club still had six players from its 1939 promotion side, but two of the best, Frank Chivers and Albert Clarke, had been killed. An experienced goalkeeper was needed when the young incumbent was called up. Like many first-time managers, Eddie Hapgood went back to his old club, Arsenal. He did not receive much hospitality, for during long and protracted negotiations he 'had to sleep in the back of his car'. Nevertheless Hapgood got his man, wartime international George Marks. Thereafter, almost uniquely, Hapgood stayed at home with his team. Marks shored up the defence, but goals proved scarce. Excessive 'hopes are pinned' on prewar hero Len Butt, who had 'touched the heights in the promotion season', with 'quicksilver dribbles of those little drumstick legs'. But Butt had started in the 1920s and had bad knees. Soon Butt was out and Eddie Hapgood was left with 'energetic but incoherent' youngsters. The search intensified. The most bizarre of their near misses was an offer to Carlisle for Ivor Broadis, which was turned down by manager ... Ivor Broadis. At 23, a former navigator on bombers, Broadis was football's youngest manager.

Blackburn turned to Scotland. Their directors failed with a five-figure offer for a major talent, Gordon Smith of Hibernians. Into the New Year, more bad results, no goals, and Rovers directors were willing to pay 'fantastic prices' for the more mundane: Jock Weir, Hibs' ex-Royal Navy centre-forward, and a reserve. 'Negotiations broke down at an advanced stage … the last word being left to the players.' As the major target it was Weir's word that mattered. But Rovers were soon back again, closing the gap and signing him alone for £10,000. Now the local *Blackburn Times* wanted goodwill extended to Weir, whose football persona was in any event to be 'mustard keen'. So Weir was described to have 'made up his mind to come to Ewood at all costs … it was no fault of his that he did not come when the deal was first in the air.'

Blackburn suddenly went wild in the market, buying two other forwards for £10,000, and a non-league centre-forward. Finally they signed a true successor to Len Butt, a Scottish international in his mid-30s. From famine to feast, and food inevitably provided the imagery: Rovers' supporters had been 'hungry for new forward talent. Now before they have quite digested the heavy meal put before them, they have been served with an extra course they scarcely expected.'

"It's for you, Mr. Matthews, from the Big Four—they want to know how you arrived at your peace settlement!"

Stan,
a tower and
a stick of rock

11

A Clash of Lesser Strifes

'The thunder of war is past, but the clash of our lesser strifes is insistent to our ears and brings uneasiness to our hearts.'
'Tell me if there is another profession to equal football finance – outside the black market of course.'

For ten minutes on Monday, 14 October 1946 the footballers of England were on strike, their 'stewpot of grievances' finally come to the boil. The decision, taken by a small group of men in Room 4, Grand Hotel, Manchester, was swiftly aborted by His Majesty's Government. It was a day of strikes: hotel strikes, restaurant strikes, railway strikes …

The footballers had every reason to strike. Football was booming, 'more than ever a mammoth money making machine.' Massive interest, windfall profits, soaring transfer fees. The clubs had more money than they knew what to do with. Real football had come home, but so had the scandalously low wages and a challenge seemed in tune with the times. The war and the new government had changed social relations and made for a new economic order.

The group was the Players' Union Executive: all experienced in the underworld of professional football, fed up with their poor deal and immersed in its bitter day-to-day realities. Secretary Jimmy Fay, JP, had run the union single-handedly throughout the war from the flat above his sports shop in Southport. His twenty-year career as a professional footballer had gone from ten shillings a week to England selection. His six years took Oldham from Lancashire Combination to First Division, missing just one match: 'when the wind carried the roof off the old stand whilst he was in his bath … the Oldham ground-staff ran into the dressing room shouting: "Come on Jimmy, you're going to be killed," and in his haste to get dressed before he was properly rubbed down, Fay caught cold.' He was always a zealous worker for the Players' Union. A founder member in 1907, when he joined Bolton he quickly enrolled 35 Wanderers. Fay had been secretary since 1929.

All committee members had difficult autumns. New Chairman Jimmy Guthrie was still fighting Portsmouth. Claiming his registration, they tried to prevent him playing for as well as coaching his new club. Jimmy aimed to reorganise the union within the context of Labour's 'massive programme of economic reform', of freeing footballers from his own fate: 'a few days after my seventeenth birthday I became a bondsman, a serf, a slave' (Guthrie, 1976, Preface).

Another committee member, Middlesbrough's ex-schoolboy international, Bobby Stuart, was given the run-around by Tom Finney when he returned from the Executive meeting. The home crowd so barracked his efforts that Stuart announced an irrevocable determination to leave the club he had served for sixteen years. Initially Stuart had treated Finney cautiously: 'ignoring frequent injunctions to "tackle", preferring to "wait" for his opponent'. Stuart changed tack after the break, and Boro's 3-0 lead evaporated. Stuart's tactics became the talk of the town: 'so many varied opinions have been expressed.'

Norman Low travelled to Manchester with his name all over the Sunday papers – 'the dirtiest thing I have known in football'. Low was steeped in the game – his father Wilf was a Newcastle star in their Edwardian heyday: the days of the last union challenge. Norman had captained Newport to promotion in 1939, but now that team was gone. Newport started badly and got worse. Low did better than most, 'stood alone' when West Brom won 7-2 on County's own ground, trying to cover the many gaps. However the defeats encouraged local mischief makers and, after the 0-13 loss, Low wanted away: 'rumour mongers ... have been spreading stories about me and even writing letters to the newspapers criticising my conduct on and off the pitch ... The crowd have singled me out on several occasions for unsportsmanlike demonstrations ... it is just as well for me to get out straightaway.'

High-flying Cardiff wanted Low for their promotion team, but Newport would not transfer him to neighbours, so instead of the leaders Low moved to the bottom club.

Frank Broome was also the subject of rumours: 'Don't pay any attention to those whispers that Broome's position as a committee man of the Players' Union made him unpopular at Villa Park. Players can stay too long with clubs they serve well.' Whatever. Most unusually Villa took the initiative in proposing Broome's transfer to Derby, home of outgoing Union chairman Sammy Crooks. Before the war Frank Broome – 'the footballer with the greyhound legs' – had experienced within 24 hours both responses to Nazi Germany – appeasement and resistance. Frank's first international was in Berlin when England players were instructed to give the Nazi salute before beating Germany 6-3. The following day Frank turned out for touring Villa, who beat another German team (including the best from Austria, which Germany had just annexed) 3-2. The Villa pros refused to Heil Hitler.

Like the others, Joe Mercer's motivation had been questioned. Joe's last game as England's captain that April had ended with accusations of his not trying after a knee injury. Mercer was hurt, and Everton secretary-manager Theo Kelly added insult by querying Joe's commitment. Mercer was debating his future now that he had joined his father-in-law's grocery business. Joe later described his transfer request as a personal rift, although contemporary journalists-in-the-know hinted at something more material. Fans, it was said, wanted Everton to 'immediately settle what is really a small point of issue'. Instead they dropped him, citing the attention Mercer was giving to groceries. Notwithstanding public disillusionment and apparently imminent retirement, this respected England captain was co-opted onto an Executive deciding the future of real football.

'Farmer' Joe Wilson had known many ups and downs since signing for Newcastle in 1927. The Saturday before the Executive met, his Barnsley went four points clear of their Second Division rivals – a notable achievement given that most players, like Wilson, lived and trained elsewhere. Wilson had reached his pinnacle: the previous Saturday he 'blotted out' the vaunted young Trevor Ford, and 'saved his side a trouncing'. In some eyes the season had so far had been a question of 'thank heaven for Joe Wilson'. However hell beckoned on Wilson's return from Manchester. After a series of 'grotesque failures', in which Wilson is 'often beaten', there was a shoal of letters regarding Barnsley's 'toboggan' down the table. Wilson was dropped and his humiliation complete when Barnsley paid a record fee for his replacement, a 6ft 3in former commando who had toes shot off in the war, and who promptly put through his own goal in each of his first two games. Wilson wanted a move.

This then was a battle hardened group. They had the mandate of a vociferous AGM, an overwhelming ballot and London players issuing a 'no compromise' clarion call. Yet they faced formidable difficulties. First, they were already too late. A season's beginning was the best time to act: clubs were vulnerable following a summer without a cash flow; and neither players nor public would be deflected by the emerging events, results and momentum of a new season. One reason the Executive did not call a strike earlier – they were dispersed throughout Europe on summer coaching jobs – mirrored fundamental weaknesses: players were scattered, and they had different interests. Anxiety about whether new professionals or part-timers would support action lay behind a damaging split in the Union Executive. 'The seed of great bitterness was sown' in the abortive strike of November 1945. Executive members as well as Tommy Lawton had resisted the false dawn of that settlement: 'unfortunately the union delegates did most of the arguing amongst themselves.' In particular 'Farmer' Joe Wilson was angry at 'Grocer' Joe Mercer's 'soft-soaping the management' and the latter's fear that new recruits would not hold solid. This disunity carried over into 1946, 'a basic split working against the union's strategy' (Harding, 1991, pp.213-16).

Wavering was acknowledged. Membership now stood at 2,300 (an average of 26 per club), but some fell only hesitantly into line. Players complained that, unlike other unions, the Players' Union required 'a guinea to renew their membership on returning from the Forces', but these objectors eventually crumpled. At their own workplace, Jimmy Fay suggested 'the players of each club opposing Sheffield Wednesday on the field will point out the advantages of joining the Union.' In other workplaces around Sheffield: 'why should trade union workers support non-union footballers.' Wednesday players soon telegrammed for membership.

The dispute was dissected and debated in Saturday Football Specials throughout the land as it rumbled over the autumn of 1946. What were footballers worth? What were they really paid? The circumstances of men like

Middlesbrough's George Dews were cited by those sceptical of headline figures. During 1945-46 Dews had had to travel 500 miles from his base to play. But on demobilisation he found work with Middlesbrough corporation. So Dews had three jobs: his council post, training evenings with Middlesbrough (which included summer wages when 'they weren't even playing'), and summer employment with Worcestershire Cricket Club.

The League accused the union of being intimidatory, then said they would play with amateurs or take the opportunity to throw overboard players 'who have not turned out as well as expected'. The Players' Union proclaimed the support of the country's biggest unions, and observed that amateurs would be unionists too. No strike pay was possible, but most players had other jobs anyway. Jimmy Guthrie lobbied energetically with Labour MPs and newspaper columnists in the battle for public support, a battle that the newspapers were unsure the players were winning: 'the threat to strike has not produced alarm or sympathy from crowds.' Executive members were surprised at the public's lack of sympathy. Perhaps supporters were too parochial, or too angry with the threat to real football or with the D-Day Dodgers.

The dispute also prompted columnists to give masterclasses on the structure and history of professional football. They explained that a key grievance concerned the lump sum benefit payable after five years. The trouble was, benefits were discretionary and thus subject to the rollercoaster of club finances and power relations. Clubs used benefits as sanctions to hold a player in line or agree to a transfer (out of which a benefit might effectively be paid). Clubs' deviousness meant only ten per cent of qualifying professionals received a benefit: Bill Shankly never did, despite fifteen years sterling service. Bill was no 'yes man' and ended his Preston career in dispute: a common scenario.

One 'old get out' was to offer veterans reduced wages, and when they refused, hold them in breach of requirements. Veteran England player Jack Pickering testified to the transfer scam, recalling when Sheffield United tried to sell him, 'pointing out finances were so low there was little prospect of me receiving any benefit money, much as they desired to pay.' Pickering resisted until United reached the Cup final, when 'four or five of us were paid benefits'. The FA Cup might have had a special place in public affection, but Depression era players had very material reasons for hoping success would persuade clubs to discharge responsibilities they otherwise resisted. Birmingham players remembered their 1931 run: 'after each tie we quietly shook hands with each other, and scanned the newspapers eagerly and maybe apprehensively to see if our luck in the draw still held ... When we got to the final, we knew our benefits were in the bag.'

The League's pre-emptive strike that spring indicated they meant to run things as they had before. They reneged on promises to consult with the union. Using as an excuse the high levels of Entertainment Tax (soon reduced) the League determined a £10 maximum wage, £2 shy. And in the spring the players, not the clubs, were vulnerable. Not to accept meant no summer pay, a reprise of the old prewar dilemma: 'if the man signed they saved money on his wage packet, if he did not sign until the start of the following season they saved the summer wages' (Guthrie, 1976, p.52).

The union asked players not to, appreciating that acceptance undermined further resistance. A crucial moment but a futile hope, and they soon reverted to their initial 1945 strategy, proceeding 'under protest'. Thereafter, the League always threatened not to accept even government-sponsored arbitration, but go to court for enforcement: 'there is nothing upon which to arbitrate, as the players signed contracts running to the end of the season, agreed to the wages offered them and would be guilty of breaking their contracts by "downing boots".'

Otherwise, the clubs' distinctive tactic was to prevaricate, to finesse the gap between the Management Committee as a negotiating body and the governing executive of all clubs. Such prevarication had the effect of: diminishing players' momentum for industrial action; giving time for differences to emerge and dissatisfactions with their Executive; and above all allowing the rhythm of the season to exert an effect. As a last resort they could call upon the FA to jeopardise players' livelihoods through their essential power of registration. This was what broke the century's previous challenge, and was remembered as a warning for 1946.

In 1907 the period's greatest star Billy Meredith initiated a new union with expansive aims – 'freedom of contract, access to the law of the land, an end to wage restraint' (Harding, 1991, p.128). The crunch came when they joined the Federation of Trade Unions and used a new law designed to protect workers against the loss of their livelihood through industrial injury or illness: 'we wanted footballers to be recognised as workmen within the meaning of the Compensation Act.'

This was too much: a challenge to the FA's authority and also to their assertion that footballers were primarily sportsmen, not workmen. The authorities saw their very power over the players at stake. The FA granted clubs an amnesty over previous illegal payments; and made their acceptance of a player's registration conditional on a loyalty clause, 'effectively disowning the union and declaring specific loyalty to the Football Association and its rules.' As in 1945 and 1946, the players' best chance of challenging the authorities successfully had lain in not starting the 1909 season. A strike was called but outflanked when the FA called its own mass meeting and vague promises were enough. The football authorities then prevaricated until the union came into line. Their challenge was effectively broken and the inter-war period saw a disillusioned Meredith dismayed that the players were 'content to live a kind of schoolboy life' (Harding, 1991, pp.138-43).

But the League's ally proved to be the Government, not the FA. Footballers had every reason to strike but, under wartime regulations, no right. The system of regulating industrial disputes through requirements to give notice and submit to arbitration was a wartime measure looking fragile. 1946 was a year of unofficial strikes. Like the footballers, workers sought to remedy old grievances or hold on to wartime gains, and would not leave change to government or union. Footballers were literally surrounded by these actions as many bus crews chose match Saturdays as a good day for an effective strike. Those crews in Bury demanded double time: 'many men leave home at 4am, work until about 2pm, snatch a hurried meal, then carry on with football specials. It is 6.30pm before they can get home.'

All this was much to the chagrin of a government advocating industrial discipline. Footballers, symbols of wartime solidarity, provided an opportunity to demonstrate the system had not lapsed. What would the footballers do? How could they, amidst an unprecedented boom, honour their unfair contracts? 'With crowds, gate money soaring to new heights, and cheque waving managers in a transfer queue, disgruntled and disappointed players meet this week to discuss strike action.'

Nevertheless after only ten minutes Grand Hotel porter Herbert Braid knocked at the door and relayed the message – 'long distance call for Mr Fay'. The Ministry had activated arbitration and the strike was off. Initially the process proved chastening: League President Will Cuff would not negotiate and left for an early train, saying it was impossible to get hotel accommodation in London at such short notice. Another meeting, scheduled for 4 November, became the key moment.

In the interim, both sides reconsidered. The League realised the dispute was not going away: the players were angry and the contrast between clubs' burgeoning incomes and their meanness was unmistakable. They would lose the mandatory arbitration consequent on a further breakdown. A new compromise, or delaying tactic, was needed. Where did it lie: in relaxing the maximum wage and allowing players to receive some of their transfer fee, or ensure the minimum and the conditions of the poorest paid?

The union made the same calculation. They were finding it difficult to contain all the interests and expectations raised. Without resources they represented many causes. They inspired campaigns by other sports professionals benefiting from the spectator craze to gain greater reward and to wrest back some control from employers. Speedway riders went on strike. Great Britain's Rugby League squad returned from a successful Ashes tour, threatened strikes and like Scottish professional footballers saw the Players' Union as a model.

The campaign also confronted a decline in footballers' relative wage position. The *Ministry of Labour Gazette* indicated a 74 per cent increase in average weekly earnings between October 1938 and January 1946. Mining earnings, including the many absentee workers, had gone up 104 per cent to £6 8s 5d a week. The Players' Union wanted a 50 per cent increase on their 1938 maximum of £8. The wage was greater than other working class occupations, but there were hidden expenses: 'an international footballer explained to me today where his £10 wage goes to, and I must admit it is an eye opener. He sends his wife £5, pays his landlady £2, income tax takes 15s, his rail fare home at weekends claims £1 5s. So by the time he's met his newspaper bill he can't even change a pound note.'

How many professional footballers received the maximum? Only a few: 2-3 per cent was claimed as 'common knowledge'. £6 was a common wage for a full-timer, whereas 'an unskilled labourer gets £5 10s or £6 these days'. Another journalist suggested 12 per cent of players received the maximum wage, with young first teamers progressing from £7 by £1 a week annual rises. The official parties to the dispute were circumspect. The League stayed mute, and the union offered 5-10 per cent. On the eve of the strike Jimmy Fay flourished 'the wage sheet of a headline-making First Division club, which chalked up big profits last season ... 50-odd professionals on the books and only eight of them are getting £10 a week in the playing season.' Thirty-nine professionals only received £5 appearance money if they played: 'in idleness, many of them receive "nowt".'

Whatever the true percentage, it was low. Therefore the need to pay the stars according to their drawing power gave the claim prominence, but mattered less than appeared. The union had changed since Billy Meredith pursued a driving message of freedom of contract that would benefit star players most. The first ten years of Jimmy Fay's secretaryship, the Depression years when the League refused to discuss wages, saw membership rise from 434 in 1929 to 1950 in 1939, and now 2,300. The union's threat was now more potent, but its agenda had changed. The 1946 campaign was based on a thousand-word 1943 Beveridge Scheme for professional footballers, except now 'the argument about maximum wages were of little interest to the general body of players, but the fixing of a minimum concerned all.' This campaign would also command more public sympathy: '£12 maximum demand ... is taking wage-talk into a realm unknown to the average club follower. Life on £3-£5 a week is a problem too well known to the man-in-the-street.'

Ex-pros who were now managers reinforced this theme with a warning that 'ordinary rank and file players will eventually have their wages depressed to balance the higher pay for the top-notchers', or worse, 'we shall have to cut the number.' This 'mute multitude of the unsung' also suffered from seasonal contracts: a player who was released in May had no income until signed in late August.

The public case increasingly carried the powerful argument of player as victim. Clubs continued to act as if they could have the best of both worlds: pay as little as possible, and exert maximum control. Those which made handsome wartime profits threatened that unless players gave up their other jobs, they 'would not be paid a penny piece' but could not leave. Similarly when the clubs asked for time to see if the attendance boom was going to last, Jimmy Fay knew his men could not wait: 'the lads who are playing now and have been doing so for the past two or three years have made the money for the clubs.'

Fay was thinking of John Eves, representing those many whose match-by-match payment made the big profits of 1944-46, but now sitting idle on swollen staffs. After a month without a penny to show, he gave up the unequal struggle: 'John Eves' contract at Sunderland was on a match basis and as he has not had a game he has not received anything for all his training. He goes to Darlington but will work and train at Sunderland.'

The inherent ingratitude was palpable: 'not much of a reward for his wartime service. I think I know what I would say ... if I were expected to train and then get paid just when they thought they would play me.' The union worried whether such part-timers, who made up two-thirds of the professional ranks, would support the 'top money full-timers'. Would their other job make them more, or less likely to strike? Then there were marginal pros like Kenneth Speak. The married former Marine rejected Bolton's 'reasonable terms' after a month's trial and signed for Portsmouth. A mundane event, which surfaced only because Wanderers' meanness 'caused feeling in some quarters ... Apparently he left over £1 a week which Portsmouth were and Bolton weren't prepared to pay.'

The campaign risked becoming merely incremental. A more radical approach sought freedom from the restrictions of professional sport, deemed anachronistic in the postwar social climate. Commentators found echoes in American football's 'draft': 'a human slave market extends from the Atlantic to the Pacific; from Canada to Alabama. Day by day young men come to the auction block for sale to the highest bidder. Bidding is bitter, determined, unscrupulous.'

English football needed a William Wilberforce to 'free the good game of the taint of slavery which disfigures it ... the pernicious system which enables a club to nail down young players on professional forms that may bind unwary youngsters indefinitely ... What is the difference between such a system and that of the slave market.'

1946's newspapers recalled the events of 1919 when the League sold a disbanded club's registrations to the highest bidder at an 'auction'. Players had to play for whoever paid the most. It was a logical outcome of the importance given to registration when professionalism was established, but the slave imagery was irresistible and retained its resonance: 'a sale of human flesh and blood ... an immoral and disgraceful affair.'

The 1946 dispute veered between the bread and butter of wage levels, and a turnaround in footballers' self-belief – 'in the bad old days the public paid the piper and the directors called the tune whereas now footballers everywhere are making stands for what they considered to be their rights.'

For this to be translated into each player negotiating his own individual contract, a further obstacle needed to be surmounted: different pay within the same team. The justification of this disparity today is that in a competitive sport each player hopes to become a star. Gordon Taylor, the union's Chief Executive, restated this credo in April 2000: 'the PFA from the days of Billy Meredith onwards has always wanted to achieve, that the latest trainee could make it to the top.' Such individualism was more problematic in the immediate postwar world. Higher wages might be a matter of natural justice, reflecting a star's pulling power, but it was rarely articulated how this could be squared with a team sport.

Billy Meredith's arguments in the Edwardian era were essentially laissez-faire: a worker had an unrestricted right to work for the highest bidder. In 1909 opposing forces had been too strong. Then there was no alternative to the League's cartel, no Colombia, no hole-in-the-wall, and the FA asserted that laissez-faire need not apply in sport. In 1946 the official ideal was that of the collective, of which the experience of war and the triumph of the Labour Government were but two expressions. Football's 'good war' had been based on tapping into the collective spirit.

Today differential pay seldom threatens ideas of teamwork: football is managing the tension. Just after the war, the tools to integrate the grievances felt by all, and team spirit as a basic football concept, with the freedom of a few to earn unlimited amounts, were not available. There could be plausible references to outside equivalents, to film and music hall stars, and to American sportsmen, but to articulate how such a freedom could be integrated into football's existing structure and assumptions went beyond what either top players or union could grasp: 'don't you think the maximum should be wiped out, so that stars can command their box-office value?' The international: 'No. I think team spirit would be effected.'

This remained the strongest argument within the game against the removal of the maximum wage. On the very eve of its demise in 1960 the manager of champions Wolves still felt the same: 'for the sake of team-spirit, a manager could not possibly have a large differential in the wages of individual players' (Cullis, 1960, p.181).

The union thus suffered from a surfeit of interests: full-timers or part-timers; players being transferred or staying with their club; returning servicemen, or those who played at home and produced the profits. Above all, players in difficulty needing the minimum wage raised or the great stars wanting the maximum wage abolished. How to act without jeopardising the financial viability of Third Division clubs and therefore the livelihood of present and future generations of journeymen professional footballers? There was a lot to be said for all these strategies but it was hard to pursue them all. And the expectation to deliver was high.

So the Executive grasped at straws when the League was conciliatory at 4 November's arbitration. Jimmy Guthrie announced: 'everything went well for us … it is the best offer we have ever had. I think you can take it the matter is settled.' Although there was no agreement on the maximum wage or compulsory benefits, the League was 'sympathetic': to the minimum wage; August to August contracts; 'granting a free transfer to players not offered a living wage; and players on the transfer list receiving some payment for the period when unsigned.' The League had previously resisted defining a minimum, sticking to a 'reasonable wage', so Jimmy Fay was jubilant at a £7 winter, £5 summer recommendation.

But Fay was guilty of wishful thinking. 'Sympathetic' meant clubs were committed to nothing. The League still denied the War-time Emergency Powers Act applied to football (because not an industry); still threatened to go to court, and insisted that any agreement had to be accepted by all clubs. It refused to convene this meeting before February, but agreed to recommend backdating a settlement to 1 January.

What justified union optimism? Had the League yielded enough? All their instincts must have warned against prevarication. Yet the Press were so persuaded by an anticipated generous settlement, that worried Third Division clubs publicly complained they would be unable to afford the increase and would be forced to employ only part-time professionals, and privately lobbied the Management Committee.

The reality emerged with Machiavellian timing when, on 28 December, clubs received their Committee's 'elaborate booklet'. The recommendations contained few crumbs of comfort. Perhaps they thought the players would be too exhausted to notice after a Christmas spent criss-crossing the country in cold, unreliable trains to play three matches in four days. Fay and Guthrie bitterly linked the three million people who watched the footballers over Christmas with this 'niggardly paring down': '£6 and £4 limits are no use to men in their twenties.' They regretted 'the long hours spent arguing and explaining' and realised 'we would have done better by going to arbitration'.

The Executive had thrown away their earlier momentum. Furious members again wanted to act, yet the union was committed to a long wait until February and certain disappointment. A season was being lost. Members blamed their Executive for falling into the trap of 'kidding' tactics. Jimmy Fay tried to revive the cause that had seemed so vibrant by claiming players were 'heartily in favour of calling a halt to football any time now'. It was unconvincing, and extraordinarily the very opposite became true. The dispute now ran into 'King Winter's sharp right hook', in which stoicism replaced discontent. In contradiction to everything that had been said since the season's beginning it soon seemed as though the footballers were the only people who were working.

The weather too conspired to challenge the main plank of their case – the clubs' 'happy financial position' – in the most unexpected way. Players' hardiness playing in virtually any conditions meant that there had only been one year in its history, 1933, when the weather significantly disrupted the League programme, and therefore cash flows. Now 1947's great freeze up meant clubs went six weeks without playing; York City seven, a League record. In addition, the efforts to make grounds playable cost money: Sheffield Wednesday spent £800 employing 150 men for over a week in several failed attempts to clear 5,000 tons of snow for one cup-tie.

However, protestations of sudden poverty cut little ice, the players realising that clubs 'made their money before the bad weather came along. The players mean business. They feel they have been patient too long.' On 24 February the clubs had their long-awaited meeting. It was now deep in an icy winter, in which shortage of coal meant no fuel. Thus in the unheated grill room of a Manchester hotel, the League delegates 'sat in overcoats and mufflers in an ice cold room lighted with flickering candles and smoky hurricane lamps.' Or storm lanterns, anticipating the players' likely reaction. Jimmy Guthrie found the decision-making 'rigmarole' pretty chilling too. The President submitted the union claim and the Management Committee recommended its effective rejection. In fact their only recommendation not carried was that the settlement should be backdated to 1 January.

For some, the terms of the conflict itself was all just a matter of time: 'those who profess to see farthest into the future say there is only one solution and that it is bound to come, either in this decade or one other. That solution is to scrap all wage restrictions between clubs and players, and allow each club to pay each player what the club itself considers the player to be worth.' But the players could not wait for the future and knew nothing would come without a struggle. They called their own delegates meeting on 10 March. Following another great blizzard that cut the country in half, only half the delegates made it. But there were no qualms about their mood: 'the Union Committee was roundly condemned by delegates for allowing the League constantly to play for time' (Harding, 1991, p.227).

All had had enough: some wanted to strike immediately; but the law required they give notice again – effectively back to where they had started, in October. This time, unless the Ministry of Labour acted further, they would strike in ten days, on 21 March. This time nothing could stop the strike, unless the Government called a halt to football, and that couldn't happen, could it?

12

King Mud was determined not to be beaten

'Hundreds of supporters stayed after the match at Roker ... Topic – that man Matthews. Stan astounded those who saw him for the first time and there were thousands.'

Stanley Matthews was back. The 'Prince of the Potters' was mesmeric in Stoke's 1-0 win at fourth-placed Sunderland. The return of national competition gave many fans their first chance to see the legendary prewar star. Almost an hour before kick off the gates closed on 57,290, who generated record receipts of £4,980: Stoke got £500 and Stan himself the maximum £10 wage plus £2 win bonus.

Stan Matthews was a touchstone figure of 1946, inspiring crowd records at eight grounds with music, magic and fantasy: 'Matthews is the supreme virtuoso among footballers. He is the great extemporiser of cadenzas. The game stops, the opposition falls under hypnotic influence; Matthews has the ball this way and that and back again' (Young, 1950, p.68).

Matthews was revered for his hat-trick in the 5-4 win over Czechoslovakia which preserved England's increasingly neurotic undefeated home record against continental opposition, and for sealing England's greatest-ever win over Scotland, 8-0, with a mazy 70-yard run, 'then working the ball right up to the unhappy Crozier popped it into the net. The brilliant effort brought the house down.' But Matthews was not universally admired – in his own words he was 'a headache to play with'. In particular, his club manager Bob McGrory was 'never a Matthews fan' (Seed, 1957, p.43).

Stan Matthews was a reluctant celebrity: a reserved, private man. There were two occasions, in February 1938 and October 1946, when he squirmed uncomfortably within a media storm. In 1938, soon after his Czechoslovakian triumph, 'browned off' Stan asked for a transfer. Seven hectic days followed, with protest meetings attracting thousands. Stan was 'staggered by the limelight' and fled Stoke, unable to walk down the street without being dragged into arguments. Industrialists from local pottery factories brokered an outcome that Matthews described elegantly: 'difficulties began to be smoothed out. I was given an assurance that efforts would be made to make me more comfortable in the future.'

During his wartime RAF service, Matthews established his family in a new home and business, a hotel on the Blackpool promenade. The 1946-47 season brooded under the question: when would Stan cut his prewar roots and move his football there too?

After his brilliance in the Bolton Disaster international, Matthews' 1946 autumn faltered: twice injured, he felt sorry for himself missing England's internationals in Ireland. The relevance of his genius within the new all-action style was questioned, especially as neither club nor country missed him – his replacements, Tom Finney and George Mountford, exhibited 'new and devastating directness'. Matthews-less Stoke became a vibrant, resurgent team: 'what gives a relish to watching Stoke just now is the feeling that almost at any moment goals might turn up.'

Stoke's Chelsea triumph, their sixth successive win, made them the toast of the football world, but a destructive controversy laid them low. Matthews declared himself particularly anxious to play against Arsenal that Saturday, for the first time since 1939. Stoke chose a 'problem of extraordinary difficulty' to show who was boss. The directors instructed McGrory to ask Matthews to prove his fitness in the reserves. They resented his freedom from surveillance: Stan had not been seen since he limped out of the Manchester United game three weeks before.

Journalists avidly echoed the steadily more acrimonious phone conversations between Matthews and McGrory. Stan dismissed the very idea of playing in the reserves: 'I immediately replied "Of course not. I am 100 per cent fit." If City wanted to retain a winning team, he preferred "another week's rest".' He remembered another time when 'I got up out of a sick bed and played'. That January, Matthews went straight from RAF night duty to his record 44th appearance for England and promptly caught a cold. McGrory was loath to accept his absence from Stoke's cup-tie (the run culminating in the Bolton Disaster) against the leaders of the Football League (North), Sheffield United. McGrory had him take 'pep pills used by the Luftwaffe before taking off to raid England'. Matthews dozed off after the win, but then awoke, alarmed and disoriented, when the high kicked in.

Relations became stormy when Matthews suspected McGrory of planting the story that Stoke players would challenge the directors if he replaced George Mountford. Matthews said 'it has been very badly handled by manager McGrory' and he 'had been dissatisfied for some time': 'Matthews to all intents and purposes has left Stoke.'

How much was Matthews worth? Now nearly 32, 'obviously the best part of his playing career is over,' and a record £15,000 meant £100 per match if he lasted another three seasons. The issue was the individualist versus the team: his style; his international status; and now he asserted personal interest over club authority – Matthews' newspaper column argued that playing in the reserves would gravely affect his prestige and commercial status. So, whilst not a vocal union campaigner, Stan's actions in holding his own chimed with the prevailing context of asserting footballers' rights.

Poison pen letters and constant calls forced Matthews out of his hotel to eat meals: just like 1938. That Saturday he was famously photographed on the terraces supporting Blackpool to a top-two win over Manchester United. Provocative, moi? Matthews said it provided 'a little peace to recover from constant telephone calls'. Perhaps from Bob McGrory, who announced Stan would meet the board. Stoke players denied any complaint: 'We are all the best of friends with Stan.' He 'was glad to hear that. I have no quarrel with the City players and could not imagine them quarrelling with me.' But Stoke remained 'wild with rumour at this time. There was the pro-Matthews group and the anti-Matthews group, and there were those people who spent their time inventing bigger and better stories ' (Franklin, 1956, p.67).

At Highbury, the Stoke players issued another 'clear the air' communique, stating both their every confidence in the management keeping an unchanged team, and how highly they thought of Matthews. The gates were closed on a crowd of 62,000, with huge queues of 10,000 still outside. A battery of press photographers besieged George Mountford: it was all too much and Dr Kevin O'Flanagan gained struggling Arsenal's first home win with an 'amazing screw shot'.

The crisis was resolved the following Tuesday. McGrory expected the directors to take a strong line, and insist that Matthews train with the club twice a week: counter rumours hinted that he would follow his friend Jock Dodds through the hole-in-the-wall to Shamrock Rovers. Portents were bad when Stan found the club offices locked, but he carried the negotiations. Matthews got his week's holiday – because of the publicity – and continued to train at Blackpool, the board knowing 'they could rely on him to train as conscientiously as at Stoke'. He was 'glad it is all over … the past week has been a nightmare'.

McGrory celebrated Matthews' comeback as the team, 'with sandshoes under their arms … took a tram to Roker and had an hour's frolic on the beach.' Then on to the ground, where Stan lived his favourite moment: 'in the dressing room before the match. Tension. The butterflies. You know there's fifty thousand there … if you won you would have a good night's sleep. If you lost you couldn't sleep … to me that was something. You couldn't beat it.'

His magic triumphed as Stoke won at Sunderland for the first time ever. After a quiet first half – 'I was beginning to find my legs' – Sunderland's biggest crowd were soon 'roaring with laughter at the ease with which he beat his man': 'I have never seen a player exercise so much influence on a game. The surprising fact was that he was only once really tackled throughout the game.'

In their Sunderland hotel Stan found it harder to escape: 'Mr Matthews, please' … non-stop … 'Telegram for Mr Matthews … Will Mr Matthews come to the telephone' … 'Mr Matthews wanted downstairs' … 'Mr Matthews please.' Stan himself was less than stoical: 'what can I do to stop it.' Bob McGrory did not go home but on to Scotland, demonstrating a welcome dry wit: 'Don't say a word to anybody … I'm after an outside right.'

AUTUMN PROGRESS IN THE FIRST DIVISION

Matthews' return was one moment, and any season has many such. The immediacy of the last match, and the next, is one of the essential time elements. Another is form, the sense of connections between matches, measured invariably not in terms of the many might-have-beens but tangible results. A long season of 42 matches inevitably carries rhythms of swells and eddies for every team: each match has its own urgency; but each has its history of preceding wins and losses and carries the promise or threat of future ones. At the heart of form is confidence, as Neil Franklin remembered: 'once the run starts, you get tremendous confidence and can do no wrong' (Franklin, 1956, p.66).

As the 1946-47 season unravelled, the early leaders Manchester United, Blackpool and Sunderland came under pressure from form teams like Wolves and Stoke. City's run attracted national publicity to their magical black cat, and when they lost, darker forces were suspected: 'I have been unemployed and have wanted a job as a gate steward at Stoke for a long time ... I went to see if there was any chance of a job. The cat followed me into the office, and stayed when I came away. I had been given the job at last, so I said "It's brought me luck. I'll let them keep it and see if it brings them any." They needed it – four games without a win. It did – six wins in succession. On Saturday my wife saw a woman in a fur coat, who had come in a car with some Wolverhampton supporters, stroking Blackie at the club entrance. It's my belief that went to Wolverhampton, like the points.'

A new mojo was needed, so Matthews was resurrected. He was a 'forward line in himself' at Roker; then 'slippery Stanley danced and jigged' to another away win, before another huge crowd, at Portsmouth. But at home, like many clubs, Stoke had become intimidated by critical crowds: 'more than one player admits to not feeling so happy playing at home as away.'

Nevertheless, their crowd roared City on to a disputed last-minute winning goal in fading light against Everton, whose furious players swarmed around the referee in protest. The goal stood, and when Stoke were still contesting a uniquely tight championship finish the following June, Merseyside had cause to remember when George Antonio handballed City's winner. Antonio admitted the offence, and Stoke fancied an omen: 'there's no doubt that terrific roar won us the match. Wouldn't it be a strange thing if that late goal won us the championship.' Antonio was long gone by then and, having been driven away, was amused to hear calls for his return: 'that means nothing. They would be the same people who used to give me the bird.'

A long run through the early winter eventually took Preston into second place. In September 'they didn't look like a First Division side with a gaping hole in defence which pulled the backs out of position, and forwards who might have just reported for August training.' Bill Shankly, 'enjoying a brilliant thirteenth season,' commanded their reviving draw with Manchester United and victory over a team going in the opposite direction. Brentford's controlled football had impressed on the opening day, but now, dropping fast, they adopted desperate measures: 'get to the ball and get it away in the quickest possible time ... The amount of vigour and recklessness in subsequent scrimmages went beyond reasonable heartiness and robustness of spirit ... exceeded all fair bounds in aggressiveness.' Brentford's local paper agreed that good play was as out of place as a 'fancy waistcoat at a funeral', and poetic justice demanded that Shankly 'crashed the ball into the net' from 20 yards for the winner. That's for the programme calling him Sankly!

As Preston prospered, others declined: among the early leaders Manchester United's eclipse was temporary, Sunderland's more long lasting. Nevertheless the north-easterners inflicted United's only home league defeat of the season, 3-0, and set off home as quickly as the 48,388 crowd: 'ten minutes after the match Sunderland were in the bus having been in and out of the bath. Manager Billy Murray lent a hand dashing around with the towel. It took the bus fifteen minutes to Exchange Station and 25 minutes after the match they were on their way.'

Manchester United went five matches without a win in wet, inhospitable November. The team absorbed more demobilised servicemen: commando John Aston and tank-crewman John Morris. Morris had recently returned from India to become a warehouseman and Matt Busby welcomed his fresh attack: 'in the mood, Johnny Morris could demoralise, disintegrate and completely demolish the finest defences with his speed on the ball: he would dart here and there making a pass like a genius, or coolly slipping the ball between the legs of a mesmerised goalie' (Busby, 1957, p.87).

Jack Stelling remained ever-present for Sunderland, although after his 6am-noon shift as a mining plumber he had a 'hurried snack and makes a dash for the ground' before every home game. And home games became indigestible. It started in mid-October when third-placed Sunderland introduced international Jack Robinson against third-from-bottom Grimsby. Town's forward change was born of desperation after a worrying start: ex-soldier Tom Blenkinsop switched from half-back to centre-forward. Blenkinsop scored twice in an unexpected win, and altogether six goals in four matches as an unbeaten run took Grimsby to mid-table. Meanwhile Sunderland endured an unprecedented series of successive home defeats: Grimsby were followed by Matthews' Stoke; Lawton goals inspired Chelsea; Shankly scored Preston's winner; then Liverpool in December; Wolves at Christmas; and Arsenal in the New Year.

Abnormal November rainfall and gales created a parody of 'English conditions'. The wild weather caused floods on a mile-wide Thames and the Trent bursts its banks so that Nottingham Forest had to play, and lose, a league match at Notts County's ground. Players did not see anything resembling a normal pitch until the following April. Some clubs traditionally favoured the heavier going – Sheffield United's programme welcomed leaders Blackpool optimistically: 'When the grounds become heavier, when stamina and sweeping attacks tell their tale, we think United will shake some of the top-sawyers. Time will show.'

Sheffield United duly 'frolicked' in the mud: Jimmy Hagan, now so good he 'wandered across the field unseen by his opponents', beat three Blackpool sawyers running from the halfway line and inspired a 4-2 win. Blackpool had been leaders for six weeks but were now stuttering. They defended a perfect home record against in-form Grimsby. Blackpool led 1-0 into the last twenty minutes but, amid a plethora of goals, penalties, and 'innumerable offside decisions' (Ellis, 1954, p.51), Town won 3-2 after an almighty goalmouth scramble. Blackpool lost the leadership.

Albert Stubbins inspired Liverpool to a twelve-match undefeated run. His presence especially benefited 30-year-old Jack Balmer. Just before his purple patch Balmer had lain on the sacrificial altar of crowd scorn, and its consequence, the transfer list. One player's wife recalled 'the crowd used to get at him an awful lot', and a teammate remembered: 'it's funny but the only time he was popular with them was when he scored three hat-tricks in three games running' (Taylor *et al*, 1993, p.53).

Perhaps in defiance, Balmer was elected captain by the team, scored all three at home to Portsmouth and then four in seventeen minutes away at Derby, aided by the meteor-like Stubbins and other 'joyous extras'. When Balmer completed a hat-trick against Arsenal, Liverpool went top, and Anfield was briefly grateful: 'as memorable as the never forgotten one when Dean scored his 60th goal against Arsenal at Goodison Park ... Surely there has only once been an occasion on which a Liverpool crowd has risen to a son of the city with such fervour.'

Even when top, Liverpool, in the ancient scouse tradition of understatement, issued a protective request to the Anfield crowd: 'Not so much advice to the players please.' Without effect. Next Saturday the new leaders took on the old, at Blackpool. A journey in a train carriage 'completely upholstered by followers of Liverpool had its joy and pain ... the old harshness towards a very good club servant was still evident.' The match was lost 2-3, and on the way home: 'already there is talk of blame ... Stubbins is pilloried.'

Not even Wilf Mannion, 1946's unofficial 'footballer of the year', was immune: 'he shoots goals that look so easy the terrace morons scoffingly brand them "soft".' Middlesbrough became the 'dream team of post-war football' by inflicting Wolves' only defeat. 45,522 at Molineux watched Mannion's 'sheer, impudent brilliance: scheming and operating without wasting a second: controlling, cajoling, cementing his forwards into a quality-plus quintet.' Mannion's hat-trick put Boro 3-0 up against Portsmouth, but one man cannot make a team and Middlesbrough found consistency difficult. Portsmouth fought back to 3-3. Next, 'Trojan' Wilf was 'forever in the coils' of Sunderland's gallant defenders, whereas Sunderland's Jack Robinson was a 'flawless artist'. It was of course a Sunderland *away* win.

At the other end of the table salvation was already being sought. Reigning (1938-39) champions Everton had sought theirs in a new centre-forward: twice they named AN Other as their No 9 in anticipation ... He came from across the sea, as FIFA denied Jock Dodds' registration with Shamrock

Rovers. Jock negotiated hard: 'don't forget. I want a big pair of shorts.' Within three games he was top scorer.

As Jock arrived Joe left. Joe Mercer's sixteen years with Everton ended in mutual disaffection when he was rested 'because he was working so hard at his business'. Notwithstanding his vulnerable knee, Arsenal's Tom 'The Healer' Whittaker hoped Joe could turn their troubled season. As Joe Mercer caught the midnight train to London to make his debut, his new club was in a relegation place. Highbury's mud saw a 'great struggle', saved for Arsenal by Dr Kevin O'Flanagan's wonder shot from 25 yards when Bolton decided against a wall: Mercer was not prominent – it was 'a day for plodders, not for artistes'.

All four London teams were struggling. Brentford's first win in seven matches was achieved at home to Bolton in fading light: 'for the 23,268 spectators I doubt if it faded quickly enough.' So Brentford sought to buy their way out of trouble with £25,000 worth of Scottish talent, 'providing a team like the Milky Way – brimming over with stars.' Sadly they moved as slowly as a galaxy when giving Charlton a rare win, 4-1.

Chelsea provided the usual music hall joke, building upon the autumn concern that footballers had insufficient food – 'Tommy Lawton deserved the extra rations available to heavy workers because … he carried the team every week.' His winning 'shot that did not lift an inch' at Sunderland was typically inspirational. In his only full season, the 'genius' broke Chelsea's First Division scoring record: 'that autumn he showed what separated him from your general, knock 'im 'in, bash 'em aside centre-forwards. He had something else – an amazing balance, for one thing, and a quickness off the mark … above all there was the headwork from the famous groomed Lawton "nut", those high bounding leaps a fraction before the opposing centre-half, connecting with the ball as the poor rival was going up or already spinning back towards the turf' (Moynihan, 1982, p.55).

Huddersfield Town needed 'a captain' to harness the potential of their younger forwards. 'My car knows its own way to Manchester,' said manager David Steele as, having been outbid for one, Tommy Walker, he closed in on another. Peter Doherty's Derby was not a happy club, rather a place of 'continuous groans and sighs'. After he joined in December 1945, Doherty scored 33 times as the Cup was won. The vast crowds spilled into 1946-47, and saw 'almost a surfeit of every good thing except goals'. County slumped to twentieth, their magic persuasive only against southern softies: Carter and Doherty 'sawed the Brentford defence in half with the nonchalance which Horace Goldin used to divide his partner in the music hall.'

Derby lost badly to no-nonsense northerners: 1-4 to Jack Balmer; 1-4 to Manchester United; and 1-5 to Bolton. Wanderers' Willie Moir in particular returned from his seaside cures 'to plough through the mud', get a two 'goal tonic', and end his 'psychological ills'. Derby suffered their own psychological disorder, jitters' in attack and defence. It was no consolation when Derby's 'superior style' was recognised: 'County worked some fine quality stuff, as intricately patterned and colourful as Crown Derby ware ... [Stoke's] plainer workmanship ... chipped, but did not crack.'

Repairs were needed throughout the team: veteran England goalkeeper Vic Woodley, 'sticking to a good job' outside football, was evidently 'feeling the strain in factory work and First Division football'. So Derby were deep in the mire when they faced Chelsea on 30 November: without Cup final hero Jackie Stamps, injured playing for his Army unit; without full-back Parr, barracked into opting for the reserves; and, above all, without Doherty, captaining Ireland in Scotland.

The Derby match was an eye opener for Chelsea's new signing, Swiss international Willi Steffen, the 'best left back in the world', who found the Baseball Ground a very foreign place: 'oh, the mud. I have never played in anything like it. We do not get that sort of pitch in Switzerland.' 'Down came the rain in a solid sheet, making the already sodden pitch even more glue-like.'

Whilst commentators watched Frank Broome 'jitterbug' his way round him, mud-bound Willi was more impressed with Raich Carter's illusory speed: Carter 'has the knack of seeing moves ahead. He gets into position, and has so much working space that it is easy to imagine he must be quick.' The following week Raich set up another goal with the 'finesse and simplicity of a chess master', his artist's delicate touch putting the ball 'into a marked square of turf'. During December a new direct and forceful Derby, without Doherty, rose to tenth: the poetic potential of Carter and Doherty still appealed, but the tough world of real football allowed only one 'cheeky pranks'.

On the dismal, drenching afternoon of 30 November, the top four shared ten goals opposing one another; Liverpool at Blackpool and Manchester United at Wolves. That Saturday morning the leading and struggling positions were – *Top Six*: Liverpool 24 points; Wolves 22; Manchester United 21; Blackpool 21; Stoke 20; Middlesbrough 20. *Bottom Five*: Everton 11 points; Portsmouth 10; Derby 10; Arsenal 10; Huddersfield 9.

TELEVISION AND THE CUP

As the mud deepened, football on television took some hesitant steps. The FA gave the BBC provisional permission to televise selected games whilst the question of copyright was resolved. There were some who warned: 'dangerous. Open at your peril.' Stanley Rous, the FA's clairvoyant Secretary, produced 'the startling theory that television may be used as an excuse to rocket admission prices ... very expensive seats at actual events. The cheaper seats would be in cinemas ... as they happened.' Transpose for cinemas the local pub transmitting BSkyB broadcasts and you have football watching in the modern day.

The cameras attracted 5,000 to the first televised match, at Amateur Cup holders Barnet, but gradually lost sight of the muddy ball. Tommy Lawton saw no danger, only a joke: 'a complete blur out. Commentators were scared of mentioning players' names in case the screen proves them wrong. He little knew the only players recognisable were two with bald heads ... [TV] is more likely to drive 'em to matches.'

The captains of the varsity match, chosen for the next broadcast, forestalled further experiment when they refused to use the white ball that could be seen on television! In fact touring side 'Norrkopping will be the first football club to be televised when tomorrow the players will wear their kit in the BBC London Studios and give a demonstration of their prowess by using a ball indoors.' In the New Year, arrangements were made to televise the fifth round tie between Charlton and Blackburn. No fee, but 'BBC will pay laundry fees if technicians want a change of non-photogenic muddy pants or jerseys.'

The first two rounds of the Cup were a 'Cain and Abel business', as Third Division and non-league brothers knocked each other out for the privilege of challenging the 'bigwigs' after Christmas. Increasing muddiness made outcomes uncertain: Hull won through, but referee Arthur Ellis remembered New Brighton leading 1-0 when their 'centre forward shot past the Hull goalkeeper only to see the ball stick on the line in the mud' (Ellis, 1954, p.111). Army vehicles had made their ground behind the Tower Pleasure Fair a quagmire: the ball had to be excavated when 'only a small portion' was visible. Things reached 'shocking proportions of muddiness' before matches were postponed: 'attempts to launch a horse and roller came to a sticky end when the horse became mudbound.'

Mud made for goals. 'Southend believe in Southend mud for luck and brought some with them in a small box.' Most appropriate, as they triumphed 6-1 at Loughborough and 9-2 in Barnet's 'special' Underhill mud. Norwich drew 4-4 with QPR: their offices were promptly robbed and £270 stolen, but the game's record receipts (£2,100) from a record crowd (26,317) had already been banked. Oldham thought their thrilling cup-tie with Doncaster was twilight robbery. When the referee allowed Clarrie Jordan's equaliser, Athletic 'were so incensed about the ruling that for some time they would not centre the ball for the restart. After the game the home defenders said the ball had not come within a foot of the line, and the Doncaster forwards said it was a yard over ... the line was as imaginary as the schoolboys' definition of the Equator owing to the churned up mud.'

The mud, the light, whatever, it was hard to see. Oldham missed a penalty in the dying minutes: 'I don't think I have ever seen a game finish under conditions of near total darkness.' Elsewhere that day, the crowd placed their own ironic slant on proceedings: 'the last two goals were impossible to see ... spectators were striking matches in humorous comment.'

There were two ways of attending these midweek replays: bury a distant relative, or work late afterwards. Two female enthusiasts returned to their office to make up lost time, to find colleagues had left an ironic message: 'In affectionate Remembrance of Ipswich Town Football Club, whose aspirations to the FA Cup Died December 18th 1946.'

AUTUMN IN PIONEERLAND

Football feared that the autumn invasion by the continentals signalled the end of British supremacy: 'we have little chance against the foreign visitors ... British sport suffers humiliation after humiliation.'

New priorities were called for. Norrkopping's final opponents were in-form Wolves, but they would lack Billy Wright, due to appear for England against Wales two days later. Wright was very busy: the previous Thursday he had played for the Army against Cambridge University; on Saturday in the First Division. Now Wright was needed to 'launch the lifeboat and rescue a bit of Britain's prestige ... It's more important for the Wolves to beat the Swedes than for England to beat Wales.' On a Monday afternoon 32,857 saw Wolves draw 1-1: the Swedes were lucky, puzzled by traditional British qual-ities of first-time tackling, but also tired: 'banquets, sight-seeing, dancing – so little sleep. We've been treated like kings.' Sweden listened to the match on the radio and King Gustav indicated the Brits were not alone seeking nation-al prestige from football: 'three victories and a draw – that's more than I expected.'

To their hosts, these tourists were 'sheer delight to an eye more than slight-ly jaundiced through watching a melancholy succession of kick-and-rush league games'. Their 'quick-passing, keep-the-ball-on-the-move, man-to-man style' had 'to be seen to be believed'. In contrast, the Danish tourists were unimpressed by their hosts: 'too robust ... we were naturally distressed ... such vigorous tackling ... our spectators would be indignant if they saw a team making two footed tackles as certain Wanderers made at Highbury.' The continental sheen of modernity was given an additional dimension: 'as sweet an exhibition of positional play and ball control as I have seen in this atomic kick-and-rush age ... Norrkopping's Hungarian coach Czisker revealed they always take the field with a pre-arranged plan.'

After a month watching British clubs, Czisker concluded they lacked 'a single preconceived notion of attack or defence'. This reluctance puzzled English commentators. For example Bolton's Ray Westwood used a copyright 'quick return' pass to score countless match-winning goals: 'a sure way of bypassing the opposing "stopper" centre-half ... I frequently wonder why other teams have not copied it, for I firmly believe the plan could be operat-ed in any class of football and by any class of players.'

Pioneerland's greatest anxiety concerned its national side. Before the war England had played ten home matches against continental opposition and won them all: away, since 1929, they had won seven, lost seven. Then, in May 1945, France achieved the first continental draw in England, and won in Paris a year later. The tide was turning, but England's trio-to-die-for remained defi-antly off-the-cuff in beating Wales: 'Mannion secured the ball from a bounce-down, and sent a quick pass to Carter. Two dancing steps, then a short ball inside for the fast-moving Mannion to pick up. Lawton was, as usual, in the right place for a pass, and the centre-forward, canting over, hit the ball with his right foot to Sidlow's "wrong side".' (Swift, 1948, p.114).

The team had received every local assistance: 'an SOS for partners was sent out for girl typists in nearby offices to attend a tea dance to which the England players were invited. The girls quickly seized this opportunity of dancing with soccer stars they had previously seen only in pictures, and stayed late at their typewriters to offset the loss of time.'

Holland presented the autumnal challenge to England's unbeaten home record, but found themselves training on a waterlogged school pitch, with 'no dressing accommodation' and 'no football': 'they are staying in the same hotel as England, who would have rendered every assistance had they been called on … Our men changed in the hotel, put on their track suits and coats, and took half a dozen footballs.'

Things did not improve. Perhaps retaliating for unfavourable copy about their town, Huddersfield officials refused 35 Dutch journalists a half-time cuppa (their tickets were the wrong colour). When sorted out, the tea had run out.

By then Holland's luck had run out. Taking inspiration from the Dutch traditions in painting, England's 'exceptionally gifted' forwards – 'at the height of its powers' – earned themselves the title of Old Masters. England scored five goals in thirteen amazing minutes; their 'scheme of positional movements and crisp passing calculated to baffle all but themselves and tear any defence to shreds' (Swift, 1948, p.114). The win, the display and the imagery combined to soothe the panic of continental superiority: 'the rout of the Dutchmen by their English masters … a final lesson in craft and culture.'

It was a mood with which the graceful Mr Lotsy, President of the Royal Netherlands FA, was happy to affirm: 'Britain is our father and mother in football … We thank you for this lesson in how to play … In the Occupation we kept our honour, and we feel we have done so today in this match without a foul.'

Honour eluded England's clubs. Vaas Wilkes' would play for the Rest of Europe against Great Britain in May 1947, but First Division clubs already swarmed around the Dutchman with a 'mania for dribbling'. He signed for Charlton as one of Jimmy Seed's amateurs. Rumour and innuendo fed jealousies and backlash. London players complained to the union: 'A First Division club with a big professional staff offered a job to a star from the continent if he would stay here and play for them – as an amateur of course.' Jimmy Fay went further: 'Why should these men play in English football? They are taking the places of professionals … preventing young footballers getting their chance in the first team, earning an extra £1 or £2 a week.'

Others went further; the lazy embrace of overseas players was an 'admission of bankruptcy', the outcome of easy money searching for quick results and the squandering of our 'backyard genius'.

THE SECOND DIVISION

The early leaders Barnsley collapsed spectacularly. Even when the small Yorkshire club sat proudly on the top of the Second Division, the giants of

London, Manchester, Birmingham and Newcastle in their wake, their local community was sceptical, and critical: 'certain people deliberately set out to barrack the home side.' Barnsley dropped one point in their first five matches, yet manager Angus Seed likened his position to a besieged war leader: 'Mr Churchill received much advice on how to win the war. I have this past fortnight received similar advice on how to win promotion ... at least seven of our players should be dropped.'

Success may have gone to Angus's head, because he gave his 'Anthony Eden' hat to struggling Grimsby manager Charles Spencer: 'since then, Barnsley have done nothing right and Grimsby nothing wrong.' When Barnsley were four points clear, supporters thought only one player was good enough, and that Angus Seed should go too. Then the club started losing: 'Barnsley, three goals down, came out for the second half [but] there was booing by a considerable number of onlookers who, I suppose, would claim to be "supporters".' When the promotion wheels did come off, the town was rife with 'malicious rumour mongers' attributing the decline to 'bad feeling among the players'.

Five straight defeats sent Barnsley back into a pack which remained tightly bunched until Christmas: for several weeks the first six were within two points, and four points could cover the top half of the table. Inconsistency was endemic: clubs had 'more moods than a spoilt child.'

Manchester City were the moody giants to break out of the promotion logjam. Although City's new manager received a salary four times greater, Frank Swift proved the inspiration. A six-month undefeated run started when the football gods favoured them over promotion rivals: 'short of being held up at pistol point, Coventry City were robbed at Manchester.' Minutes from time former tank-crewman George Ashall headed the likely winner. However Manchester appealed fiercely and the referee disallowed the goal: 'Swift, who had defied Coventry all afternoon, slammed it hard over the Coventry players, half of whom were still congratulating the scorer.' George Mason, the veteran centre-half, was fouled 'twenty yards from the ball' and Manchester scored: 'sheer hullaballou. All the Coventry players ... clustered and clamoured around the referee. Mr Bryan slammed the ball down on the centre spot and signalled play on, but not the slightest notice was taken. The ball was kicked off the spot, returned to the middle by a Manchester player, and kicked away again.' The final confrontation, and reluctant resolution, was between the respective captains, Swift and Mason: 'we have been robbed. That was a good goal of ours.' 'I know George, but you will have to carry on, you know that.'

Newcastle were irresistible when Len Shackleton was in the mood: 'putting a trap, a swerve and a left-about swivel into one bewildering movement he sold a dummy on the edge of the penalty area and crashed home a glorious 20 yards shot.' 65,979 – 'the thousands turned away looked like the crowd leaving a big match' – saw United beat Manchester City at St James' Park. Even Frank Swift could not deny Charlie Wayman's last-minute winning hat-trick. Wayman was an unlikely hero: only 5ft 5½in, he had played in India and Ceylon with the Royal Navy before returning to work in the mines. By 1945-46 he had become the man United fans loved to hate – there was one, at least, at every club. As Stubbins' replacement Charlie scored all four goals against Sheffield Wednesday. He had the 46,916 crowd spellbound, but watching Norrkopping were unimpressed: 'first half bad, second half good, technique wrong.'

Nevertheless, Newcastle's 'gold-studded, glamorous £80,000 team' was a tremendous draw, and their next away games captured the drama and theatre of football in this early winter: 'no match in Luton in recent years has fired the imagination of the football fans as the one with leaders Newcastle next Saturday.'

Another near record crowd saw Newcastle take a three-goal lead. Veteran writer Capel Kirby rated the best goal of 1946, Shackleton beating 'five men in a corkscrew run before enticing the goalkeeper to become victim of his remarkable dribbling effort.' But when Newcastle had to defend the end with the thickest mud, Luton's recovery was the biggest thrill of the season: 'for sheer guts on gluepot pitches I've never seen its equal in first-class football.'

It was as memorable in Luton: 'some football matches are forgotten as soon as the final whistle blows, but this was one which will remain in the memories of all who saw it. It had everything … brilliant football, thrills by the score, an amazing recovery by an apparently beaten side, and a late winning goal that sent the local fans into a frenzy of excitement.' In a rousing finish their £8,000 record signing Allen Driver scored an ecstatic winner, and provoked a very contemporary celebration: 'so excited were the Luton players when they scored their winning goal that an unparalleled scene in English football was witnessed: Driver, the scorer, was kissed by his colleagues.' Newcastle took it hard: 'the team dug for themselves their own grave.' After this 'heartburning' defeat, Jackie Milburn sulked into the reserves, and United went 0-2 down at home. Roy Bentley came to the rescue with a second-half hat-trick. And so to Leicester.

The amazing crowd scenes made the front page. Wartime damage to the grandstand prevented a record, but the ground was closed on 34,630. Thousands 'clamoured at the turnstiles hoping against hope the gates would be reopened.' 'A couple of doors were broken down and a few got in,' the frustrated '10,000 people outside the ground adding to the din of constant encouragement'.

Earlier the visiting players were among those denied, their coach so stuck fast in the throng that they had to take out their kit basket 'and struggle with it, with the aid of police, through a crowd of several thousands to enter the official gate.' Inside, the crowd 'held a note of danger … 60 people climbed upon the roof at the popular side. From their precarious positions these 'squatters' joined the first roar of the afternoon, as a Newcastle fan ran onto the pitch to welcome his side – only his 'feet slid under him and he slithered along the mud in a semi-sitting position'. The fun continued as the crowd's biggest boo was reserved for 'Military Police looking for Forces men at the match without leave passes.'

The match turned, as many did, upon injuries. Leicester went two up, then Joe Calvert, City's veteran goalkeeper, was concussed saving a certain goal at Shackleton's feet. Serious injury was an occupational hazard for 1946-47 goalkeepers. Unstable pitches, a wet, heavy ball, and attackers with licence to put in a hard-capped boot: two top keepers had died in the 1930s. That December, four others were stretchered off after kicks to the head and upper body. Two England internationals were hospitalised, one for twelve days, the other after 'going to earth like a pole-axed steer'. Boro's Dave Cumming was sent off for retaliating against a forward's kick, and West Brom's Lew Twigg fractured a skull – it ended his career.

Calvert's experiences were typical. It was the sixth time he had been carried off – '[Joe] has been knocked about a lot this season.' At Birmingham, he was kicked unconscious, given stitches, and returned after half an hour. The same on 'a ploughed field' against Spurs. Calvert faced centre-forwards who were 'the spearhead of as drastic a rough and tumble as even I have experienced'; whose reputation was that a goalkeeper who caught the ball 'most certainly would have sailed into the net'. He was the hero against Bury where the referee was 'constantly wagging a warning finger at players whilst the belligerent crowd bellowed lustily 'send 'im off'.

Joe became a boo-boy target when he objected to a Burnley forward's flying kick whilst 'he was on his knees'. Joe's resistance earned him a referee's caution and the enduring hatred of the home crowd: 'hooting and booing him for one long spell, during which he was struck on the back of the neck by a stone.' Despite police protection, a spectator invaded the pitch and 'still remonstrating, was escorted off by three officers'. The crowd remained in an ugly mood and the situation on a knife-edge. One policemen said: 'I don't know what will happen if Leicester score.'

Scoring became increasingly unlikely as players sank deeper into the mud: 'a series of rugby scrums in the goalmouths.' Burnley v Leicester said everything about late 1946: complete commitment demanded by an edgy public, in appalling conditions and fast fading light: 'continuous rain before the match and a driving, icy storm turned the pitch into a series of miniature lakes. Some players were near to physical collapse when the gruelling game, which was played at a cracking pace, despite the waterlogged condition, came to an end in semi-darkness.'

Without Joe Calvert, and Don Revie injured, Leicester's 'nine men and a cripple' were overhauled by Newcastle, who scored four times in twenty minutes and stayed top. Calvert, who had already broken his collar-bone three times, went to hospital, recalling the fate of another Leicester goalie, who was told he required minor surgery: 'I found out I had had 200 stitches put in to hold me together. I'm glad it wasn't a major op.' No break for Joe, so he was back twelve days later, on Boxing Day – and his season still had six months to go.

TOP OF THE FIRST DIVISION

The 'howling Wolves' proved the strongest of the First Division titans. Twice behind, twice they fought back before beating Manchester United with an 'amazing' Johnny Hancocks volley. Feelings ran high: Hancocks got hurt, the 46,704 Wolves crowd threw bottles, and at the death goalkeeper Bert Williams won the day, hurling himself painfully at Delaney's feet. Next, Wolves went to leaders Liverpool. Anfield's biggest crowd of the season, 52,512, saw Wolves' half-back line of Wright, Cullis and Galley show 'prodigious power' – Tom Galley went full length in the mud five times in the first twenty minutes. Then in 25 stunning minutes Westcott scored four goals, Wolves won 5-1 and took the leadership in style.

Merseysider Dennis Westcott, 29, now had the golden touch. Four goals at Anfield, then four against Bolton, added to the two against Manchester United – amazingly he had equalled Jack Balmer's ten goals in three matches at first opportunity. Wolves were now the epitome of modern football, just as British inventions would fuel her future prosperity: 'a grand team, well dubbed the "jet-fuelled squad" ... the sparks fly from these jet fighters.'

Shell-shocked Liverpool travelled to Sunderland. Captain Jack Balmer remembered it as a moment when their season could have washed away: 'early on it looked as though Sunderland were also going to mop us up – the lads responded with every ounce to my call for an extra effort.' Jack's own 'lightning shot' set his team on the way to a 4-1 win and Sunderland were 'well and truly whacked'.

Blackpool hit the wall. A lorry smashed into their taxi doing a mandatory tour of the pottery factories. Six men shaken up, they lost 1-4 at Stoke after floundering in Stan Matthew's wake on a waterlogged pitch: 'Matthews' goal will be talked about for years, and those who saw it will describe how he progressed by acute zigzags half the length of the field, with four or five Blackpool players trotting at his heel like a pack of dogs, until finally he made even the goalkeeper go the wrong way and tapped the ball into the net.'

13

Three Festivals

Dennis 'hat-trick' Westcott was the hottest player in football: fourteen goals in his previous six matches. But like everyone else he froze on Saturday, 21 December. Freezing fog, distorting ground and travel conditions, replaced the incessant rain: fog that prevented Dennis joining Wolves on the morning London train. He set off by taxi, missed another connection and continued until one o'clock. Then, 60 unseen miles short, and still faced by icy roads and fog belts, Dennis gave up. His teammates arrived in London two hours late. A quick meal, and then a dash for kick off. The victorious return journey was equally long: train delays meant arrival back in Wolverhampton at 1.15 in the morning.

Footballers were the central figures in two ancient festivals marking the turn of the year. First, the country was desperate for a normal Christmas, but disappointed: turkeys especially were very thin on the ground. Football filled the gap. Second, these frantic endeavours were followed by the return of an old tradition, the third round of the Cup. A third festival symbolised the intended shape of the country's future: the nationalisation of the mines.

Christmas meant four matches in eight days. At least. Lincoln City zig-zagged England from Wednesday, 18 December until Saturday, 28 December: six matches in eleven days. Tough journeys, hard matches, scarred pitches. Yet in the process Lincoln scored the 'perfect goal', bringing together English resilience and continental style. It was a Cup second replay for which a neutral venue proved elusive – clubs reluctant to batter further grounds disfigured by November's heavy rains. In the end the luckless Maine Road pitch, host to both Manchester clubs and two England international fixtures already, drew the short straw. 2,600 souls, including 80 huddled on the vast terraces, braving mucky weather on Monday afternoon, two days before Christmas, witnessed 'the most perfect goal I ever hope to see … a wonderful goal in the best Norrkopping style. It started somewhere near Lincoln's penalty area, was carried along by players going at no more than gentle trot and the last pass of all ripped the defence wide open.' Veteran commentator Archie Ledbroke, later killed at Munich, saw 'no reason, except unimaginative managership, why more goals of this type should not be scored, and I am convinced that, properly coached for six weeks, players of only average ability could carry out such moves.'

Westcott had been one of many missing men. Eddie Shimwell had joined Blackpool during the week for £8,000, when Sheffield United would not countenance his taking a pub in the Peak. He made an inauspicious start, his train being so late into St Pancras that it was already half-time at Charlton: Shimwell went straight back. At Accrington, bronzed Tom Hutton, fresh from the Middle East, his new demob suit on his back and his wife on his arm, strolled into Peel Park to say hello to his old Stanley team-mates: manager Jack Hacking told him he had five minutes to get changed – he was playing against Hull City!

The most serious injury occurred to the 'best full-back in Europe', a title earned when Wales' Billy Hughes subdued the previously rampant Tom Finney in the international. But plaudits cannot provide a home near Second Division leaders Birmingham: Hughes commuted from Wrexham. Whilst Dennis Westcott peered sightlessly out of his taxi somewhere short of London, Hughes was a lasting victim of the fog-shrouded, icy roads when a 'windscreen visor gouged out his forehead'. Two square inches of skin were taken from his thigh and grafted onto his head. Hospitalised for weeks Hughes did not play again for three months, three months in which Birmingham faded from the promotion stakes.

As usual, lack of food was a metaphor for defeat. Promotion challenging Bristol City lost at Southend on an empty stomach. Their train was too late to have lunch, they had to fight their way, bags and all, through the London Underground, and afterwards they missed dinner because they were attempting the long haul home.

The west's other promotion hopefuls, Swindon, were stranded five miles from QPR's ground, kick-off imminent. Manager Louis Page 'ordered them from the train, a sharp trot to the bus stop [there were no taxis] and obtained seats on a trolley.' Over 10,000 awaited their arrival, 'stamping their feet and clapping their hands in the bitter cold.' Kicking off 25 minutes late, Swindon lost 0-7 on a foggy 'skating rink' in which their goalie couldn't see the ball. They continued to protest as the referee dispensed with an interval and played only 80 minutes. Swindon then rushed back to Paddington where they finally got a break: their 4.15 train was delayed, and they got a meal.

Millwall did not make it at all. They spent eighteen hungry hours travelling to and from Swansea where a crowd of 30,000 waited in vain. Liable to a £500 fine, Millwall had to pay £20. Northgate Athletic, earlier fined for playing an unregistered Dixie Dean, risked another by calling off a Cheshire League match because their brewery workers team were 'too busily engaged with the Christmas brew to spare any time for football'.

Deputy Mayor Stranger helped Southampton v Fulham to start: 'to break up any small clods which might form between their studs, [he] brought along a number of pointed wooden picks, placed handy for the players near the touchline. The referee said "This is a good idea".' Saintly fans developed the idea by throwing stones, and one 'threw his hat on the grass' before attacking Fulham's full-back.

Stoke softened the impact with an 'all-in thawing-out offensive': '25 braziers, five tons of sand, and the prodigious exertions of a steam roller.' These

'Herculean labours' achieved the task of allowing the match to go ahead – 'with frozen pot-holes the size of pint mugs' – but even the most skilful player could not control the ball: 'a capricious object which periodically went into a freakish spell against which even the magic of Matthews could not prevail.'

For Christmas itself, the strength-sapping mud returned, 'churned up into a clinging, slithering, unstable mess reminiscent of Blackpool sands after a Bank Holiday'. Last-minute goals were scored by players 'indistinguishable in a coating of sand and mud'.

All fixtures comprised the same two teams meeting each other on successive days, Christmas morning and Boxing Day afternoon. Distance often determined how gruelling it would be. Plymouth lost to Manchester City home and away then were beaten at West Ham on Saturday: three defeats in four days, and over a thousand miles travelled. It was also logistically demanding. Chesterfield contacted 40 hotels without obtaining Christmas Eve accommodation in London. Thinking they might have to resort to air-raid shelters or police stations, Chesterfield appealed through the national press. Fifty readers responded, and finally an inn was obtained for the night, although it is unreported whether any star had to use the stables.

Travelling was a nightmare. Wolves, Sunderland, West Brom and Newcastle had all 'fixed up to travel on the same train back' after their Christmas Day matches – only it was cancelled. Thus, 'fresh' from their eighteen-hour ordeal on 21 December, Wolves spent a further nineteen travelling to beat Sunderland twice – Dennis Westcott scored twice in the last five minutes. 53,834 spectators were in Roker Park, 10,000 outside. Christmas induced panic on the Tyne and Wear. Sunderland continued their slide, and Newcastle lost all three games, twice to West Brom before a combined crowd of nearly 100,000.

Injuries took heavy toll and a much-changed Wolves came to London again to defend their burgeoning reputation at an Arsenal made resurgent by the goals of new signing Ronnie Rooke. Earlier, toothless forwards, even Reg 'Lewis Gunner', had scared no one: 'If I'm condemned to be shot, please put me in front of that Arsenal firing squad.' Arsenal versus Wolves was another great set-piece: 63,000 were officially inside but hundreds managed to climb over the walls when the gates were closed and 20,000 were left outside. Weakened Wolves drew 1-1 on a 'glue-pot' pitch – and went five points clear.

The saviour was late at Huddersfield. Peter Doherty, a 'mystery man' all December, became positively messianic at Christmas. Blackpool, where he still lived, were favourites to re-sign him but Huddersfield 'refused to take no for an answer'. Doherty was listed in their team on Boxing Day and Town's biggest crowd, 39,606, turned up. But there was a 'last minute hitch'. Doherty managed to be in two places that day. He described how a youngster to whom he gave a lift 'to the ground surprised me for a moment by telling me Huddersfield's new star would be turning out that day' (Doherty, 1948, pp.69-70). However he also recalled being hauled in by the police as a late 'Christmas gift to the crowd at Derby'. He did not disappoint, scoring two of five goals in his first game for a month – and then signed for Huddersfield for the 'small fortune' of £9,000. Peter became the most expensive footballer in history, his combined transfers costing £29,000. From the start he created 'chance after chance', but somehow Huddersfield lost:

'Doherty could not have played better had he purposely wished to demonstrate his value. For half an hour he played in a fashion which no inside forward in my recollection could have bettered … No wonder the crowd told the Blackpool players, in no uncertain voice, not to be afraid of him. No wonder the Blackpool teamwork was cut to ribbons. No wonder one of the finest half-back lines in football floundered and gasped in an effort to stop the game running all one way.'

When Derby County sold their prize jewel, three directors resigned, knowing that the money could not compensate for a season gone to waste: 'Poverty's patches and frayed edges were plainly and pathetically visible … Cheque for Doherty was accepted by the bank, but bounced at Villa Park.'

On Sunday, Tommy Lawton uttered football's 'universal sigh of relief', 'Well, it's over,' and complained of matches lost to 'railway train cramp'. However, commentators foreswore any 'moonstruck moans about the hard lot of professional footballers:' compared to the uncomfortable 'spectator, who pays, the professional footballer, who is paid, seems to me to be on a good thing.' Even 'punch drunk' players were criticised for 'sit down strikes' when they were still 'fresh' from Boxing Day: 'worse conditions could hardly be imagined. Hours of torrential rain from midday converted the ground into a veritable swamp, in which the players slithered in uncontrollable fashion in pursuit of a ball that took an impish delight in doing the unexpected … bouquets for superb exhibitions of human endurance.'

The deep need for football over Christmas meant crowds topped three million. Third Division Cardiff attracted 48,000, Ipswich set a ground record (20,267) and at Port Vale the turnstiles failed and a fan collapsed and died. Of many, many injuries Chelsea's Bobby Russell's broken leg was the cruellest. Russell had played against Moscow Dynamos in 1945 but not this season as he was in the Middle East. Demobbed, the Boxing Day game was only his second match back. Russell missed his wedding, due two days later.

The turn of the year was a time to reflect, and it all felt bad: 'The Year 1946, which opened so full of promises of a Post-war Paradise. These promises, unhappily, have turned to dust and ashes; the fruit that was to be so rare and refreshing proves to be just Dead Sea fruit – all brine and bitterness – the Land of Promise has turned out to be the Land of Promises unfulfilled.'

Yorkshire columnist Candide tried to capture the spirit of this 'year of disillusion'. At the Leeds v Preston match he found 'the shouting of the masses silences the men of judgement and constructive criticism'. Yet a 'supreme artist' could transcend parochial bitterness. Tom Finney made winning look 'ridiculously easy', until he was sent sprawling, in pain, out of the game. His return was hailed by the whole ground, a 'deep throated roar'. Finney's reward for this act of redemption? 'if you are a genius at football you get the basic minimum like all the rest. Somehow it seems all wrong: just like paying George Formby the same as a member of the chorus line.'

Football was experiencing its own disillusion after the heady August days. Club programmes were now challenging the 'unpardonable brutality' of excessive competitiveness. 'Conservative managers and dull directors' were blamed for the poor quality of play displayed even by title-challenging Preston on New Year's Day: 'of football quality there was precious little, and well might our foremost experts have sat there, head in hands, almost audibly groaning.'

Aggression was now well established: 'there is nothing unduly genteel about the upper crust in soccer society. It is a virile, hairy-chested crowd whose table-manners are primitive. Snatch what you can off the other man's plate is the general idea.' It must be the referees' fault: 'a well known ex-referee [observed] that a defender punched an opposing forward on the jaw in view of the referee and got away with it.' But when clubs blamed referees they were undermined by hypocrisy: 'in programmes Directors are full of righteous indignation. In private, their reports on referees are childishly biased.'

Whose ever fault, it was a heavy failure – 'these tactics represent serious threat to the future'. The authorities made a gesture of resistance: the FA warning referees to stamp on 'too much rough stuff' and warning players against 'bullying referees through intimidation'. Refs immediately became tougher: of the twelve players sent off in 1946-47, six came that month, four on 28 December, that day players reached the ends of their tether. Coventry's Jack Snape was warned the day before to desist a tendency to 'harakiri' methods, to 'rid himself completely and forever of animosity in his football'. Remarkable prescience, which Jack, like many lads, did not heed.

After Christmas the FA Cup brought renewed licence: 'All-in wrestling note introduced by two players who rolled over and over in a Hackenschmidt grip [a famous wrestler in the Edwardian era] ... a cautionary word, a handshake and all was forgotten.' Differences did not always end so amicably: 'one of these soccer-thugs spat full in the face of a player who remonstrated with him after a particularly vicious foul. Later there was a dressing room brawl in which one footballer k'o'd another.'

The anger towards referees was pervasive: 'go to any match you like, and the after-the-game inquest almost always touches on the referee and linesmen, and as often as not, players and spectators alike go away dissatisfied with the kind of justice that has been handed out to them.' Many league matches ended in direct action: 'the crowd gathered outside the dressing rooms and protested the referee's decision: they would not disperse until forced to by the police!' Sometimes the protection was unavailing: 'as I came back into the dressing room I felt a blow on the back of my neck ... [the secretary] was struck by a blow intended for me, and one of the players who came to assist was also struck.'

Another referee felt the wrath of home fans after Finchley 4, Wembley 5: 'Players warded off blows as they escorted him to the dressing rooms. Mud was thrown and Wembley players became involved in a fight with a member of the crowd. Some spectators tried to invade the dressing-room of the visiting team and police were called to clear away angry people round the players' exit.'

388,000 Germans were targets. Clubs still assiduously enforced a prohibition on PoWs as spectators – those excluded from Derby included members of the 1943 German champions, Dresden – and railed against fans who 'erred' in helping them avoid the ban. PoW games were officially restricted to five miles, but Bert Trautmann's Camp 50 team played 90 charity matches all over Lancashire, attracting average Sunday gates of four thousand. Attempts to join the English leagues were rebuffed – a Sussex FA member responded acidly to one application: 'Let them play on pitches they bombed.'

Women were another target. The FA chose Christmas to prohibit female matches on affiliated clubs' grounds. One victim was Farsley Celtic versus girl operatives of Woodhouse and Co., just as a crowd gathered on Boxing Day. Mrs Edwards of the Committee felt 'very incensed over the matter. The ban came as a last-minute bombshell.' Another was in the Forest of Dean, where a King Canute of Gloucester's FA celebrated his victory: 'Women are in everything nowadays. Let's try to keep them out of soccer for goodness sake.' There was uncertainty everywhere. Little could be relied upon: 'times of violent upheavals, when institutions hallowed by time fall like ninepins.'

In these circumstances football self-consciously sought refuge in reasserting old ways. Portsmouth revived a prewar tradition of directors toasting the League in the New Year: 'Portsmouth entertain well, the loving cup with its complement of champagne, and the clubs toasted each other like old friends should.' The players received more modern treats. Chairman Vernon Stokes, part of the booming Butlins holiday camp firm, took them to the circus at London's Olympia. The team had just won three successive First Division games to climb off the bottom and were rewarded by a 1946 form of Christmas bonus: Stokes 'assured the players a long time ago that the board were wholeheartedly behind them, but people looked for action … Then, in a flash, the board decided that the club would pay their staff the maximum benefits.'

Portsmouth's veteran manager Jack Tinn mediated the pressures on all southern clubs to improve their staffs: 'to those who were calling for new players he would say there was such a thing as the Essential Works Orders. He could have signed two or three good players but he could not provide a mine in Portsmouth.' Portsmouth's change of fortune began with two local servicemen: Jimmy Scoular and Len Phillips. Len, who had never kicked a ball before he joined the Royal Marines, had landed on the D-Day beaches at 7.30am. Both would feature in back to back championship sides 1948-50, but their initial contribution to Portsmouth's 1-0 win at Blackburn was unimpressive: 'it was just 90 minutes of aimless kicking, with not a suspicion of a constructive move.' Blackburn themselves sought supernatural inspiration, 'in the present disturbed state of mind of all friends of the Rovers.' Blackburn could not get a goal to save their lives. They needed something to get them in touch with the club's heritage, with the promotion team of 1938-39, with their war heroes killed. At lunch before their next match, 'someone – I believe it was Bobby Langton – passed round a signed portrait of the late Frank Chivers. Everyone, those who knew him and those to whom his name is only a legend, gazed at it thoughtfully, and in some reverence.'

Championship leaders Wolves lost unexpectedly, 1-4 at struggling Brentford in front of 34,791. Liverpool hit a slump: after their unbeaten run, they won three and lost seven. Defeats against Sheffield United and Chelsea were due to the virtuosity of mature talents. United's Jimmy Hagan dominated their match: 'if there is a finer inside forward playing today, I am the Emperor of China.' And Tommy Lawton gave a towering performance before 58,000: 'the finest football seen at Stamford Bridge for many a day, Chelsea literally tore the boots off Liverpool ... [Lawton] leapt head and shoulders above defenders.' But 'quite a lot of spike' crept into Liverpool's home defeat to Bolton. Their centre-half Laurie Hughes broke an ankle, whilst Wanderers commented acidly that 'if there was a sliding tackle championship Liverpool would win it'.

Blackpool were 'pathetic'. Autumn star Jimmy Blair could no longer get into their side and north-easterners inflicted a second 5-0 home defeat, Sunderland's Jack Robinson scoring four. Only their away form was keeping Sunderland, seven points from fourteen games, afloat. They managed to scrap their way to a 'temper frayed' win at Bolton, which pleased their devoted if unlucky followers and solicitous manager Bill Murray: 'Sunderland have two women football fans. They turn up everywhere sporting red and white. They were at Bolton. Left home at 7 o'clock; arrived five minutes before the end of the game. Fare 33s each. Consolation was an invitation to dinner with the players on the train extended by manager Murray.' Bill's ministrations were not confined to females. He came up with homes for three more players, then introduced diminutive ex-soldier Tom Reynolds as left winger. But Tom weighed only 8st 10lbs, and needed building up, so Bill did what mothers up and down the land were being urged to do: 'often seen carrying a small paper parcel containing cod liver oil.'

Others were finding consistency elusive. An inspirational two-goal performance by Wilf Mannion put Middlesbrough second, and next they faced two season-defining matches against championship rivals. First the chance to end Stoke's title hopes for good and all: 'anything short of a victory over Middlesbrough will mean their disappearance.' Boro had the country's most in-form forward 'brilliant Mannion ... dominating in midfield and directing a stream of passes. His feinting, stationary or at speed, is one of the greatest things in football today.' Middlesbrough led 1-0 until stand-in Bert Mitchell became an unlikely hero. Only recently demobbed and playing his first game Mitchell got two quick goals. His success tested even his nearest and dearest: when he got home, his wife doubted he had played at all, and knew he was kidding when he said he scored.

Next Manchester United won 4-2 at Ayresome Park. For Boro, this was 'not a mere stumble ... rather a very bad fall'. Likewise for United goalkeeper Jack Crompton, hospitalised for ten days following concussion. So only Preston, featuring Tom 'curly from top to toe' Finney, were matching Wolves' pace.

By 25 January and the great freeze up, the leaders were: Wolves 37 points; Preston 34; Manchester United, Middlesbrough, Blackpool 31; Liverpool, Stoke 30. At the bottom: Portsmouth, Charlton 19 points; Huddersfield 18; Leeds 16.

With Christmas over, football moved on to its own unique festival – T'Owd Tin Pot, or the Football Association Challenge Cup, and in particular the third round where the big clubs join the survivors of the original 438 entrants, each paying ten shillings entrance fee. Most clubs revived an ancient tradition of going away: 'this morning dawned with the stars of the more fashionable Soccer clubs stretching a pyjama-sleeved arm from beneath the eiderdown to take the morning cup of tea in the room of some cosy coastal hotel. Special cup-tie training invariably starts like that.' In 1946 this traditional picture of lazy comfort had an edge of envy: players even had 'extra meals at the clubs' expense to tone them up for the big game.' Some clubs went further: Bolton provided glucose and Port Vale 'pep pills' and 'halibut oil capsules'. Supporters sacrificed coupons so players had steaks and Southend 'a barrel of oysters'. Sunderland men put on four pounds from the high living.

But 'feeding the brutes is not enough'. The week presents an unprecedented opportunity to revive and update football's paternalism: to relax and pamper players and prepare for further challenges. The main drawback was the New Year 'mixture of snow, ice, gales and fog, followed by torrential rain'. In these conditions a trip to the hills was an incautious sanctuary. Hull were caught in the snow, although they managed some 'light training on a farm'. It was almost too much of a good thing: 'it has been possible to assemble all the first team together for a few days for the first time.' Spas were revived as a favourite and traditional preparation. Sheffield United champion Droitwich – 'the most powerful and concentrated brine in the world'. West Brom felt no need to leave home: 'there is something about the North Country air.' Snow mainly. Their opponents Leeds United took the air and the tonic baths at Harrogate Spa – except inside-left Short, left at his Essential Work factory: 'take him away from his bench and the Services would have immediate claim.'

'Cup tie fever gripped Yorkshire,' and despite the snow falls their clubs escaped to the hills: Barnsley took a five-mile walk on Penistone Moor; Huddersfield, getting to know Peter Doherty, went further – 'a long walk over the moors between Huddersfield and Sheffield'. In this battle of moor or less, Barnsley had the last laugh – miner Jim Baxter, his fractured jaw 'encased in plaster', getting their 4-3 winner at Huddersfield. Arsenal's 'week at the seaside' and Swansea's in the country were more candid acknowledgement 'of what goes by the name of special training', 'after all the exertions of the

Christmas week it was just as well for some of the players to have a rest. They do walking exercises and a lot of hill climbing.' It was too much of a good thing for Trevor Ford, 'bored silly' in Swansea's 'lonely farmhouse' in Cardiganshire for their league match with Newcastle. When they decided to return for their Cup preparations Trevor said 'I'm not going to that place again. I hate it,' and instead transferred to Aston Villa (Ford, 1957, p.34).

'Special training' was a case of anything but kick a ball, in fact: 'the majority of club managers are sedulously guarding their players from any sight of a football.' Except for the odd 'Edwardian throwback' trainer who 'might chuck in a few balls on to the practice field and says in his uncouth way "Get stuck into these, lads".' Some had little option. Third Division Rotherham, asked if they had done any special training to prepare them to face favourites Wolves, replied: 'Yes, lad, at the bottom of several pits.'

These efforts received a ready response. The fuel shortage led to the cancellation of special trains and dense fog further 'dislocate[s] transport' but still the 32 Cup-ties were watched by 974,915 fans – a third higher than any previous Third Round – paying over £94,000. Lincoln, Bournemouth and Northampton (where 50 German Prisoners of War cleared the snow) established ground records.

There were many absent fans who could not wait for the local *Pink 'Un*. In the days before club calls and mobile phones, even before radio's Saturday Sports Report, communities used an earlier technology: 'every match day at St James' Park, Newcastle you will see miners carrying into the ground with them baskets containing pigeons. Quarter-time, half-time and three quarter-time scores and the result are sent out by 'pigeon post' to various collieries in the district.'

Club officials, ever sensitive to accusations that football was disrupting coal and industrial production, argued its compatibility with work discipline: 'a good idea, for it keeps those at work in touch with the game.' Geordie Bill Dodgin, Southampton's modern manager, tried something similar when his team visited Newcastle in a cup-tie for which 'somebody was offering £6 for a 7/6 ticket' (the 62,000 attendance produced £6,340 receipts). Bill had watched Newcastle the week before, telling all who would listen that 'our boys will shake you'. Informed that in his absence his boys had lost 0-6, he answered quick as a flash: 'That's alright. The boys are saving themselves.'

Bill's pigeon post was 'half-hourly phone calls' to stricken Bill Ellerington, left behind in their Whitley Bay Hotel when he developed serious respiratory problems. Ellerington was initially cheered by Saints' opening goal but subsequent calls brought news of Charlie Wayman's winning hat-trick for Newcastle. The illness kept Ellerington away for ten months. His misfortune had a very significant effect on the future of English football: it gave a prolonged opportunity to an unsung reserve, Alf Ramsey.

Without a pigeon in sight, 300,000 watched eight London Cup-ties: the biggest crowd, 70,195, saw Chelsea draw 1-1 with Arsenal. Demand was far higher. Stamford Bridge was filled in only 80 minutes: when closed, those jamming the entrances struggled with mounted police; some scaling the main gates, others clambering over the Underground's railway embankment. The football was at 'breakneck speed, no skill', a 'roaring tie' in which the two goals were 'bright lanterns'. Undaunted, 53,350 attended the midweek afternoon replay. There was greater pressure on replays to be all-ticket because of the FA's concern to limit interference with industrial production.

Arsenal thought it an impossible project, and 'would play into the hands of the ticket racketeers'. Arsenal had Dr O'Flanagan standing by to play despite a broken wrist in plaster, but the teams drew again. Denying Chelsea's proposal of Wembley, the FA directed the third match to Arsenal's wartime home, White Hart Lane for the following Monday – and stipulated there would be double extra-time if necessary i.e. a match of 150 minutes! The gates were closed again: some dodged police, smashed down a factory fence, climbed a ladder onto its glass roof, dropped twenty feet into a small passage, and over a six foot wall into the ground.

Arsenal's chances came very early. 59,590 watched Jimmy Logie 'alone in the world, a few yards from goal' … miss. Then an even better chance: 'in that moment the afternoon was exquisitely balanced, and as Lewis approached to take the penalty time stood still.' It went 'yards wide': Reg Lewis was inconsolable about his first ever miss. Tommy Lawton scored twice, one a 'feverish left foot volley' (Moynihan, 1982, p.44) and the 'Pensioners shut up like oysters,' thus deciding the season's biggest London match. The overall gate for the tie was £20,100: Arsenal's Midas touch was back – a quarter of a million people (£24,000) watched them in ten days.

65,681 watched Matthews at Spurs. Stoke perversely went north beforehand for a short break at Stan's hotel in Blackpool. As they left in a blizzard and faced treacherous road conditions, Spurs' choice of Brighton looked wiser. For the replay Spurs had the accommodation problems: manager Joe Hulme found it impossible to book a hotel 'near' Stoke for the Tuesday evening: 'I tried Manchester, Derby, Birmingham, Nottingham and half a dozen other places, but no luck.'

Wednesday morning early: 7,000 tickets went on sale at the Victoria Ground, attracting queues of 20,000. In the recently nationalised Staffordshire coalfields absenteeism that day was up to 42 per cent higher than normal; and there was 'permitted absenteeism' in the pottery factories, i.e. the workers worked through lunchtime and returned afterwards. The 38,639 crowd saw Stan strike the winning left-foot shot: 'Matthews beat almost as many opponents as he liked with his usual bewildering ease … One Spurs player, so deceived that he could not keep his feet, resorted to grabbing the Stoke player by the ankle with both hands … When the referee on another occasion adjudged Matthews to have committed a foul (the second against him in the memory of this writer who saw him on his first game for Stoke) the crowd showed its disbelief by a roar of laughter.' Others were following Stan closely. Liverpool's safe was blown out after Stoke's visit there on Boxing Day, but the receipts had already been banked. Now, after their Cup win, an 'expert gang of safe breakers' burgled Stoke's offices, ate half a large cake presented to manager McGrory by grateful supporters, and stole £600 – £250 of McGrory's, and the players' wages. Well, not everyone's: 'the only pay packet which the thieves failed to get was that of Stanley Matthews, who drew it before returning to Blackpool.'

The football was 'win at all costs:' 'tackles which made me shudder'. Higher bonuses spurred players on to 'feats of recklessness', and commentators lamented an annual 'Kilkenny catfight': 'far outshining the sane, staid League championship in magic and money ... It glorifies the brainless regime of kick-and-rush. It drives crowds to the verge of mayhem. It imbues its protagonists with the fanaticism of Indian fakirs ... fans bayed with delight as a visiting player buckled like a bent matchstick after a foul tackle ... men degenerate into kicking, hacking hoodlums.'

Club programmes confronted aggressive home crowd behaviour: 'opposing players, referees and linesmen ... spat on, pelted with orange peel or called vile and abusive names. Offenders will be ejected and spectators are asked to restrain hot heads.' Warnings went unheeded. Already a Bournemouth fan had 'stripped off his overcoat, ran on to the pitch and attacked an Exeter player' – 'it took several policemen and club trainers several minutes to restore order.' At Bristol City, 'it comes a bit thick when players get kicked when they leave the field.'

Now the frisson of the Cup provided additional temptation. Liverpool's defeat of would-be giant-killers Walsall was an exciting encounter: 'only the action of the boy who kicked Bob Paisley as he left the ground marred the aftermath.' Austerity produced a double-edged effect. Cartoonists advised supporters to adopt a New Year's resolution of 'not throwing the kids' orange ration at the opposing goalkeeper,' whereas lemons were 'eagerly seized by the players'.

Even a small fair-haired girl of four, collecting her cup-tie ticket with her father, gave unheeded advice to Blackburn Rovers: 'Tell them to shape up today.' Instead Hull's tigers fought 'tooth and claw' to set up a replay on their 'peat bog' new ground. City established a record crowd of 37,263 but the £3,355 gate did not beat the record established at the old ground in 1921. A Blackburn debutant was George Higgins, a former Commando who had made 'several eventful runs into Northern Russia' during the war.

Rovers won the replay 3-0, having overcome uncertainties about current military commitments – their RAF players 'may be called upon to play in a services match, and that would take precedence even over an FA cup tie.' One was Corporal Jackie Campbell whose feelings for the East Lancashire club were coloured by resentment that he had transferred from Liverpool in 1944 'without a cut' of the fee; and his first impressions: 'a bigger dump than Bootle.'

In the servicemen's old camps, squatters, the summer's symbol of despair and resistance in the face of official disinterest, were now suffering anew as the winter bit: 'children, their faces swollen with cold, are living in smoky, unhealthy Missen huts … A widow was burning old tarpaulin for fuel and awoke Tuesday to find a pile of snow at the foot of her bed. An official said: "We are simply not concerned with squatters … They are not our pigeon".'

The third festival, intended to signify fundamental change, was celebrated with a resounding tinkle. On 1 January the National Coal Board took over the mines. Prime Minister Attlee chose cricket to indicate the difficulties ahead: 'the Coal Board is a fine team going in to bat on a distinctly sticky wicket.' Mine nationalisation resonated through Labour Party history as well as carrying its hopes for the future. The grandeur of the symbolism – encompassing war, monarchy and the nation itself – had been captured on Christmas Day, when the King's address was introduced by a Kent miner. Now the coalfields were the Spitfires and Hurricanes in the Battle of Britain 1947. 'King Coal has been enthroned,' and 'it is no use hoisting flags unless we hoist the coal as well.'

January 1st was a working day … or meant to be. Absenteeism meant several Yorkshire collieries were idle. A manager explained: 'a long time ago, a man was killed in this pit when working New Year's Day and since then there has been no work here on that day.' Ten days later, the National Coal Board had its first mining tragedy – fourteen men were entombed in a shale pit – and days later its first dispute as one thousand miners near Glasgow struck against the dangerous use of explosives. The Minister, Emmanuel Shinwell blamed consumers when it was learnt more electricity was used in Christmas week than ever before: 'It simply cannot go on. There has got to be some curtailment.'

Despite families running out of fuel, children were sent home after sitting in cold classrooms; factories and mills were closing or going on two and three-day weeks; exports were reducing. To move the coal, passenger trains were cut – the government targeted the cancellation of football specials – to enable supplies to travel more easily. The FA respond to a Government appeal for intensified production by limiting officially sanctioned midweek games, but the professionals were not affected … yet.

An unofficial transport strike started in Smithfield Market. Soon, Londoners were on half meat rations, and only then by 'long queues … for dwindling supplies of tinned stewing steak and spam'. When troops were sent in the strike became nationwide and led to the ultimate sacrilege: '17,000 dock workers leave food ships half unloaded.' The Government described the economic situation as 'extremely serious' and said the next six weeks would be decisive.

This was the social and economic climate as the country, and football, entered the legendary winter of 1947 – blizzards and heavy frost and ice binding Britain into sub-zero temperatures for week after long week, without light, warmth and work, until the thaw flooded the land. The country nearly closed down. Football carried on regardless, only to suffer at the end the untimely blow of bearing the cost of recovery. Football as scapegoat.

14

Up for the Frozen Arctic Cup

'February 1947 may go down in British sporting history as a red letter month in the calendar of Association football' (29 January 1947).
'White February – blackest month in Football League history'
(25 February 1947).
'Goodbye to February, good riddance too, in the opinions of most clubs'
(1 March 1947).

February was the point of no return for real football. Until then the game might still have overcome its difficulties: the League might resolve the players' dispute, and was 'practically certain' to expand to 110 clubs. This optimism disappeared under the ice of 1947's terrible winter and the blackness into which the British economy stared.

The cold descended just before the fourth round on 25 January. At home, 'the only place to keep warm at home is in bed with a hot water bottle back and front.' Where homes lacked fuel, workers went into work early to get warm.

Not all work. Len Shackleton had finally moved home and changed jobs. He lost his Bradford club house as Mrs Shackleton was in hospital having their son, and as the home promised by Newcastle remained elusive, so the family lived with his parents. They moved north in the New Year, and Shackleton was free of life underground – 'a terrifying experience: it is like being suspended on a piece of elastic'. As a United player he was offered 'work at practically every pit' in the north-east. Having had enough of the 'torture boxes' that were pit cages, 'I soon started investigating ways and means of "dodging the column"' (Shackleton, 1955, pp.61-62).

Unsuccessfully at first. 'The highly skilled and artistic Shackleton' became 'skivvy' to future Tyneside legend Jackie Milburn. A 'smashing job', Jackie had called it. On Len's first day, still pitch dark, 'the two of us waded through the snow and ice, eventually reaching a half-submerged pile of steel girders. Our "smashing job" involved lifting those girders and carrying them across the field. Nowadays, whenever I want a good nightmare I just go to sleep thinking about Hazelrigg Colliery' (Hutchinson, 1997, p.122).

Life was becoming more and more uncomfortable. Yet many thousands willingly embraced an unsheltered 'weekend of snow, gales' and ice to see Len, Jackie and 350 other players: 'the hold Cup-ties has on the football public is simply amazing.' Fellow miners, straight from their shift, followed

Sheffield United to Wolverhampton, arriving at 4am, and started clearing the snow off Wolves' pitch. 43,277 were rewarded by total commitment: 'Referee Barrick all but blew the bends out of his whistle trying to check the series of reckless and unnecessary fouls that ruined the match as a spectacle.' The replay was also typical. They were going to play on a bed of snow, but another heavy fall meant it had to be cleared. Despite terrible cold there were long queues, high black market prices and favourites Wolves went out.

The sixteen ties attracted 670,088 people (average 42,000), producing receipts of over £60,000. A ground record 82,000 was anticipated at Stamford Bridge to see holders Derby. Queues started before dawn in 28 degrees of frost. Variety star Arthur Askey gave an impromptu show to distract the crowd from the heavy snowfall onto exposed terraces, and redundant mounted police listlessly walked their horses. The 'ballyhoo', i.e. concerns over crowd safety, and the intense cold kept the crowd down to 49,484. Ticket 'sharks' got £10 for 10s stand tickets at first but not even face value at kick-off. 'Serve 'em right,' said *The People*. The match was a heady brew: 'Carter cocktail … an intoxicating draught with such a kick in it that people were sent reeling dizzily away from Stamford Bridge – Rams supporters well lit up, Chelsea fans in a stupor.' Tommy Lawton 'wriggled free' to put Chelsea ahead late in the game and the Cup seemed destined for a new home: 'one could almost hear the crackle of the wrapping paper in preparation to send back the Cup from Derby in a neat parcel.'

Raich Carter equalised with the whistle in the referee's mouth. Chelsea histories still say he handled, and contemporary accounts were intriguing: 'neither foot nor head could be used, with defenders converging upon him Carter swept the ball over the line with a flick of his right thigh.'

Two Derby fans – a railwayman and a miner – had been killed in a coach crash on icy roads en route to London, but in the midst of death there is new life. Everton captain Norman Greenhalgh was the latest footballer about to become a father. When he could wait no longer he crossed the desolate Pennines alone, to play Sheffield Wednesday, relegation-threatened in Division Two. Everton's soldier Eddie Wainwright was also delayed and frozen, both from guard duty at his army camp and a hundred-mile journey. Wednesday's win was the biggest shock in front of the biggest crowd – 62,250.

Preston's plumber Tom Finney scored the first of six second-half goals against Barnsley and a joiner, John Spuhler, got a last-minute winner for Middlesbrough. Here was the passion of the Cup and its do-or-die finality, the willingness to challenge authority when 'almost every verdict assumes a major significance'. Both teams had moments of grievance. First, 'at least half a dozen players, including goalkeeper Cumming, who ran up the field' protested that the ball had been 'a yard out of play' before Chesterfield's goal: 'I have never seen Boro make a more emphatic protest.' Not to be outdone, Chesterfield's 40-year-old Geordie captain Billy Kidd fumed about Boro's equaliser: 'I'm not in the habit of making silly protests, but there was the imprint of the ball on Spuhler's arm.' At least little Chester, deprived of an equaliser as they besieged Stoke's goal at the end, heard the referee's reason: 'I was right up with play. I don't care whether Mould was over the line or not. The ball certainly was not.'

In Birmingham, former pros watched 'players crash over the touchline to plunge knee deep into snow' in amazed tones: 'never in my many years' experience do I remember the players being at such a disadvantage.' Portsmouth felt doubly disadvantaged: 'The Birmingham goal was frequently lost in a smoke-screen during the second half and when the final whistle went the players were reluctant to leave the field. I learned afterwards that Jennings [of Birmingham] handled in the penalty area and the linesman was waving furiously when the referee blew for time.'

Another draw, and another crash, at Brentford. Eleven Leicester supporters were injured when their coach skidded and overturned. Brentford typified the many footballers given a 'raw deal' by 'the fates'. Against Leicester, the hard, frost-bound 'boomps-a-daisy' surface caused three back injuries. Thursday's replay went ahead when 50 men, a tractor and a snowplough worked from dawn, producing the 'worst conditions we've known'. Another goalless draw, after extra-time, and less than two days later, on a layer of snow covering frost-bound Griffin Park, Brentford lost to two goals by Villa's Trevor Ford in the First Division. It was said that, conscious of Monday's second replay, Brentford played with 'exaggerated caution'. The replay was at Villa Park after another 'dawn patrol' cleared deep snow, and throughout the 'swirling snowstorm eddied through the iron beams of the half-empty stands'. A 7,000 crowd was further entertained by elements of a comic opera: a lone trumpeter sounded at intervals, a sports-coated entertainer walked on his hands in the snow and posed for movie cameramen at half-time, and the lines were kept clear by 'two men who painstakingly pushed brooms throughout the game'. Appeals to end the game were in vain and Leicester won 4-1. Within days Brentford's changing-room pipes froze: luckily 'the local baths are only a few yards away and the players just continue with their running, pass out of the ground, straight into the baths' ... and down the drain. Exhausted Brentford lost seven successive league games and sank inexorably towards a relegation from which they have never returned.

The most evocative tie was at Bolton, scene of March's disaster. Police set a limit of 58,000 but decided against making the tie with Manchester City all-ticket. They worried that serious congestion might result from simultaneous arrival at the site of the spring tragedy. The public was reassured that the embankment was limited to 5,000 less than in the 1933 ground record crowd of 69,912. Plus, ten new turnstiles would operate, 'thanks to rush work carried out this week.' In general there would be 'comfortable and good seeing for every person'.

However 'every person' meant a certain type of person: on the notorious 'railway embankment a man will be able to take out his tobacco pouch and light his pipe with ease'. This example illustrated a folk lesson of last March:

'the popular terraces on these occasions are no place for young boys, or for women, either.' But there was a residual distrust about taking your chances on the haunted terraces: either the reassurances to men were insufficient, or the warnings to boys and women were too scary, for the crowd was 41,286: lower than recent league matches, and recalling archaic memories of famous Pie Saturday. When Bolton had hosted the 1901 FA Cup final replay, an expected 'monstre' crowd did not materialise – only 20,470 attended – and thousands of meat pies were left in the hands of the caterers, and given away.

The FA despaired of 200,000 workers deserting industry to attend mid-week replays, but still pressed to make replays all-ticket in the wake of Bolton. This 'colossal task' was always touch and go for the printers, and ticket distribution was a disaster. Everywhere, queues formed in the bitter cold of the early hours. Police haul reluctant club secretaries out of their beds to start selling early. The queues became unwieldy, and eventually those far back realised there is no hope for them. The queue broke, the police were overwhelmed and a battle for the gates began. Thousands jammed them outside as those inside desperately shored up the barrier.

And all this for a paltry few tickets. In Bolton itself, it became the most destructive 'topic in town ... harbouring too much resentment and bitterness for the good of the Wanderers ... widespread grumbling, bitter criticism and vilification throughout the club's area of support.' Derby County, that 'very unhappy club', ran into problems for favouring insiders. They received 1,500 tickets for their tie with Chelsea and sold them in half an hour. Or, as letters to local papers angrily denounced, 400 were sold – the 'other 1,100 tickets just vanished'.

For some it was a matter of special pleading, such as at Northampton's record crowd: 'some people are claiming tickets on the grounds of infirmity, short sightedness, and one official was overheard to remark "You'd think it was a hospital".' Or for semi-final tickets: 'I think I have received more applications from men who say they have just returned from Burma than the total number sent there during the war.' A Birmingham fan returned the club's letter of thanks for donating clothing coupons towards players' kit in angry 'protest at not securing a ticket despite three weary hours of waiting'. Nottingham Forest ran into different criticism for giving just two tickets to each player. As a result one 'actually stood in the queue at the City Ground, only to be refused tickets when his turn came'. This was 'bad psychology ... the players got the club there ... their interests should be served before all else. I know that several of them feel they were let down, which is all wrong.'

January 25th was the precursor to over two months that would define the age. In the coming days blizzards raged, temperatures dropped as low as 41 degrees of frost and German PoWs were 'out in great numbers clearing the roads of deep drifts' that marooned many villages. The Cup replays stood like beacons in a world closing in on itself: 'Snow was falling last night at Stoke, Sheffield, Derby and Manchester, where fourth round replays are due to be played today. Grounds are frozen.' The 29th was the coldest January night in

London for 66 years, with 17 degrees of frost. Next day saw the whole country snowbound, with new blizzards in the south. Fuel cuts – 'the worst there have ever been' – people fainting in the food queues, and transport chaos. Football carried on, negotiating a frozen landscape in delayed and unheated trains. Laurie Brown made a weary journey through a snowstorm to referee the Bolton tie and his return was delayed until 3am: 'there were no taxis to take him to Barnes, so he spent the night drinking tea in a snack bar, got home just before seven, and in half an hour was off to Newport, where he found the conditions unplayable and called the match off. Then home again.'

At Bolton the coin spun to decide choice of ends was lost in the snow. It was not only the pitch, weather and journey that tested Mr Brown's spirit. Its last leg was, according to the pre-eminent social commentator JB Priestley, 'characteristic of the British industrial landscape: between Manchester and Bolton the ugliness is so complete that it is almost exhilarating.' Football historian Percy Young thought Priestley had understated the ugliness (Young, 1950, p.31).

Chelsea's replay at Derby attracted another big crowd on a freezing day, including some who battled up from the capital: 'among Chelsea fans was four-year-old Kenneth Blackwell of Balham, dressed in a tail suit made up of Pensioners' colours. During the war he was an evacuee in Darley Dale near Derby.' The match was distinguished by a fall on the icy surface after only four minutes by ex-RAF flight sergeant Alec Grant, the Derby goalkeeper. Despite a dislocated elbow, Alec resumed on the wing, his initial uncertainty providing welcome light relief: 'Grant raised a laugh when from force of habit, he put his hands to a high pass and gave Chelsea a free kick.' But soon he was demonstrating unexpected abilities: 'With the ease of an experienced winger, [Grant] slipped past Winter and fired in an oblique shot which skidded across the goalmouth.'

This was truly remarkable. Not only was wounded Alec opposing an international, he was literally unprepared. Like many demobbed servicemen Alec was training as a teacher and since his autumn transfer he neither moved to Derby nor stayed at Leicester – he trained on his own! But who should go in goal? Raich Carter asked Frank Broome: 'How about it?' Broome replied, 'It is up my street.' Derby survived, and extra-time loomed in the coldest conditions possible. Veteran trainer Dave Willis rushed on to the field with a bottle. Before the referee could order him back, Dave was besieged by County players: 'What was in the bottle? From the knowing look on Willis' face, I have a good idea.' Thus fortified, Derby's extra nip won the match: a Jack Stamps winner, courtesy of ... Alec Grant. Chelsea complained: Tom Lawton said his extra-time header had been nine inches over the line: Frank Broome said the save was his greatest moment in football. Lawton also bemoaned going out in two rounds after playing enough to win the Cup: 510 minutes, watched by 251,698, paying £28,000. Meanwhile, the next day Derby's future England defender Bert Mozley played in an RAF inter-station match – his fifth game in eight days of dreadful conditions.

Groundsmen pitted their arcane remedies against pitiless weather and pitches that 'would have done justice to St Moritz'. Birmingham's Harry Green employed a 'secret mixture' 'of three chemicals, salt, peat and sand, 'and something else I'm not going to tell you about'. Leicester despaired of playing their already postponed replay with Newcastle. The pitch was 'a slab of ice, frozen for more than a month'. Five tons of salt did the trick, but destroyed the texture underneath. Leicester 'lost more than a cup-tie – they lost a football pitch'.

'The situation gets worse and worse.' Life became more fragile in the coldest weather, the biggest electricity cuts, the heaviest snows since ... For both families and industry the supply and communication system was breaking down, with coal uppermost in every mind. Mills and factories were closing for its want. International footballer Neil Franklin put the dilemma in a nutshell: 'industry demanded power. So did the harassed housewife, who could only gaze at the empty coalshed' (Franklin, 1956, p.46). Three hundred thousand tons lay in thirty thousand wagons in West Riding sidings. The weather was preventing coal movement by rail or sea: 57 loaded ships were unable to leave the north-east coast.

February 4th saw the worst road conditions yet, and it got worse. Discontent and criticism mounted: 'we were ambling along to disaster and men in public places did not seem to be taking too much notice.' Footballers also had private responsibilities. Middlesbrough's Alec Linwood returned to Scotland where his sister was 'dangerously ill': he did not play again until the quarter-final replay, extra-time and all, when he had not kicked a ball for two months. Irishmen like Portsmouth's Jimmy McAlinden fled to Belfast where his three children were ill, and talked of a transfer to somewhere nearer, say Lancashire, where he might be able to visit more often. Coventry manager Dick Bayliss became ill, and died. Footballers and their families, like Bill and Nessie Shankly, suffered along with everyone else: 'forced to huddle round half-empty fireplaces. 'It was terrible. There was rationing, no coal, and we had young Barbara. They were difficult years for all of us.' Such children had 'to be kept warm and bathed, and many was the time Shankly would return home with a few splinters of wood' (Kelly, 1996, p.47).

Illness hit government too. Aneurin Bevan went down with pneumonia and two other leading ministers, including Education Minister Ellen Wilkinson, entered hospital. The blizzards came south again: on four successive mornings, from 5-8 February, there were around 30 degrees of frost in London. On 6 February, Wilkinson died. Foreign Secretary Ernest Bevin, immersed in the unfolding Palestine crisis, received delegations in cold unlit rooms.

A Cabinet meeting on 7 February, called to discuss Palestine, instead dealt with the grave supply difficulties caused by the breakdown in rail and road transport, and of course the fuel shortage. The Government's emergency plan was announced on 8 February, the morning of the fifth round. The Air Ministry forecast that day: 'very cold conditions will be intensified by the stronger Easterly wind, which will reach gale force.' 'The Arctic conditions kept the crowds down' – to an average of 39,000 per match!

Before closing down for the crisis, BBC television broadcast London's sole survivors, Charlton Athletic, play Blackburn Rovers. Blackburn MP Barbara Castle was there, along with another Labour MP George Tomlinson, the school leaver at twelve who became Minister of Education.

The match was a turning point for others too. The reign of Rovers manager Eddie Hapgood, England's record full international, had become increasingly acrimonious. First wooed in July 1944, he did not arrive at Blackburn until demobbed from the RAF early in 1946. The extended courtship did not endear everyone, because negotiations concentrated on resolving the housing needs of Hapgood, his wife and three children after their wartime separation. Of the new generation of managers, he had the toughest job. Matt Busby had a ready-made team, little was expected of Cliff Britton at Burnley, but Eddie inherited the Football League (North)'s bottom club. He gave Rovers defensive backbone, but when results worsened criticism mounted: 'The accent was too much upon fighting zeal instead of skill, and reliance was placed upon youth before it was ready. Week after week we saw converted wingmen striving energetically in the key inside forward positions, when the need was for shrewd calculating scheming.' Conflicts, already 'fairly well known' locally, became public when wartime international Walter Crook 'did not see eye to eye with Mr Hapgood'. Crook was the heart of the promotion side.

Change came abruptly. Like many others, Eddie Hapgood became 'confined to his bed with a serious cold'. The directors recalled Crook, attracted Rovers' biggest crowd, won and retained control. A 'sweeping change of policy' brought in new players for whom Hapgood denied responsibility. The match at The Valley began badly when 'Crook wrenched a stomach muscle skidding on the ice in the first minute'. Effectively with ten men, Rovers fought 'tigerishly' on a 'veritable skating rink' and were still level into the last minute. Then, Charlton goalkeeper 'Bartram, advancing to meet a back-pass, took a tumble on an unsanded patch of ice'. Jimmy Baldwin raced past the 'prostrate' Bartram but, faced with a 'gaping, open goal', 'blazed his shot wide – an incredible miss.'

The goalkeepers survived several mishaps on the dangerous surface. Blackburn's George Marks was treated twice and Sam Bartram had already been 'laid out when his head hit the bone-hard ground'. Three minutes and thirteen seconds into added time Charlton scored. Eddie Hapgood resigned. Walter Crook never played again for Rovers. Also 'dumped unwanted' was 'a large brown paper parcel', containing Charlton's quota of tickets for a replay that never was.

Whilst two thirds of League matches were postponed, each Cup ground had an army – some paid, some volunteer and some, like players and German PoWs, impressed – working day and night on the pitch. But £600 spent on putting 50 tons of sand on Sheffield Wednesday's wasn't enough – it was the one tie postponed because the removal lorries left deep ruts. Visitors Preston were for a while 'lost' from communication: their train over the Pennines was cancelled and they waited two hours in the cold of a Manchester station, before finding the match off when they finally arrived. Criticised for not travelling earlier, Preston's reluctance recalled a clash in 1888 when the Invincibles resisted visiting 'the plague spot' on rumours of small pox raging in Sheffield. Wednesday's scorer in that far-off match, Billy Ingram, was among the disappointed 1947 fans.

Stoke versus Sheffield United was confusing. City tried to avoid ticket controversies – notably, employees taking time off work to queue – by allowing factories block allocations. However the fuel crisis made the pottery factories idle anyway. All 50,000 tickets were sold, but 10,000 United fans did not turn up, foiled by cancellations of both trains – to ease coal transportation – and coaches – because of dangerous road conditions.

The match carried uncomfortable echoes for Stoke, who had been knocked out of the Cup by a man named Brook in 1934 before a record crowd of 84,569. Now there were record receipts (£5,686), and a man named Brook beat them, after 'a combination of good football and courageous disregard of injury on the most dangerous playing pitch I have ever seen ... The players who stood out were those prepared to take the biggest risk of broken bones.' Sheffield played tough, with Scot Alex Forbes aiming 'wild kicks' at Stan Matthews: 'the crowd would have buried Forbes if he'd connected.' Stan mostly 'swayed out of the way like a hare evading a coursing whippet' (Miller, 1989, p.88).

Then Forbes connected: 'Matthews lay on the floor and the referee raised a beckoning finger to Forbes, red-haired Sheffield left half. Many thought the finger was already pointing to the dressing room. There was a hush after Forbes walked slowly to the referee and then a storm of booing when it was seen that he was not going off ... the most booed player visiting Stoke this season.' Stoke had all the play, raining in shots, but with 90 seconds to go came the winner. Stoke manager Bob McGrory was bemused. He later took his players out to view the place from which Harold Brook had hit his 'bombshell' winning shot – an 'impossible ... freak ... acute angle'. McGrory told his players that they would have missed from that position 'five times out of six ... with no goalkeeper in'. The clubs would meet again in another decisive encounter.

Holders Derby had very disturbed preparations for their match on Merseyside, where 'never in the history of the Liverpool club has the demand for Cup-tie tickets been so great.' County were marooned, Dickensian-fashion, in Mrs Muggleton's Guest House 'Haven' in the Peak, when the League required them to play a rearranged home game with Arsenal only days before the fifth round. To get out, 'four vehicles, specially equipped to fight the snow, had to make a perilous, but successful journey ... The rest cure proved anything but restful.'

The League insisted both teams attended the Baseball Ground even though everyone knew the match would not be played. The Arsenal party, travelling the day before the match, found that their reward for initiative was to get their supper. They had left St Pancras at 4.20pm, but the train engine broke down. Abandoning the wait for a replacement, Arsenal commandeered taxis and got to their hotel in Matlock at 11.15, to find that their dinner, which had been prepared by 7.30, had been 'kept warm for them'. Inevitably the game was postponed and Derby crossed the Peak to defend their Cup.

Referee 'Smiling Jim' Wiltshire had a more pleasant preparation: he had been 'walking along the Rosea in Lisbon' (Wiltshire, 1948, p.45) when he heard of his Saturday assignment. 'Smiler' had stayed on after refereeing Portugal v Spain, where he was presented with diamond cuff-links and a gold cigarette case and had a confusing conversation with the Spanish goalkeeper about his habit of swinging on the crossbar. After warnings in French and German were not understood, Smiler exploded in English: 'Well, I don't want you hanging on to that bar, see.' 'Why didn't you say so? I speak English. I played in Southampton for two years.'

Anfield presented a Christmas card scene, and Smiler 'never saw Vic Woodley play a more inspired game'. Woodley, a regular prewar England goalkeeper who was only playing because of Alec Grant's injury, was 'miraculous' on the 'snow and ice crusted Anfield pitch'. The match was decided when Derby neglected the Liverpool captain. Injured Jack Balmer had gone on the wing but suddenly reappeared in the centre to produce a 'glorious header' for the only goal: '... and the Liverpool crowd roared, and roared, and roared.'

The slogan for the 44,493 fans who had braved the elements could have stood for any match during the freeze-up: 'if they can play, we can watch.' For players and officials there was a comradely exit. Smiler shared a taxi as they passed by the leading football commentator of the time, Raymond Glendenning, fresh from delivering the radio broadcast: 'with Vic Woodley and Cyril Sidlow the respective goalies, we were making a dash by taxi to catch the London train. I glimpsed through the window one who looked to be an Arctic explorer. He was none other than Raymond, complete with snow boots and a terrific scarf' (Wiltshire, 1948, p.125). Derby's journey home was as miserable as last spring's celebrations had been joyous: 'the packed train from Manchester stopped at every solitary station around the Peak and Peveril [reporter] has rarely felt less at home among the Derbyshire hills.'

Goalkeeper Larry Platts, star of Forest's unexpected fourth round win at Manchester United, couldn't make their Middlesbrough tie. An Army sergeant about to be posted overseas, Larry could not get leave for only his third game of the season. At Nottingham, even the referee helped clear the pitch after the coldest night many had experienced. The 2-2 draw was notable for Wilf Mannion scoring for both teams. Wilf's face after his first own goal in any football was a sight of the season, but he resented the attention: 'the next thing I knew was that a Forest player was clapping me on the back to congratulate me, which I didn't appreciate.' Photographs suggest Mannion's predecessor as England's inside-left, 'waddling warrior' 'Sailor' Brown, was the author of this gamesmanship. Or Sailor, the 'driving force' behind Forest's surprise win in Manchester, may have been simply trying to keep warm: "never known such a cold day in all my forty years' experience in the game" ... Despite the terrific pace at which the game was fought, we witnessed the unusual sight of those players not engaged in chasing the ball, dancing up and down to keep the circulation going.'

It was a particularly sensitive time for an afternoon football game. The Prime Minister had just told the country that coal supplies had absolute priority: there was no fuel for most of industry and no fuel for domestic homes for large parts of every day. Yet 200 workers toiled from the early hours to clear Ayresome Park of six inches of snow. Among the 'astronomic prices' being asked for tickets was the most astronomic of all: 'the most fantastic bait offered was that of a ton of coal delivered free for two stand tickets.' Mannion's revenge was only delayed. Boro trailed at home in the replay, but Forest went down to ten men, and Wilf scored a brilliant hat-trick in incessant second half attacks: 6-2. The Forest fans didn't see their beds from Monday to Wednesday night.

But the weather had enabled the Government to shift the agenda. Until now the focus was on government competence in not anticipating a fuel crisis most commentators had forecast; or cowardice in denying the inevitable; or impotence in lacking the economic means to achieve its ends. Now the Government could mobilise the country behind the Battle of Britain 1947, and focus on the obstacles to all-out production: 'once again production or sport is the vital question.'

15

Coal before Football:
A Moral and Economic Panic

'If domestic and industrial consumers decline to co-operate we find ourselves in the next ten days in a condition of complete disaster ... we should not have any fuel for electricity at all.' Emmanuel Shinwell, Minister of Fuel and Power, 8 February 1947

The 'winter of discontent' in 1979 that preceded Margaret Thatcher's rise to power reached its apotheosis when industrial disputes prevented burials. In 1947 weather and illness produced the same effect: 'so much interference with normal public services is arising ... Two brothers dug the grave for their sister ... volunteers opened up old graves for the large number of funerals that took place last week, and many were impossible.'

Prime Minister Attlee announced a 'great switch off' of electricity, with exceptions made for mining areas, essential services and 'continuous industrial processes'. The plan proved incomprehensible and unworkable, and the Ministry of Fuel and Power, besieged in its offices on Sunday, were overwhelmed by queries. In a return to wartime conditions, camp beds littered the building. The Minister, Emmanuel Shinwell put in an eleven-hour day, fortified only by a spam sandwich. His exhausted minions chose another sustenance: 'the Civil Servant in battledress jacket, flannel trousers and gum boots has just croaked into his telephone: "Block this line for one minute please. I want to light a cigarette".'

The whole basis of a technological society was in jeopardy: industry paralysed; millions out of work; passenger trains withdrawn, to move coal. The Government brought forward British Summer Time. The BBC halted television and limited radio to five hours. Papers 'must cease publication' or be limited to four pages, a ban 'responsible for the absence of programmes' at football matches. The black market reaped a 'rich harvest'. Food became ever more basic: with supplies critical, queues lengthened and lengthened. Life reverted to a previous century: in a nicely poetic, but sadly apt image Britain was now 'washing in snow by moonlight'.

The weather, the morale and Britain's economic distress all went hand in hand. School children of the time remembered these as epoch-defining events: 'so cold we're allowed to stay in the school hall at break and dinner-time, huddled over the iron radiators, drinking our warm, near-curdled milk. Outside, as well as the ice and snow, is immediately post-war Britain: rationed, exhausted and grey' (Duffy, 1995, Prologue). The world outside the Armed Forces suddenly seemed a bleaker prospect: 'I'm to be demobbed in May – but perhaps I'll stay in after all.'

Then the fightback began in the Coal Battle of Britain. Barges broke the ice on canals. The 'keep-the-coal-moving-weekend' of 15-16 February was achieved by miners, soldiers, dockers, seamen and railwaymen all working extra shifts. A hundred coal trains headed for London. Coal ships, 'encased in ice from bows to stern,' arrived at beleaguered Beckton, the world's largest gas works. Exhausted crewmen hoped their effort was respected: 'Tell 'em to watch every flick of those gas taps.'

Sport had 'a graveyard smell about it', and needed light relief: 'A man invaded the pitch at the interval and with shirt sleeves rolled up proceeded to amuse the crowd by paddling round on the snow on his hands with legs in the air. Three constables persuaded him that St Andrews was hardly the place for such antics, and he left the field to wild cheers.' Crowds had a new weapon: 'snowballing was not altogether a pleasant pastime at Charlton. Before the start several spectators received facial injuries needing treatment and the referee and linesman, too, came in for a share.'

Meanwhile there were desperate measures to supply isolated snowbound communities. Halifax bombers, equipped to drop bread from bomb racks, were ordered up 'whatever the conditions' until, flying blind through thick, low cloud, one hit a Derbyshire hillside, killing all eight occupants. New blizzards, whipped into great drifts by strong winds, blocked roads afresh despite the work of bulldozers, snowploughs – even flame throwers – and thousands of troops, Poles and German PoWs to clear them or free stranded villages. They failed, and further falls mocked their efforts.

Throughout the industrial shutdown, the domestic misery, the warnings of worst to come, footballers travelled an unforgiving country, often to play, sometimes not, but anyway on the unplayable. At first the League required clubs to travel even when postponements were inevitable. Thus Bradford City, minus four players who could not even get to Bradford, made a six-hour journey on the dreadful Friday of 7 February just to view the foot of snow on Wrexham's pitch. Portsmouth made an even grimmer trip that same Friday: all the way to Sunderland.

The terrible winter had hit the south first. Frost shattered the glass windguards on HMS Vanguard and snowploughs cleared the path of the Royal train as it took the King, Queen and the princesses out of frozen England for the sunnier climes of South Africa. Portsmouth, like most southern clubs, had over a foot covering their ground: 500 lorry loads of shovelled snow in 24 hours, and the help of 200 Royal Marines, cleared the pitch but the ground underneath was 'as hard as steel' and as slippery as a 'skating rink'. League leaders Wolves went home. A week later it was Portsmouth's turn. The odds against play were 100-1 but still at noon on Friday they set off. It was the coldest day of the year in County Durham: 'the countryside was scattered with the jetsam of war: anti-aircraft posts in cornfields, banked with dribbling sandbags; concrete tank-traps lining the roads, like idols left by some gloomy, extinct race' (Cooper, 1986, pp.26-27).

It felt like a wild goose chase, a metaphor for the mood throughout a cold, dispirited country: 'Portsmouth had a singularly trying and dismal journey under particularly depressing conditions, and the further north they got the less the prospects seemed.' In Sunderland dockers were refusing to work, 'their hands and feet numbed.' Hundreds were gathering gale-strewn coal from Roker beach to heat frozen homes. Sunderland manager Bill Murray and hundreds more were at Roker Park clearing the football pitch. It was bitterly cold, the ground was again as hard as steel, but rough, and they played: 'to turn 22 players out in thin jerseys and knickers in a wind which lashed your face like a whip was, in my opinion, wrong.'

Grounds posed constant risk of serious injury. Tommy Lawton confirmed players 'were absolutely scared to move when they played their last games'. He made his disapproval evident when a full England team, masquerading as the Football League, beat the Irish at Goodison Park. The pitch was dangerous: one half was 'a snow covering over concrete, and the other half was shear, shining ice, broken here and there with sharp toothed tufts of turf.' 36,000 turned up, so the game went ahead: 'if Goodison was fit for football no match should ever be cancelled in the future.' The cream of England's footballers became 'ice stars'; the 'ball looked like an inebriated reveller trying to work his way round a lamp-post.' Lawton scored twice, then became a 'looker on', unwilling to risk life and limb. His attitude did not go unnoticed – 'some stars risked their reputations rather than their necks' – and his subsequent criticism led to a 'disciplinary measure', being dropped against the Scottish League.

A pattern was set. Home players battled to clear the snow whilst away teams battled late-running trains, 'prepared to make a dash on the pitch,' but found the game off. Barnsley's cold bus took five hours to travel 35 snowbound miles to Bury: 'a noticeboard was sent round informing the crowd that Barnsley would arrive ready changed for the match for a 3.15 start.' Unsurprisingly, in nine minutes Barnsley were 0-3 down. They began a heroic fightback, and a more exciting match than anyone had a right to expect ended 4-4.

On Friday, 21 February new snowfalls, whipped up into great drifts by strong winds, blocked roads and rail-lines afresh – but the football went on, with consequent misadventures for leaders and stragglers alike. Wolves, playing their first match in a month, were delayed, stripped on the bus, and withstood both a figurative footballing blizzard from a Leeds team fighting desperately against relegation and a real one from leaden skies. Wolves missed their return train and arrived back in Wolverhampton in a bone-chilling dawn, twelve hours after the final whistle. Mansfield's team of working miners were now on a 'slow, but remorseless slide' down the Southern Section of the Third

Division. So many players with two physically demanding occupations was proving too much. Their additional geographical obstacles were figuratively illustrated by a midnight return from defeat by QPR (described as the sequel to the Immortal Bard's Comedy of Errors). First the London train was very late: then their bus 'battled its way through deep snow drifts' until 'the road was blocked by a bus and a car stuck side by side and the players had to pile out and push the car through before the way could be cleared.'

One group of intrepid workers undeterred by this frozen white landscape of disappearing trains and non-existent accommodation was the football managers in their never ending search for new players. Swansea manager Haydn Green still had the money for Trevor Ford and perhaps other items burning a hole in his pocket. Haydn went north, and had his offers 'laughed at' in Scotland. He came south, and found himself sleeping in a Bolton barn. He crossed the Irish Sea, got nothing in Dublin, and headed for Belfast, until he was intercepted at the border: 'after being ordered by a Customs officer to remove his overcoat, jacket, waistcoat, boots and braces, all bought in Welsh Wales, the chocolate he was nibbling was confiscated and he was fined £3. He got the impression he was lucky to get back his braces.' In Belfast he couldn't sign the Larne blacksmith who led (Northern) Ireland's line, and failed to get Birmingham's Welsh international Wilson-Jones. Haydn returned empty handed and Swansea's season, bereft of a convincing centre-forward, faded away into relegation.

Other industrial workers walked out because heating systems failed, or were simply turned off: there were ten degrees of frost inside the railway works at Doncaster. London had 24 degrees of frost; Manchester 34; Cambridge 42. It was the longest spell of continuous frost since 1841. And then 40mph blizzards made every road in Yorkshire impassable, football cities Sunderland and Newcastle isolated by great drifts. The end of February saw the worst weather, ever.

In London the Labour Government was in deep trouble, their project almost over before it had began. 1946 had seen a growing disillusionment: 'peacemaking is hard, plenty a long way off. Government, as well as people dwelt in the clouds, has felt the bump.' Regulation had become despised – 'we are being governed to death' – and still there was no compensatory Welfare State. Its industrial policy, stressing exports and productivity yet adding substantial social costs, was condemned in apocalyptic terms: 'the world is gasping for goods of all kinds … the manufacturers' seventh heaven. But I am very much afraid that this seventh heaven will prove to be, in reality, a false paradise, for shortly, and so much sooner than we expect, we shall be cast, like Lucifer, from our paradise to a veritable hell of competition.' Now this 'devil of a crisis' had handed out 'the heaviest indictment ever brought against the government.'

Conservatives attacked with the slogan 'Starve with Strachey, and Shiver with Shinwell.' The sense of impending disaster amid a winter from hell led to panic that the precious dollar loan was being spent too quickly and, with exports now further dislocated, might be gone by the autumn. And what will we do then?

The Government's vulnerability was recalling historical precedents. The last Labour executive had fallen during the Depression and replaced by an all-party National Government. The country's crisis was more than political and economic, it was moral: to be compared with a recent Hollywood film, about an alcoholic, the depth of whose decline was captured by a weekend of amnesia: 'the nation has lost its soul – a lost weekend.'

Essayist JB Priestley addressed the nation's moral problem. The 'prevailing temper of our people' revealed that 'clearly something had gone wrong': '[they] were largely kept going through the war by a sense of collective values [which] have mostly vanished and the energy they held has been dispersed, frittered away the last eighteen months. We are ill … feel vaguely let down and depressed.'

One expression of the convergent moral and weather crisis was the successive cancelling of the Football Pools. They had permeated 'the consciousness of the people more than ever before'. In contemporary terms it would be like the National Lottery being halted within its enormously successful first year. Like our current National Lottery, the Pools' proceeds promised to solve so many otherwise intractable problems. The Players' Union wanted the money offered by the companies, or to establish their own Pools, to ensure insurance payments to injured players. The football authorities stopped them doing either. And yet, also like the Lottery, its popularity was seen as a metaphor for withdrawal from real life, as a moral loss. At times it seemed the only thing in which people were interested: 'to hear people in Swindon inquire about football scores on a Saturday afternoon made me wonder if they thought of anything else.'

Priestley continued his analysis: 'then from out of their depression or irritation, begin to behave badly … no better than "spivs". So you find everyone trying to do a bit of dodging … Notice how many people want to get out of the country … We relieve drabness by triviality. Our new world is one of packed greyhound tracks and bulging football pools.'

Priestley's was a poetic lament but others made a more prosaic attack: why were 300,000 people working in Football Pools when the country was desperate for productive workers? The Government now added its voice: 'today it is the producer who counts.' The abnormal weather provided an opportunity to retrieve a moral momentum. Their counterattack elevated mining to the status of 'a national service', a stepping stone from the wartime Armed Forces to the promised future social services.

The Government's White Paper on Employment, an immediate best seller, pointed the way forward: 'only an all out' productive effort 'will prevent an economic crisis overtaking Britain with disastrous consequences'. Now more than ever the mines would prove Britain's salvation – 'coal is the basis of the entire production process' – so more miners were needed: up 35,000 to 730,000. Leisure, sport, football were not essential like 'imported food' or 'as important as coal, clothing or housing.' So with labour shortages in the mines, textiles and agriculture, 'we cannot afford' hundreds of thousands working in betting.

Labour MPs wanted the Pools banned, and their labour directed elsewhere. Soon the Minister of Labour met Pools company directors 'with a view to releasing some labour', that is their female employees, back into the mills and factories. And what did the pools depend on? 'the industrial and business world ... maintained that professional football is a luxury which the country, starved of manpower cannot afford.' Thus the Players' Union's revival of its long running dispute met a steely response: 'this is no time to push wage claims. Somebody might want to know why they're not absorbed in industry.'

The last thing football needed was a high profile match during the working week, but 1 March saw the Cup's quarter-finals: 'midweek replays ... draw vast crowds and force a situation in important industrial areas the Football Association are desperately anxious to avoid.' The pressure upon midweek football had intensified: no longer because of occasional and localised absenteeism. The Government now sought a radical change in working hours, to overcome the economic crisis by maximising the workforce from 6am to 10pm, with staggered hours, night working and double shifts. For the next couple of years, spectator sports should be Saturdays only.

Yet midweek matches were not optional: they were essential to complete the season. The 211 league matches already postponed would normally be replayed during the light spring afternoons or early evenings. Otherwise there would be no promotion and relegation outcomes and the whole credibility of football's reconstruction put in jeopardy. Then there was a dramatic demonstration to everyone – government, press and football authorities – of football's enormous pull. If further emphasis were needed, local employers Joseph Lucas Ltd sacked 50 absentee workers for going to the match. Burnley, a small Lancashire town, hosted Middlesbrough in a Cup replay on the 'worst ever' Tuesday afternoon, 4 March.

A decade later Arthur Ellis was 'the best referee in the world' (Shackleton, 1955, p.63) and veteran of Cup finals, World Cups and Olympic Games. He told presenter Richard Dimbleby on the radio programme 'Down Your Way' that the most memorable match he ever refereed was the Burnley v Middlesbrough replay in the Arctic weather of 1947. The contemporary view was that it would have been 'declared unfit but for the need to complete the tie and avoid further congestion of fixtures'. Arthur Ellis initially agreed: 'conditions were so bad when I looked at the ground that it seemed hopeless to think about playing football.'

He delayed opening the gates until, an hour before kick off, 35,000 thronged the cobbled streets outside 'snow-bound, wind-swept Turf Moor'. Eighty police were struggling to stop them breaking into the ground. The Chief Constable got Ellis to stand on a police horse and look out. He found the police 'rightly concerned about the safety of the mass of people congregated ... it was an awe inspiring sight.' 'Among the vehicles from Middlesbrough was a lorry filled with miners straight from the pit.' The application of brine and sand, not to mention men with picks and shovels, 'worked wonders' – most of 'the jagged iced corners and ridges' had been 'levelled off': and twenty minutes before kick-off Ellis gave the go ahead. But trying to cram 50,000 people into Turf Moor quickly risked disaster and, uniquely, the referee delayed kick-off by 40 minutes. The match was dramatic enough (see next chapter) but Ellis remembered the occasion, and the admission of 49,244 (£4,124 receipts) within an hour: 'without the delay I am convinced we should have had another disaster similar to the tragic one at Bolton in 1946' (Ellis, 1954, pp.60-61).

The essential message of that Enquiry was that dangerous situations 'happen again and again without fatal or even injurious consequences. But its danger is that it requires so little additional influences ... to translate the danger into death and injuries.'

The quarter-final between Middlesbrough and Burnley stood for many other near-misses. The original tie was as equally dangerous. 53,025 (creating record receipts, £5,489) squeezed into Ayresome Park – 9,000 more than the closed gates for Boro's early League matches – and created the classic dilemma: 'the people outside wanted to get in and those inside wanted to get out.'

In the crush outside, Samuel Harrison collapsed and died. Inside, as at Bolton but here with four degrees of frost, young fans broke out onto the side of the pitch: 'the boy with an open neck shirt, short trousers, no overcoat and no hat, who sat on the snow and drank steadily from the largest bottle of lemonade ever seen was typical of their toughness.' The following week's letters page was dominated by angry and scared remembrances: 'I would like to voice my disapproval at the number of people admitted to the ground. The ghost of the Bolton disaster seems to be unheeded.' As in that death trap there were spectators who could not resist the 'pressure behind me ... right through a seething mass of humanity until I finally landed on the floor.' The 1s 3d enclosure came 'near to disaster': in the two shillings stand, correspondent 'Never Again' found conditions 'appalling': 'the first half was over before the serious struggle for existence eased sufficiently to allow me to take a glance at the game ... Sheer good luck alone avoided the necessity for hearses.'

Those inside thought it 'criminal' that the gates were not closed earlier: those outside came close to criminality. Burnley supporters who had survived the 100-mile journey on treacherous roads complained about not being allowed in: 'the only sympathy we got from police was for them to send for the fire engine, who threatened to give us a shower bath.' The 5,000 outside 'threatened to break into the ground'. A fire engine arrived, but the National Fire Service credited unexpected means with cooling the crowd's ardour: 'the Chief Constable began his broadcast and what apparently had been a somewhat disorderly crowd became quite orderly.'

Middlesbrough's Chief Constable saved the day by giving a commentary from the grandstand to the waiting thousands outside. Middlesbrough's secretary defended the club from charges of not making safe its dangerous embankment: 'the contractors could not get the necessary permit and license for material ... fully expected that the job would have been started long ago, but circumstances, over which the club has no control prevented this.'

Football was days away from its lowest point. These near disasters occurred almost a year to the day of the original. In normal circumstances that replay would have been postponed. The players needed Herculean efforts just to play, yet produced an epic that ran into extra time. Players had been producing Herculean efforts all winter. It is remarkable how many matches were played. On viciously cold 8 February, nineteen matches were played and nineteen postponed. The following week 21 were postponed and seventeen went ahead (only one in London), and seventeen games were played on 22 February, 23 being called off.

The only other comparison is with the terrible winter of 1962-63, when in similar circumstances five successive weeks saw only single figure matches. Footballers were entitled to think that Burnley marked the end of the nightmare. But no, the match had barely finished when the blizzards resumed, the 'worst yet' in the West Midlands, creating chaotic road conditions and 24 miles of snowdrifts on rail track in Oxfordshire. Cotswolds houses disappeared. In Wolverhampton, home of the First Division leaders, it was already the seventh week of cold, the 43rd continuous day on which snow lay on the ground, and the 46th night of frost.

BLACK SATURDAY, 8 MARCH 1947
'Never before in history has a football season started with more promise ... What a sorry change we have witnessed in this last month.'

The 'blackest ever day in football' recalled the farces of Laurel and Hardy: 'soccer is having its full share of "sticky mess".' Everything was going wrong. Any question of expanding the League was now off the agenda: rather the winter had proved there were too many clubs, too many games. The blizzards meant that more were postponed that day – 27 out of 44 – than in the whole history of the League. Those remaining – some with snow on, some off, others studded with freezing lakes – each averaged twenty thousand spectators. Portsmouth used steam jets just so their reserve match could go ahead, and over 11,000 watched. Conditions were farcical: at Spurs, 'the ball often stopped dead in the icy slush,' but the players kept going: 'they fell yards from the ball, slid astonishing distances on their backs, and some might have "sledged" out into White Hart Lane had there not been a snow bank around the touchline.' Such scenes produced a laugh a minute – especially when 'one pair of shorts came completely unstuck' – but did nothing for the status of those performing in impossible circumstances.

The further postponements confirmed the Government's 'forbidding attitude': football and other sporting authorities were summoned to the Home Office on Tuesday. If midweek football was banned, the season would be wasted because the FA Council had reaffirmed that the existing extension of 10 May was final.

And before Tuesday there was Monday's union meeting, where 'smouldering unrest burst into the flame of a strike'. Jimmy Fay's letter mountain from players angered by the League's intransigence and threats was echoed by all 53 delegates who braved the journey to decide to strike on 21 March. But 'now things were different', the loss of so many weeks' revenue providing an 'ideal opportunity for clubs to plead poverty'. If the postponements were never played it spelt disaster: prewar, many clubs would have already gone under.

The Government met sports authorities on 11 March threatening all non-Saturday sport for two years. The parallels with an earlier crisis were evident: 'the whole business [of sport] has gone back into the melting pot, just as it did at the beginning of the war.' Although football was easily the sport most threatening to production, Will Cearns, West Ham's chairman, ridiculed a ban as 'too fantastic': 'the moral effect on the people would be disastrous. The whole idea is incredible ... forcing too much austerity on to the public.' The Government faced a storm of disapproval for tactics threatening to destroy its compact with a people who 'survived the greatest war in history and feels that it has earned whatever pleasure these bleak days of scarcity allow. What was tolerated in wartime will not be countenanced in peacetime. A stranger might think we had lost the war.'

Some thought the Government was panicking, and would not legislate if its bluff was called. However the League had second thoughts. Here was an opportunity to pressurise the FA, which had just rejected their request for a further extension, and sweeten the Government. The Chancellor, again pursuing clubs for not reducing their admission charge, was threatening higher tax levels in the forthcoming Budget. And on the same day that the football authorities met the Home Secretary, the Ministry of Labour announced a National Arbitration Tribunal to consider the Players' Union's appeal. So Will Cearns, the League's representative, went the 'whole hog' in accepting the government wish for sport on a Saturday-only basis, not only for this season, but next as well. There would be no further midweek football matches in 1946-47.

The implications were profound. The world was falling in on football. The urgency of real football derived from competition. Competition was given texture by promotion and relegation, the 'life blood of soccer in this country' (Ellis, 1954, p.49). The outstanding fixtures could not be played in the nine Saturdays left. A season of high promise was ending in 'stalemate' and chaotic anticlimax. Desperate measures were needed, although not as desperate as Jimmy Fay's suggestion, that matches be played behind closed doors. Nor, to their old guard President, desperate enough for another 'thin end of the wedge': 'Football League matches on Sundays will not be tolerated.'

As so often before in this strange and eventful season the contrasting treatments accorded footballers and miners indicated their respective social value.

Footballers were now official pariahs, almost condemned to ply their trade away from the public gaze: miners were society's hope for survival. They were often one and the same. Footballers represented the temptations of the Devil of Absenteeism. Special trains were long gone and now their ordinary ones, cold and forlorn, limped along in the wake of coal wagons. Miners were feted. Extra food, vegetables, sugar, fats, and oils went their way – any incentive to increase their production was worth considering. This was not universally applauded: when a miner's daughter wrote complaining about the quality of her breakfasts, 'Tasty and Sweet' of Harrogate replied, in true Monty Python style: 'I should be glad of bread and dripping for my breakfast if I had any dripping.'

The FA Council also drew a line when they turned down the National Coal Board's request 'for Cup final tickets for 250 miners and their families as an incentive to increase production, and to attract new entrants'.

Footballers could be useful though. Bolton's new star Nat Lofthouse finished two years underground as a Bevin Boy miner – and was promptly hired by the NCB for public relations work to increase recruitment. Ambition even encompassed a National Coal Board Football League proposal, to rival the existing one. On the day the ban was announced Wheldale Colliery had an important midweek cup-tie, normally the occasion of some absenteeism. But not now. 'Coal before football,' said the miners who stayed on shift and missed the match.

Mind you, others described the ban as Hitlerite. Everywhere, the new working arrangements were forcing a re-appraisal of what football meant in postwar England. Even in rural Ipswich the 'six largest engineering firms' not only adopted the double shift system from 6am to 10pm, but they took turns so only one was free from work Saturday afternoons: 'like a bolt from the blue we are informed that we are again to give up in the words of the shop stewards 'our luxury of watching a football match on a Saturday afternoon.' In mine, and lots of other opinions, it is not so much a luxury, but like a glass of tonic wine.'

And still the weather would not relent, on footballer, miner or anyone. Five, six, seven frozen weeks. A thaw was forecast, but instead a 'great blizzard' on 6 March cut Britain in half, with thousands of workers still fighting the battle to keep the coal moving through blocked roads and railway lines. One enterpriser conjured a novel way to collect fuel: his 'garden adjoins a main railway line, keeps up his coal stock by placing bottles on the fencing posts. Few drivers or firemen can resist the appeal of throwing coal to knock off the bottles.'

The snow had one last ferocious fall on football. There were blizzards everywhere on Saturday, 15 March. New Brighton goalkeeper Alec Corbett couldn't get a train, so 52-year-old manager Neil McBain created a new record by becoming the oldest Football League player. By contrast Norman Evans had one of the shortest careers: he signed on the spot just so New Brighton could put out a team. McBain's record beat that of the great Billy

Meredith and would in turn be challenged by another legendary right winger, Stan Matthews.

Stan himself had been in the 'worst yet' blizzards that swept Scotland and closed 38 railway lines. A strong Football League side, featuring a forward line of Matthews, Carter, Westcott, Mannion and Kippax, beat the Scottish League 3-1 before 80,000 on 12 March. That evening a terrific snowstorm cut Glasgow off by road and rail. How to get back? Stoke advised Matthews and Neil Franklin to try Renfrew Airport, but they found VIPs had booked every seat on the only plane going out. Footballers had to wait. Friday dawned, and their train crawled out of Glasgow. Franklin recalled: 'our progress was painfully slow, and not very sure, but as we looked out on a world of snow, nobody could grumble ... I must admit that I began to wonder whether we would get stuck in a drift ... We seemed to creak our way through Carlisle, and groan our way up the forbidding Shap' (Franklin, 1956, p.33).

They reached Preston fifteen hours later, and split up. Franklin hopped a newspaper train and got to Stoke at six in the morning, twenty hours after leaving Glasgow. He went home, had a couple of hours sleep in a chair and then travelled to Villa Park: 'I played that game from memory.' So much so that he did not recall that the match was abandoned after an hour – the only one to succumb to the blizzards. Matthews could not get from Blackpool, and his non-appearance disappointed the 50,000 crowd: 'a half-murmur, half groan came from all parts of the ground,' before questions were asked: 'how was it that Franklin got here all right from Glasgow, and Matthews did not?'

Phil Taylor was another returning polar explorer. Taylor walked in as Liverpool were going out at Portsmouth: he was spared what his captain Jack Balmer remembered as 'the worst conditions I have ever experienced, with a raging blizzard which made it difficult to stand upright, never mind run about'. Portsmouth's steam jet, melting ice and snow, made the pitch a 'farm-yard duckpond' even before the blizzard arrived: 'I have known Fratton Park since 1899 ... but never have I seen it in a worse state.' Extraordinarily the Liverpool team who inflicted Portsmouth's only defeat in their last fifteen league games produced the best football of the season.

The blizzards of 15 March were followed immediately by a cataclysmic storm. First, 100mph winds killed fourteen people 'by crashing houses, walls and trees in gale-swept Britain'. Then the century's worst flood-waters were hurled loose, bringing wartime echoes: 'ancient motorboats and river craft which made the trip to Dunkirk are being used in rescuing families from the flooded Thames villages.' The floods affected 31 counties: the Severn reaches successively higher record levels each day – beating 1770, 1852 and 1886; the ubiquitous German PoWs fought the floods in the Fens; the Metropolitan Water Board introduced wartime emergency measures as millions went without water, ironically because the floods overwhelmed London's filter beds in the Lea valley. Threequarters of the Army Northern Command's four thousand flood fighters were German prisoners of war. Back in Germany, 100,000 were involved in riots against food shortages.

The Minister of Agriculture pronounced the agricultural losses because of snow, frost and floods, an 'unparalleled disaster to the nation'.

Top Line: a Celtic Fringe – the garrulous Bill Shankly, 'aggressive, strong and occasionally a little wild, with excitement getting the better of him;' All-Action Alex Forbes, the most booed man in 1946-47; and Kevin O'Flanagan, the doctor who attended to your wounds once he knocked you down. Bottom: To Transfer or Not – Jimmy Hagan, 'not enough money in football;' Albert Stubbins, chased by most of the First Division, and cornered in a cinema; Len Shackleton, six goals on debut; thereafter, 'like a brilliant actress, he preferred to play alone.'

16

Promotion and Relegation are off

'How do we stand now? Up to the neck in muddle, it seems. The ban on mid-week sport rubs in the austerity ointment. It smarts. Inevitably it will leave sores that cannot be cured.'
'The blow has fallen ... It means the end of the Football League as a tournament for this season.'

There were only six prizes for the 88 League clubs in 1946-47: the FA Cup, the League Championship and four promotion places: the Second Division champions and runners up; and the champions of the two Third Division sections. The ban on midweek football put all but the Cup in jeopardy. Football folk were unimpressed: 'This government has done something Hitler couldn't do.' Ironically, this imminent threat fell upon promotion candidates from coal-producing areas. It was a 'cruel blow' to Cardiff City, and Doncaster Rovers 'feel very upset to say the least'. Aborting Burnley's heroic challenge for a Cup and promotion double is 'nothing short of tragedy'. As the sun came out for the first time in months, Torquay lost 1-5 at home, but their crowd taunted promotion-chasing Swindon with the meaningless of their win – 'Don't worry. It makes no difference now!'

In effect the pressure was back on the Football Association, which had been put in an impossible position by the Government and the League. Postponed matches now comprised 216 out of the 583 fixtures outstanding. The FA's role as custodian of the ancient spirit of football included protecting its identity as a winter game, as something in tune with the rhythms of the British way of sport, and preventing incursions on to cricket's territory. But their denial of a further extension was no longer tenable: they would take the blame for rendering this season, and the reconstructed professional game, 'useless and unprofitable'.

The League, so often wrong footed during the war, had turned the tables and were on the side of the government angels. All the FA could do was bow to the inevitable and agree an extension to 14 June: 'this season, one of the most momentous in the history of the game, has been saved by Sunday's decision.' The FA thought about retaliating. Defenders of the summer-winter sporting divide proposed that leagues with more than eighteen clubs should not be recognised. But the FA no longer had the Army on their side. It was too late. The clubs muttered about missing a season of the Cup, or setting up their own, or withholding international players, and the proposal failed.

· The league programme had stuttered through the great freeze-up. By April Blackpool had played eight more games than Sheffield United and ten more than the club that had played least, York City. Not that Blackpool had it easy: 'the playing pitch covered with hard snow, had black patches where water was coming to the top and large pools lay in the penalty area at the Tower end of the ground … After this, I believe our soccer professionals, often labelled namby-pambys, could play entertaining football on a glazier. Lofthouse once tobogganed ten yards on the undercoating of ice … [others] splashed in and crawled out of a black pool near one of the corner flags in a hectic series of tackles and counter tackles … Every man challenged and no man refused a challenge.'

After the close race before Christmas, Division Two became a procession. Maine Road, so busy earlier, saw no match for six weeks and then 67,672 watched Manchester City outfight Burnley in the divisional decider. Their promotion gave Lancashire nine contestants in the 1947-48 First Division. Burnley's January defeats of Birmingham and Newcastle made them the 'sensation of the season' with a watertight defence and the mercurial Peter Kippax in attack. Newcastle United did not 'compare by comparison'. They were always playing catch-up, and couldn't. Only the Cup was left.

Nevertheless the winter had one last sting in its tail. Forget November, when Leicester and Burnley sank in the scrum of a Turf Moor mud-bath, or March, when Burnley and Middlesbrough slugged out a Cup-tie into extra-time on a jagged ice field, and the many in between. The day the players finally collapsed was Easter Saturday, 5 April: 'pitiless rain which swept over Turf Moor in an incessant downpour, and a high wind which rippled the water-logged surface into miniature waves … made football farcical, and it was not surprising players succumbed to the intense cold and consistent soaking.' Two Burnley players were carried off and three of Chesterfield's 'went under' as soon as they left the pitch. Kidd was put into the hot bath complete with foot-ball kit, Ottewell collapsed in the bath. Thereafter Burnley faltered and, as at the season's beginning, rationing conveyed the anxiety: 'housewives are not the only people in Burnley who worry about points.'

After their autumn failure to buy a high profile forward, glamour club Sheffield Wednesday at last found a centre-forward, outbidding another 'five clubs queued outside [Jim Dailey's] home' in the Lanarkshire minefields. However until Dailey could get digs in Sheffield, he travelled from Glasgow by sleeper, arriving in the early hours bright as a button: 'Dailey's hot stuff. He's fast, and plucky as they make 'em and a real nuisance. He should make good.'

Meanwhile Swansea were unable to replace centre-forward Trevor Ford. So Wednesday overtook Swansea and both Welsh clubs went down – Newport County conceding 133 goals in their 42 matches. Pre-season had proclaimed the 'greatest wealth of talent Swansea Town have ever possessed', so condemnation spoke for disappointment: 'for sheer ineffectiveness and lack of purpose the Swans' effort was without parallel this season.'

Third Division (North) champions Doncaster Rovers created League records that still stand – only twelve points dropped in 42 games, 33 matches won, eighteen away victories. In the South, Cardiff built a similar lead of ten points. However on Black Saturday, a ground record 30,417 turned up to see lowly Bristol Rovers inflict City's first league defeat in six months, in truly awful conditions: 'at half time the referee was going to abandon the game. "This match cannot go on. There are nine inches of water on the pitch." … I have never seen football played under such conditions and hope never to do so again.'

QPR, now featuring the appropriately named Len Blizzard, gradually hauled in Cardiff's lead. By 20 April they were together on 54 points. Cardiff – still employed 'in the pits and in steel and tinplate plants' – were tired, yet could afford no delay in getting back to work: 'straight off the pitch and into a waiting coach, the Cardiff men were stripping and changing behind the partially steamed-up window while gaping crowds poured out of the ground.'

The London papers chose another analogy to express Cardiff's evaporating status: a few weeks ago 'it was all Lombard-street to a china orange' on City's promotion, but not now. The following week 40,000 saw Ipswich visit Cardiff. The East Anglians found the *South Wales Football Echo* could fill all sixteen pages on the theme of 'what is wrong with Cardiff City'. The home team's 'state of jitters' worsened when QPR went ahead at Swindon. But Cardiff pulled through and QPR lost. As Cardiff's panic subsided, Swindon remembered their decisive September encounter: what if City, and not Town, had gone down to eight men?

In Division One, Arsenal briefly re-entered the relegation struggle, but benefited from a series of individual scoring efforts: first Ronnie Rooke got three in four minutes against Manchester United, and then all four to beat Middlesbrough. In Arsenal mythology their escape is credited to the signings of veterans Rooke and Joe Mercer. But Reg Lewis had scored nine out of their first ten goals, and helped keep a floundering, ageing team afloat. Then, still tainted by his 'unlucky' penalty miss against Chelsea in that epic Cup encounter, Lewis scored a hat-trick in his comeback match and four against Grimsby. He finished with 28 goals in 28 games.

Another comeback and goal-a-game merchant was Denis Compton. The wartime football international had been on Ashes duty since opening day, 31 August. The tour was long – he scored over 2,000 runs in Australia and distinguished himself with the ball (7-36) in the last match on 29 March – but evidently full of enjoyment and sustenance. Denis sailed home sunburnt and rotund, 13st 2lbs, and played for Arsenal on 26 April. Denis scored in a 5-3 win, and then left for his *annus mirabilis*, the 1947 cricket season.

Their 'startling entry in the inflated transfer market saved Blackburn'. The last buy was another comeback kid. Rovers first tried to sign Alec Venters fourteen years earlier but he stayed with Glasgow Rangers and Scotland. Now in his mid-30s, semi-retired Venters would only travel from 'his licencee of a hotel in Fifeshire'. Rovers were equally businesslike – Alec was a 'spare, mature inside forward': 'if he can win a couple of games now when we need the points, he will have justified the transfer.' Venters replaced their new signing from Hull, who had said he was too slow, when Rovers decided he was … too slow. Venters demonstrated the difference between the mature 1930s pro and the wartime ingenue. 'The old master' made the equaliser and then the winner on his debut: not since 1939 had there been a Rover 'with such pure football ideas and execution – his effortless way of making the ball do the work, the constant changing of the point of attack, the perfectly-timed and calculated passes.' 'The infusion of Venters' mature guile' won his couple of games – his was 'the season's one touch of outstanding class'.

Huddersfield also relied on a prewar rescuer. Peter Doherty made a definite impact, 'shooting with such tremendous power that he raised a miniature snowstorm.' 'The turning point in our fight to avoid relegation' was Town's first away win, 3-0 at Charlton on 8 March (Doherty, 1948, p.73). Some turning point: 'the most fantastic and farcical game I have ever seen. On a ground more fit for seagulls than soccer both sides slithered, sprawled and slid yards at a time. Frankly I have never seen a pitch so like a pond.' Even in normal circumstances Peter was targeted for 'pushing and pulling' and 'severe and relentlessly forceful' tackling so that against Charlton he knew what to expect: 'I fell and an opponent ground his heel (with three studs) into my hand, and broke two bones. Nobody saw it. I had to wear a plaster cast for weeks. Before we went onto the field, there were always one or two players who would say, "Who do you want me to sort out today?"' (Daniels, 1972, p.59).

Doherty had a 'flashing foot' in all the goals, and a fortnight later Huddersfield caught up with their fellow strugglers. Next Huddersfield hosted title-chasing Manchester United. Peter played against medical advice, and the game was going United's way, 2-1 with minutes left and Town supporters 'glum'. Then Doherty, chasing a through ball 'managed by a fraction of a second to reach it first and steer it into the net … It was one of the most valuable, I think, that I've ever scored – and one that I'll remember for a long time' (Doherty, 1948, p.83). In the terrible Easter Saturday weather, when 354,000 watched the nine First Division matches, Doherty scored the winner at Arsenal, Brentford went down again, and a five point gap was opened. The saviour had done his work.

For whilst others picked up the odd point here and there Brentford and Leeds sank into quietude, becalmed until they were left far behind. Brentford's crucial loss was at The Valley when they were only two points behind, and Charlton's 3-0 win brooked no doubt. The third goal was scored by debutant centre-forward Charlie Vaughan, the England amateur international who had just turned professional: 'in the space of a dozen yards he beat five Brentford defenders (including centre half Manley, whom he dribbled round twice) before placing the ball gently and coolly past the advancing Crozier.' Hard-bitten journalists stood up to applaud; manager Jimmy Seed was near-ecstatic about the 'dream goal' but frustrated that 'cup-tied' Vaughan could not play in Charlton's Cup campaign.

The quarter-final matches attracted 215,000 spectators and produced receipts of £19,271. The highest attendance, 60,000 in war-damaged Bramall Lane, generated the lowest gate, £3,863. Newcastle chief Stan Seymour only just got there, after digging his way through ten-foot snowdrifts at his home in Seahouses. The 'farmyard' pitch saw a clash between the side that cost £2,540 (First Division Sheffield United, for Jimmy Hagan and £40 for Alex Forbes) against £50,000 Newcastle United of the Second Division. Albert Cox, the latest cup warrior to play whilst imminently expecting to become a father, performed his speciality sliding tackle on Charlie Wayman but conceded 'a penalty which scores of referees would never have given'. Sheffield had their own plausible penalty claim turned down, could not reproduce the drive of their wins against Wolves and Stoke, and Shackleton-inspired Newcastle won 2-0.

All the ties were dramatic and controversial. Liverpool's 4-1 win against Birmingham on an Anfield snowscape in front of 51,911 was a personal triumph for big money Albert Stubbins. He had brought the balance and coherence that enabled Liverpool to go top before Christmas, contributing hugely to Jack Balmer's rich haul. Now it was Stubbins who was scoring and in this quarter-final he got a famous hat-trick. A diving header has stayed long in the folk memory: 'literally horizontal ... like a Harrier jet ... I've seen many great games at Anfield but that stands out in my memory. I'm sure a lot of other Liverpudlians will tell you the same' (Taylor *et al*, 1993, p.54).

The contemporary reference is now more obscure, if just as colourful: 'Liddell tried a shot which travelled like a bullet beyond the far post, and as it seemed, out of play. The crowd's disappointed roar of "Oh!" was stopped in the split second in which it appeared to take Stubbins to make a full-length Annette Kellerman dive and ram the ball home with his head.' But earlier, City had equalised through a disputed penalty and it was controversial decisions as much as memorable goals that distinguished the quarter-finals.

Chief among them were the two Burnley v Middlesbrough matches, watched by 102,269 and producing £9,613. Burnley's preparations were typical of the weather's effect on training during the long cold spell. The snow kept players Mather in Bolton, Bray in Accrington and Chew in Blackburn, and Peter Kippax only got an hour's grace from his father's mill. Those who made it were greeted with burst pipes in the dressing room. Travelling to Middlesbrough was equally hazardous. Mather and Chew took a bus to the rendezvous but were held up by a road-block. 'They then walked back into Blackburn and got a lift on the tailboard of a lorry to Accrington.' At Sowerby Bridge they found they were first, so held up the train until the rest (including their latest new father, goalkeeper Strong) arrived.

It is sad that in Wilf Mannion's biography this replay is the only 1946-47 club match mentioned. Sad because Mannion gave so many memorable performances and yet it is the bitterness which he still recalled. It is true that Middlesbrough's pre-Christmas 'team of the moment' promise dissipated at Burnley. Demoralised Boro collapsed after their Cup exit – winning only one of their last thirteen matches. At Easter Mannion missed two, and nearly three penalties: he had had enough, and asked for a transfer.

Mannion did not leave then or following his famous 'hold-out' a year later, but Middlesbrough found no further success. His bitterness persisted long but his strength of feeling was far from exceptional. Strangely, for so vivid a memory, Wilf mistook his nemesis: 'I still remember the name of that referee now. An Irish fella, he was. He was terrible … We were beat though this ruddy referee.'

Referee Arthur Ellis was as Halifax as they come, and soon to become in the opinion of Mannion's England colleague, Neil Franklin, 'probably the greatest referee the world has ever known' (Franklin, 1956, p.54). Ellis refereed Wilf Mannion many more times before having an unexpected second career as the over-scrupulous arbiter in the BBC's popular and long-running 1970s programme 'It's A Knockout'. The match was also a knockout, between clubs that were second in the First and Second Divisions. The tie's decisive moment came when Burnley scored after Ray Harrison collided with Boro goalkeeper Dave Cumming. A foul by Harrison, kicking the goalkeeper, or handball, pushing the ball illegally into Billy Morris's path, or both? Distraught Boro players 'bullied' (according to Burnley papers) Ellis to consult a linesman, but to no avail.

Mannion's biography implies that such disputes were uncommon, and therefore perhaps more likely to have been justified: 'The whole team, most unusually in those days, engulfed referee Ellis to protest' (Varley, 1997, p.69-70). Rather, throughout the season but especially in cup-ties, vigorous protests and after-match complaints were legion. In an earlier round Boro themselves had contested a Chesterfield goal – 'I have never seen Boro make a more emphatic protest' – and Chesterfield objected long and hard to a handball equaliser. Moreover the original game at Middlesbrough 'bristled with controversial points'. The disputes and aggression together conveyed the commitment of both players and supporters to the competitive heart of British football. The contemporary judgement is truer – the protest was 'typical of Middlesbrough's refusal to accept defeat.' Half a century later Mannion still hadn't.

Back then there were sad and scared feelings as well as angry. Alec Linwood played his first match since New Year's Day. He had been back in Scotland attending his young sister – and that day it was announced she had died. Both grounds were dangerous for spectators and both pitches (played 'at a gruelling pace') were treacherous. At Boro, players floundered on thawing snow on top of ice; at Burnley, an ice rink turned into cold pot holes during extra time: 'in the circumstances the players performed wonders in giving us a football entertainment of any kind.'

Disputed or not, the Burnley celebration of Billy Morris's winning, extra-time goal anticipated the extravagance of later ages: his colleagues' 'exuberance … was so excessive that he was knocked over and then made the centre of a triumphal dance.' Arthur Ellis went from his lofty perch on top of a police horse at one of the era's momentous matches to a prat fall at one of its most mundane – Rochdale 5, Hull City 2: 'he gave perhaps the best display of refereeing at Spotland this season ... So intent was he on being "on the spot" that on one occasion he finished up on his back in the snow at the side of the goal.'

The biggest contemporary controversy concerned the defeat of favourites Preston – Tom Finney, Bill Shankly and all – despite their pre-game preparations. Goalkeeper Jack Fairbrother had come to rely on Jolson, a stuffed Scottie doll, and panicked when Jolson was missing as the team coach made its way to The Valley. The coach was stopped, and a conference ensued: some were for going back to their hotel, but wiser counsels prevailed and a taxi was sent. The Scottie duly arrived to take his place in Fairbrother's goal: 'in time to look on unemotionally while Duffy's lob dropped just under instead of just over the bar into the Preston net. It seemed to me that Jolson couldn't care less.'

North End had been warned 'to drop their fancy ideas and substitute more solid qualities ... craft, allied to team power and determination, that makes a Wembley blend.' Their star got the blame: Preston were too finicky, 'too Finney', without enough real cup-tie boots. Charlton's winner provoked reminders of the famous 'over the line' goal in the 1932 final. Preston swarmed round the referee, disputing frantically: pushing, almost pulling him to the ground, protesting the ball had gone a yard behind before Fairbrother dropped the cross. Jolson was the only one not to join in the 'referee hunt': 'Jolson was not a very good mascot.' Fans had made equally frantic efforts to see the only tie in London: 'thousands formed six deep on the platforms, trying to gain admission to the already full compartments. Porters had to pull people out to close the doors.' Among the crowd was Geordie Drummond, 78, and just retired from the Dumbarton shipyards: a Preston Invincible from the 1889 Double side.

The themes of the winter came together at Huddersfield on 15 March. Under Peter Doherty's tutelage Town were beginning to pull away from relegation. In any other year a match-threatening blizzard would have been surprising in mid-March, but on this blizzard-strewn day it was commonplace. At any other time the snow-clearers would have gone unnoticed, but at last the 1947 ones were getting recognition: after working until 'the last minute, German prisoners were allowed to watch the game'.

In another era the late arrival of the visitors would have been the occasion of censure. But football had been put in its place. The autumn optimism for football to be in a cultural vanguard, combining the best of British and continental ways of playing, had been knocked off course. The players' struggle for a fair deal had been overwhelmed by the wider world. To an extraordinary degree, in incredible circumstances, football had fulfilled its task of entertaining a cold and dispirited people, and was slapped down for doing so. The fate of the Grimsby Town party that Saturday carried a metaphor of what happened to football in the postwar reconstruction: 'It took two and a half hours to travel from Doncaster. "A coal wagon was in front of us most of the way".'

17

Endgames

THE CUP

The century's worst floods flushed the country out of its long hibernation into the 'deafening' roar of 29 March: 'the greatest day in British sporting history.' Half a million were stunned to silence by a 100-1 winner in The Grand National: Rugby Internationals, the Boat Race ... and 156 greyhound meetings. But the centrepiece was a traditional football occasion providing colour and noise to the grey landscape: the FA Cup semi-finals. The age of austerity had its treat.

Huge convoys of coaches drove through the night to Leeds: almost every bus for hire in the north-east took Newcastle's 15,000 supporters south. Charlton were London's family club, until they arrived: 'Our wives have deserted us. I am told they are running wild in the shops up here.'

The day started well. Mining parties arrived fresh from the night train to find the cafes, hotels and restaurants awash with bacon and egg breakfasts: 'Aye, it's been a real treat.' Then disappointment: the pubs were closed – 'there is an extreme shortage of beer in Leeds'. The festivities continued – 'every street resounded with bells and rattles' – with generosity: Newcastle supporter Harold 'Call Me "Hopeless"' Taylor had been off work sick for 15 weeks but still hitched through the night, and was given a Charlton ticket.

Both teams stayed at Harrogate, 'sweating it out in the Royal Turkish baths whilst the rain lashed against the windows.' Charlton players then went down with 'violent stomach pains ... food poisoning' (Seed, 1957, p.112). Their doctor pondered the pre-match diet for a culprit: 'might have been caused by ice cream.'

Newcastle management offered an illegal £25 win-bonus, and new kit replaced 'shabby grey and white well-worn shirts ... Others have not been obtainable. Stan Seymour told me weeks ago he would give £1 a strip for a new rig out for his players.' Their season was on the line, as promotion aspirations had been dashed the previous Saturday. Seymour looked on the bright side: 'We can't play another game like that. It just couldn't happen.' But the team was in a 'state of near-mutiny': 'grievances festered' as they were closeted at Seahouses for weeks, 'like a bunch of atom scientists' (Hutchinson, 1991, pp.124-25). Len Shackleton and captain Joe Harvey threatened to leave over housing complaints; and then the directors dropped the Second Division's leading goalscorer, dismissively: 'Wayman was never the complete centre forward we have wanted.' Charlie – 28 goals in his last 27 games – confronted his chairman in their hotel corridor: 'Excuse me, Mr Rutherford. I would like to be on the transfer list.' 'Nonsense. I never heard anything so silly.'

Whilst food poisoning challenged Charlton's gut functions, Newcastle simply lacked guts, and lost 0-4, ignominiously: 'Newcastle died without a fight:' their 'defenders are running like rabbits ... the wing halves didn't seem to know what it was all about and when the forwards went back to help they got in each other's way.' The manner of defeat caused messy recriminations in Newcastle: 'Now T'Worms Will Come And Ate Thee Up', ran a local newspaper headline.

Questions were asked about the weeks in purdah: who had colluded with the footballing miners in viewing their colliery jobs as 'polite fictions'? Which 'birdbrain' 'imagined kicking a ball about is more important than hewing coal?' Nothing was said whilst Newcastle were still in the Cup, but now it was remembered that 'work comes before football every time'. Len Shackleton and Jackie Milburn were posted as absentees at Hazlerigg Colliery when they went into hibernation with United. They now faced 'the plain threat that it is either the mines or the Services. Players can take their pick in more ways than one.' The colliery's Production Committee eventually accepted their explanations that they were 'called upon for extra training' and had football injuries 'from time to time'. Whilst Len and Jackie 'mean to take mining seriously – now,' the chief of the North Regional Coal Board commented: 'If the football miner plays the game and goes to his work, I am sure pit managers will give them every consideration and time off to play football.'

After the semi-final, Shackleton and Harvey protested with 'stay-at-home strikes'. Len said his club flat was 'not fit to live in'; Joe had seen his wife and three children for only '48 hours in five weeks' and Newcastle's 'top floor flat was not suitable'. They were not natural bedfellows in rebellion: the disciplinarian Harvey, company sergeant-major in the PT Corps, dismissed the free spirited Len: 'We'll never win anything with Shackleton, we've got to get rid of him.'

The two players attracted little local sympathy following Newcastle's feeble exit from both competitions. The pair were dropped and received severe reprimands when, officially, they apologised to the board – then 'the players and their wives were taken out to hunt, successfully, for semi-detached houses in Gosforth' (Hutchinson, 1991, pp.125-28). The board itself was in disarray – President Lord Westwood said Charlie Wayman got a 'raw deal' (Charlie later lost a Cup final, with Preston, in 1954) – and Stan Seymour took the 'entire blame'. Newcastle were pressurised into appointing an orthodox manager, giving each of ten short-listed candidates, including Cup final referee 'Smiling Jim' Wiltshire, a fifteen minute interview. However Seymour helpfully spelt out that 'full and complete control' meant 'full power to spend up to say £1,000 for a player without having to ask anyone's sanction'. So the rumbling of discontent remained in 'crescendo' until Shackleton's departure early in 1948.

The other Second Division team, Burnley, were also favoured to beat First Division opposition. Liverpool got away to a seventeenth century coaching inn in Clitheroe and their own shopping spree: 'bought some lemon squeezers – now I hope we can get lemons.' Ewood Park was the centre of a 'tornado of football frenzy' in which Burnleyites 'felt strangers in a strange land … where were the thousands of Burnley fans … Everywhere was a blaze of colour – red and white represented in almost every form of garb. Liverpool had come to town in force, and their supporters made themselves heard with their sirens, klaxen horns, motorcar hooters, rattles etc.'

Police pursuit of counterfeit tickets was made easier by the forgers misspelling 'competition'. Also initially subject to zealous enquiry was the Liverpool team, refused admission by an 'officious gatekeeper'. The crowd was 52,570, and risked moments of imminent disaster: 'the crowd overflowed in one corner. Extra police were rushed there, and ambulance men with stretchers were kept busy.' Wingers had to move crowds back to take corners: the match was a 'continuous clamour of mass enthusiasm', although 'disgusted' 'pocket-sized' spectators on each side 'couldn't see a thing' and settled for listening to both semi-finals, and the Grand National, on a portable wireless set.

The 'brilliantly artful Liverpool attack' could not breach Burnley's 'Maginot Line' – only seven goals conceded in their last 26 games – and 'flame-haired' Albert Stubbins was reduced to 'flicks and back heeled passes, at the art of which he is the master'. Nonetheless Burnley's Harold Mather – 'a variety of jet-propelled brick wall' – literally burst a boil with a spectacular last-ditch tackle to prevent a Stubbins winner in extra-time. A foul on Peter Kippax had led to Burnley's quarter-final winner, and he was again 'the most fouled man in both Semi Finals', but it was Kippax who decided the replay.

After Burnley's winning goal, in vain 'Liverpool flung themselves at every ball'. Next Peter was chosen for England, and Charlton prepared for the final: 'stop Kippax and we'll win.' The semi-finals had effected the careers of all four left-wingers. Because midweek matches were prohibited, Liverpool and Burnley replayed on the England v Scotland Saturday. Peter Kippax would have been the first amateur to play against Scotland since 1911 and Billy Liddell also missed out. Scotland's selectors then surprisingly preferred Newcastle's Tom Pearson to Charlton's Chris Duffy. Tom had been one of six rebels and failures dropped by Newcastle after their semi-final debacle, but now created a unique double: during the war, when a car crash injured England's left winger on the way to the game, Pearson played for England against Scotland in December 1939!

Burnley were now an enormous draw: Kippax's brilliance and their iron clad defence made them favourites. 356,513 had watched their last eight matches, paying £44,512. Burnley were adopted in Morecambe: tremendous applause followed their reception in the Winter Gardens; a dance stopped on their arrival in the Floral Hall; enormous enthusiasm greeted their appearance at the Lancaster v Netherfield Lancashire Combination match. And yet through all this excitement their followers were reassured the team were 'always in bed by ten'.

By contrast, Charlton refused access to the Press without payment, but would look their best on the big day – supporters donated 66 clothing coupons, enough to buy new jerseys for Wembley. After their semi-final mishap Charlton's dietary preparations went undisclosed but Burnley 'rounded off a fish-and-toast lunch with mugs of steaming hot coffee'.

As ever the Cup final was an occasion to assert communal pride. The Cock o' the North invaders were welcomed by an enormous sign, displayed by a migrant Lancastrian greengrocer, 'Wap it home, Burnley,' but were vulnerable to temptations in the big, dark city. One racketeer offered £6 10s for a 3s ticket, plus twenty packets of cigarettes and fifteen clothing coupons. A Charlton fan successfully offered £8 and twenty clothing coupons.

William Pickles was left behind. His eighteen-year-old son queued seven hours for a ticket, and then got run over. William inherited the ticket and took sandwiches for the ten-hour night trip. Sadly he never found his coach and traipsed home: 'I've had it – I've missed my bus.' Many young folk made their first trip to London. Orcietta Arcangeli, an Italian who married William Clough whilst he was in the Forces in Rome, had queued nine hours for their tickets. John Roberts arrived with his car bonnet painted claret and blue and reminisced about flying over the stadium every day as a Battle of Britain fighter pilot. One girl had a 'chic headscarf with the names of Burnley's players embroidered in claret on a blue background'. Other females were not forgotten: 'Ah've left a pahnd at home wi' missus so's we can celebrate winning of the Coop.'

Charlton's Jimmy Seed had the major selection headache when Charlie Revell failed a fitness test. The choice was young tyro, or old soak. Bill Whittaker, recently an RAF rear gunner, had played only six games. George Robinson had seen it all since his thrillingly vital First Division debut in 1928 for Sunderland against Middlesbrough – whichever team lost was relegated: only seventeen, he was chaired off after a 3-0 win.

The match of a hundred throw-ins matched the austerity of the times: 'too much ballooning ... like a utility suit, limited to bare essentials.' There were of course scapegoats: Peter Kippax was rarely seen, unsurprising since he was running a temperature of 103, and pulled out of the following Saturday's international. He would never play for England. Burnley's Bill Morris missed the best chances: Middlesbrough fans, remembering his controversial winner against them, thought Morris due his come-uppence. The judgement was given in true wartime, NAAFI style: '[Morris] took the sugar from his own tea.'

A season of protests and controversies fittingly had a Final one: 'Smiler' Wiltshire refused an extra-time penalty 'when Harrison was brought down from behind when he was going through'. Chris Duffy's celebration of his winning goal for Charlton, after 114 minutes, was an 'extraordinary demonstration. He wheeled away towards the touchline and 'ran full tilt at a colleague, jumping up and throwing arms and legs round him, just as a small child does in welcoming a fond parent.' Duffy himself was more prosaic: 'I want the babe to be proud of his dad. As soon as my right foot connected I knew the ball was in.'

Centre-forward Bill Robinson did not even know he was a father. It was now seven months since Charlton had broken their league programme and played a friendly against Benfica. There Robinson, just setting up home, 'struggled through the streets of Lisbon with a carpet as big as he.' Now it all paid off: after the Cup final he went home to toast with champagne his 7lb son, born two weeks previously: 'his wife, Mrs Bessie Robinson, insisted that her husband should not be given the news until after the match.'

At the team's West End celebrations Jimmy Seed dropped the Cup and broke the top of the lid. In desperation a garage mechanic soldered it on before the Mayor's reception, and the next day a silversmith did a proper job. Undeterred, Seed took the Cup north and in Mansfield's Railway Hotel passed it round full of beer (Seed, 1957, p.106).

SUNSET IN PIONEERLAND

The spring saw England's matches against European opposition, as usual preceded with anxiety about the potential loss of prestige: England's 'rear guard was as panicky as an absconding bank clerk'. England needed a magician to cast his spell, but which one, Matthews or Finney? The choice between them was a season-long controversy, one that captured two images of football. Matthews represented the individualist *par excellence*, but also the slower tactical game of the 1930s. Finney was more evidently a team man, and his direct style reflected the faster postwar football. When Stan's early 'dazzling runs' nearly won the Scotland game in August, reporter Kenneth Wolstenholme judged 'Matthews alone was worth the admission money. His was the perfect exhibition. Soon 'dazzling' Tom changed Kenneth's opinion: 'Tom Finney is the finest outside right in the country. Including Stanley Matthews ... Finney has everything.'

Stoke's poor start encouraged 'wonder at times if an average straightforward winger' rather than tantalising Matthews 'wouldn't suit them better'. The success of both City and England during Matthews' injury momentarily made Stan the Forgotten Man. Tom Finney, 'headline snatcher-in-chief,' inspired Preston's title challenge as he made opponents 'chase shadows ... rhumba-like body sway as he dodged and wriggled, with the ball working at his feet like a yo-yo.'

Finney kept his place until he played poorly against Wales. Paranoid Preston fans scented a noxious whiff: 'a downright disgrace ... a conspiracy to freeze this one player out or else a case of "If we can't have Matthews we don't want anybody".' Others said Raich Carter only 'starved' Tom as part of a deep plan. But the early-season hero now felt a press backlash. 'This little man with the long sleeves and drooping shorts' faded amidst the wintry robust tackling: 'most noticeable was Finney's indifference to foraging for a ball ...

When he was beaten he rarely tried to recover. Is that according to plan? Or is it below his dignity.' Stan Matthews was more used to provocation: crowds habitually 'hurl advice vocally and gratuitously ... 'Go to him!' 'Tackle him.' 'Don't be frightened of him.' Opposing backs were advised: if he 'watches the ball and goes for it, whether Matthews is in the road or not, he has a reasonable chance.' As the spring internationals loomed, Blackburn's press got a chance to compare current form, as both contenders scored against Rovers: 'seeing is believing ... [Matthews'] variety of ruse, and his body swerve, wielded a mesmeric influence ... left Bell in a sitting position, with a piece of close jugglery, and centred perfectly for Ormston to score.' 'The defence, goggle-eyed at the sheer artistry of Finney, his feints and swerves, retreated in front of him until he flicked the ball over the line.'

England's eventual solution surprised all: playing Stan and Tom on either wing they beat Portugal 10-0. It was a satisfying end to another explosive European tour where, in Switzerland, charismatic Frank Swift saved the day. The crowd, provoked to 'a whale of a temper' by a Neil Franklin tackle, invaded the pitch 'thirsting for blood', hurling beer bottles and an umbrella: 'With a grin splitting his face in half ... Swifty picked up the offending umbrella, and with that unfailing charm and humour of his, he did what the scores of policemen could never have done ... led the spectators back to their seats and the "riot" was over' (Franklin, 1956, p.36).

The natives took notice: 'Gigolos of the night clubs in this French border corner of Switzerland were still whirling their elderly, but wealthy patrons across the dance floors, and heatedly discussing, like everyone else here, England's Swift-saving match.'

Otherwise a trio of victories over continental opposition served to bolster the returning sense that Britain was still best, and that continental lessons were limited. First England beat France 3-0 in a usual clash of styles: 'our continental friends must be made to realise there are rules which do not allow the use of elbows, jersey pulling, pushing, obstruction and other forms of nonsense;' whereas France's goalkeeper hated being shoulder charged by the English forwards. Then the Rest of Europe's 'fine mosaic' of nine nations experienced 'an atmosphere of coldness between us', complained they never passed to each other, and 'wept and yelled with rage' at succeeding Great Britain goals – 6-1 (Glanville, 1986, pp.142-45).

England's triumphs were seen as moral. During their 0-10 defeat, vaunted Portugal surreptitiously changed two players. England's coach was worn out from an earlier fight over which size ball to use: '"Look, they've changed their goalkeeper." [Winterbottom] replied wearily: "What does it matter? He's worse than the other one anyway"' (Carter, 1950, p.190).

Portugal's 'abuse' of substitutes branded the continentals as unsportsmanlike. For years afterwards this game was used to resist their introduction. But these wins preserved an illusion of British supremacy a little longer, when really they 'marked a brilliant sunset' (Glanville, 1986, p.145). British improvisation had triumphed over both the regimentation of continental coaching, and the underhandedness resulting from letting, through substitutes, people off the field have too much of a say. Continentals might make football an 'applied science. To us it is still just another game. We play it naturally ... [They] organise their play where we more or less let it run its own course.'

The earlier autumn crisis about the quality of British football ran out of steam. The winter's weather and the economic retrenchment made such concerns trivial. Poor football still 'sent me home with a headache', and time after time the 'ire of the big crowd ... communicated itself to both sides'. But dangerous surfaces ruled out 'balanced criticism'. Matches could still be exciting. For example Arsenal hit the woodwork six times against Manchester United in the Highbury snow, and when United lost an injured defender scored three goals in four minutes to win 6-2.

The judgement stood for many games that fantastic winter: 'real football was impossible, but both sides came close to playing it.' Burnley represented the alternative model based on preparation: 'informal discussions, perhaps in the dressing room, at lunchtime, or during moorland walks.' Manager Cliff Britton master-minded Burnley's 'deadly-defence-in-depth': previously undistinguished defenders, other clubs' cast-offs, conceded the fewest number of goals since the change in the offside law in 1925.

In 1947-48 Arsenal would win the championship with similar tactics. Critics claimed it was dull and would drive people away, which eventually perhaps it did, but the defensive tactic was itself a reaction to the aggressively critical attitude of postwar crowds. Britton was a stylish international player, but a pragmatic manager: 'play first class football but lose by the odd goal, the vast majority of your supporters will go away disgruntled. But if you win, even though you play only defensive football they will be delighted.'

This only tells part of the story. Britton had listened at the feet of Jimmy Hogan and practised possession football. In the hands of an English team such continental ways could appear dull, unadventurous, unBritish – recalling the restrictions of wartime and austerity: 'precise push-passing from man to man ... the precision of a Drill Sergeant.'

The FA's crusade for coaching failed, not just because of its aloofness from the clubs and players responsible for real football, but also because it offended deep ideas about British football. So what was football about? It was about structure: the discipline of defined positions, the tension between physical challenge and ball skills, the weight of tradition and authority, the sense of sportsmanship. That was enough. Over-preparation and coaching were innovations too far. Football was natural for the British, and it was sport – the participants were not just testing their comparative skills, but also their abilities to cope with the inherently unpredictable: 'the fact that there is a strong element of luck, chance or whatever you like to call it, about the sport of football ... that has kept it so popular for so many years.'

Bravery and chance was the English counterpoint to continental preparation. One 'famous manager of a famous club' elevated this to a positive theory: 'If your wing half backs win three out of five tackles, it is 3-2 on you winning the match. But if they win four out of five, then it is any odds you like.' Bravery was essential, yet when a wartime fighter pilot made his debut in freezing fog, on an iron-hard pitch, 'my only quibble with his display would be his hesitancy on one or two occasions to jump straight into a tackle when the odds seemed against him getting the ball. An unexpectedly gained ball can only happen if *someone* tries to get it.'

Working class practitioners added something else. In Argentina Diego Maradona would embody 'viveca', a prized quality of craftiness in South American slums, transposed to the football pitch. In the back streets of post-war Britain's cities, or its mining communities, there was an equivalent – 'nouse': 'no lad becomes a great footballer unless he has football "nouse" and can sense the time when to hold or when to part, and, when he parts, see to it that the ball goes to the right man.' It was also about men at work. The individual has to fit: 'players either cog in or they don't. When they do teamwork results.' Teamwork might be mysterious and essentially unpredictable, but it was crucial.

Competitive teamwork to the end. Rochdale's last match, at Rotherham on 7 June, seemed a classic end of season game. Both had done well: Doncaster had won their championship in record style, with Rotherham second, Rochdale sixth. Yet there was something to fight for, and fight was the word. Rotherham were defending a perfect home record – twenty games, twenty wins (between 1903 and 2003 only one club won all their home games) – and Rochdale had equalled their highest ever number of away wins. The match was 'as keen as the hardest cup game ... United used every method in the book from pure force to trickery ... Rochdale replied in kind.' The two teams swapped goals until it finished 3-3: 'the excitement was as tense as it possibly could be. The big crowd roared Rotherham on to massive efforts to maintain their 100 per cent home record but Rochdale hit back just as fiercely ... The fact that the home crowd – and their directors – took the result in an extremely unsporting spirit could not detract from Rochdale's fine performance, but it is a pointer to the feelings aroused that Manager Ted Goodier had to use physical force to reach the dressing room after the match.'

THE DISPUTE

The Players' Union won a hollow victory when the National Arbitration Tribunal awarded a maximum wage of £10 (summer) and £12 (winter); and a minimum of respectively, £5 and £7 a week. Frank Swift, no radical – rather renowned for defusing conflict – entitled Chapter 20 of his autobiography 'The government give me a rise,' and reproduced the Tribunal's full judgement (Swift, 1948, pp.132-37). Jimmy Guthrie hailed an 'unqualified triumph', Jimmy Fay 'a great victory. We were not worrying about the maximum wages, because only about 5 per cent of our 3,000 members receive the ceiling scale. The fixing of the minimum means that at last footballers have been placed on a basis of security. The award of course only applies to full-time professionals.' Yet by now up to two thirds were part-timers. The emphasis on minimum and maximum left many anomalies untouched. Tom Reynolds, the ex-Army left winger so small that his Sunderland manager carried his cod liver oil around in a brown paper bag, was one of many who, as in years past, refused terms. Billy Murray wanted to pay Reynolds £7 (summer), £8 (basic winter) and £9 (first team). However, League regulations forbad it. Under arrangements drafted when new professionals would be teenagers, not mature ex-servicemen, the maximum payable after one year's service was a pound less all round.

The Union's effective disavowal of interest in the maximum wage had future consequences. Stars rarely featured on the Union Executive, which became dominated by journeymen pros from the lower divisions. The Wilf Mannions increasingly sought transfers in vain attempts to improve their lot. A few even found their way into Italian football; or the illusory paradise of Colombia. It forced 'the big-money men, to look under the boardroom table for their well-earned rake-off'. The practice was inevitably arbitrary and divisive; made both conspirators vulnerable to discovery; engendered a suspicion of widespread corruption which brought the game into disrepute; and failed to give the profession its rightful recognition and reward.

Nor did the Tribunal resolve fundamental grievances. The union's counsel had advised: 'Guthrie, this contract has no validity in law' (Guthrie, 1976, p.43). Registration, and its associated restrictions, would surely be scrutinised: 'in what light the NAT regard the sanctity of footballers' agreements.' Sadly the Tribunal shed no light, left benefits as discretionary, and shelved a review of transfer arrangements.

The union made two further attempts in the 1950s, on behalf of 1946-47 players, to challenge these constraints. Frank Brennan's wages were docked in half (Guthrie, 1976, p.74) by Newcastle after eight years, promotion and two Cup finals. A 'restraint of trade' case was prepared but a 'disgusted' Brennan quit the game instead, and the Union had to wait another decade before George Eastham's ground breaking 'restraint of trade' action.

The Tribunal officially vindicated the Union's campaign, but it was a shallow triumph. Professional footballers had lamented, 'always jam tomorrow, never jam today.' Now it was too little, too late. The moneys paled in comparison to club profits and expenditure on transfer fees. Nor was it a stepping stone to further gains. £12 remained the maximum wage for more boom years, and only increased to £14, after more struggle and arbitration, in 1951.

Perhaps because the clubs avoided a trial of strength, they felt emboldened to return to social relations which owed little to the second half of the twentieth century. The players' campaign was effectively over, yet the bitterness remained and 1947-48 saw 'unrest in football to a degree not known hitherto in your time or mine'. The same complaints reprised: the 'slave' footballers' deal is 'as raw as uncooked whale steak'; illegal payments proliferated – 'scandals of soccer are hidden by heaven-high walls of silence;' and Tommy Lawton's move in November presented 'an indictment of the whole shockingly antiquated transfer system.' Even a sad, inglorious attempt at a 'closed shop' had its effect, as Peter Kippax – 'treated rather unfairly … because I'm an amateur' – could not get into the Burnley side. Thereafter illogicality, unfairness and bitterness remained a context of British football throughout the 1950s.

Club profits and behaviour exacerbated the situation. It was said throughout 1946-47 that 'when this season's balance sheets are published profits will be an eye-opener'. Stoke set a new record (£32,207) before selling Stan Matthews and recommended a 25 per cent dividend to shareholders. Arsenal's profit was £22,247; Everton put aside £25,000 for deferred ground repairs, and £5,000 for buying houses; and but for 'legal fees over the disaster' Bolton Wanderers' profit would have been £20,000. The League and FA took over the fund to settle the claims of victims and dependants. Clubs like Liverpool contributed £500, and passed on a further £225 from a ground collection.

Liverpool, who had already cleared a £28,000 overdraft by Christmas 1946, paid £18,391 Entertainment Tax on home gate receipts up over £30,000 (to £93,742). Their semi-final matches grossed another £23,268. Players cost £26,177 (half of which was spent on Stubbins' transfer fee), far less than a quarter of their income. Maine Road, shared by City and United, grossed takings of £250,000. Matt Busby, who inherited an overdraft of £15,000, generated 'nearly £60,000 profit' in his first two seasons of management – 'figures which made the bank manager much more friendly disposed' (Busby, 1957, p.78).

Clubs fuelled an increasingly unsavoury transfer market: 'present-day prices savour too much of the black market.' The temptations were the same: 'as in many other walks of life, football folk have money to burn and little to spend it on.' Particularly in Scotland the reality of transfer negotiations kept leeching out: 'players themselves are not always shy about telling of their part in bargains, and, if the tales they tell could always be believed, it would certainly appear that something very queer is happening, practically everywhere.' And the transfer record was broken in Scotland, for Billy Steel, who suddenly starred against England, and then was preferred to legendary figures Doherty and Carter for Great Britain.

Stan Matthews took a different path, unprecedented in football – transferring himself. Easter was a parting of the ways. Stan 'exercised the footballer's privilege of not playing on Good Friday,' but for very secular reasons: 'a rush of bookings at his Blackpool hotel.' Manager Bob McGrory retaliated by leaving him out of the remaining holiday fixtures. Stan told the board secretly that playing with Stoke was causing travel and business inconvenience: he might have to consider premature retirement if not transferred to Blackpool in July.

McGrory could not wait for July. He issued another statement, being careful not to associate himself with commitments of confidentiality: 'The directors and the player made a compact that nothing should be disclosed … Now it has leaked out I can confirm …' In a one horse race Blackpool regarded Stoke's demand for £20,000 as 'ridiculous', and Stoke settled for £11,500.

Despite being one point behind the championship leaders with three games to go, they bade farewell to their most famous son: 'he had become a blessed nuisance to the Board.'

Smaller clubs were also profitable. The League's newest members, Ipswich, were never in the Third Division promotion race and had no Cup run, yet made a £9,572 profit. Nevertheless northern clubs like Gateshead instinctively thought of ways around the minimum wage, registering youngsters for North Eastern League play only: 'if they make good then they can be registered with the Football League and receive the minimum and play in the higher grade.' The Tribunal award of minimum wages did not, as predicted, occasion wholesale clearances. Staffs remained large: Wolves retained 42 of 69 professionals. Norwich, who spent 1946-47 at the bottom of the Third Division, kept 24 of 36.

The Tribunal award of August to August contracts at least meant it was the last season in which players whose registration was not retained, or who were made available for transfer, received no summer pay: 'players who have been placed on the open for transfer list I am sorry. Until another club comes along they will be out of a job.' One of many dismissed was 'completely fearless' Newcastle goalkeeper Tom Swinburne. Tom, now 30, had been with United since he was seventeen. He had been so close to glory. Even before being scapegoated for the semi-final defeat, Swinburne laboured under the handicap of suffering repeated finger dislocations, his own fans' barracking and anonymous letters. Swinburne had played for England during the war, in the Red Cross international at his own St James' Park in December 1939. He then spent five years in the RAF. He was sorry to leave Newcastle.

Lower division clubs routinely offered such small wages to retained players that many walked away. Plymouth had four: Alec Dyer was Argyle's union delegate, a twelve-year veteran who collected his benefit and left for a cattle-dealing business; Alun Watkins went to play for Glamorgan CCC (and later England) and never came back; Bill Hurst went into the Cheshire League and an associated factory job; and Thomas Parnaby, who had shown much promise at seventeen, then 'in the Services for 6 years got pretty badly smashed up, but he is all right now'.

Many were still willing to do anything to get accepted. That summer James McGuigan, 23, came from his Scottish mining village to sign for Sunderland. In his trial he wore 'odd boots, and used his left foot because the right boot was too tight and hurting him when he kicked'.

THE LEAGUE CHAMPIONSHIP

Before the snows Wolves led the table with 37 points; followed by Preston 34; Manchester United, Middlesbrough and Blackpool 31; and Liverpool, Aston Villa and Stoke 30 points. Wolves' chances actually improved during a month without playing: Preston collapsed in dramatic fashion once Stan Matthews defied appalling elements and outshone Tom Finney in Stoke's win: 'a classic exhibition of wing play more fit for skates than football boots … never once on that surface did Matthews soil his pants.' George Mountford continued Stoke's challenge when he replaced the injured Stanley, ironically against Chelsea, where his fame, and the notoriety of Matthews' exclusion, was founded. It was a sensational return: Stoke were four up in fourteen minutes and 6-1 ahead at half-time. Some coach parties only arrived then, and would not believe the score. Journalists linked Mountford's display with Matthews' previous destruction of Preston: 'in my last two visits to Stoke I have seen the best exhibitions of outside right play for a long, long time.' Bob McGrory invited sympathy for his revived selection problem: 'how would you like to be in my shoes when picking the side for next week.'

Liverpool kickstarted their title challenge with a remorseless series of away victories. Leeds, beginning to lose touch with their fellow strugglers, played ferociously: Liverpool captain Jack Balmer counted this their hardest game of the season: United 'still had a chance to escape, and fought tooth and nail'. The city was full of crisis meetings, and although Leeds soon faded away to finish the season with a record-low eighteen points, at this point they did not lack fight. Amid the snow and ice they battled against favourites Wolves until Dennis Westcott's winner five minutes from time effectively ended Leeds' season.

So when championship challengers Middlesbrough caught up, they had played three more games. Wolves were then lucky to meet Middlesbrough in 'pardonable gloom' only four days after Boro's demoralising Cup exit. Once again Westcott scored a crucial late equaliser, but the real hero was captain Stan Cullis: constantly heading away the leaden snow-and-ice encrusted ball caused another serious concussion, and the decision to end his career.

Boro's was a last effort: winning only one of thirteen matches, they slumped to eleventh. Manager David Jack, exhausted from a 32-hour abortive-transfer snowbound journey to London, accepted defeat when he presented gifts – a gold wrist watch, a smoker's cabinet and a large action photograph of himself – to Wilf Mannion: 'we missed the bus this year.' And every other year. Wilf went elsewhere for glory, a hat-trick in 'Mannion's Match,' Great Britain's 6-1 win over the Rest of Europe. On his return 'the expected has come', Wilf's transfer request was made, but not granted. Mannion stayed until 1954 although never again did Middlesbrough challenge for honours as they had in the snow and ice of 4 March, on the brink of their first ever Cup semi-final, and 8 March, when, second in the First Division, they were within minutes of beating the leaders.

The leading places in the First Division after the 15 March blizzards were – Wolves: played 30, points 44; Liverpool: 31, 40; Blackpool: 34, 40; Middlesbrough: 31, 38; Manchester United: 30, 37; Stoke and Preston: 30, 36.

AROUND EASTER: 22 MARCH TO THE END OF APRIL
Sheffield United, whose challenge was delayed until Jimmy Hagan ended his hold-out, literally lost it at his hands too. United had games in hand but time to play them in, when they met Bolton on Good Friday. Arthur Ellis was the

referee, at least until a defender 'cleared the ball – right into my face. I felt as if I had been hit by a Churchill tank'. Ellis's stand-in gave one penalty, and on his return Arthur gave two more. After 75 minutes United were winning 2-1, and the title was still within their grasp. Then the Sheffield players appealed for hands against Bolton's Lofthouse. The United players stopped and Ellis 'turned round to see Jimmy Hagan standing with the ball in his hands' (Ellis, 1954, p.52). Previous penalties had been missed, but this wasn't. Bolton then got a last-minute winner.

The stuttering leaders, Wolves, lost to Manchester United. Maine Road saw chaotic scenes outside the biggest crowd of Wolves' season – 66,947. Still it seemed 'nothing less than a complete collapse' could deprive Wolves of the title. They shrugged off another defeat, by Derby, by winning the return 7-1, and then beat Chelsea 6-4. Liverpool fell back to fifth when, 2-0 up at home, they conceded three late goals in 'nine minutes of sheer football drama'. With a daunting run-in – five of six remaining matches away – the collapse seemed terminal: 'I'm afraid we may have to wipe off their championship hopes.'

WEEK 36: SATURDAY, 3 MAY

What remained was an 'intense four-cornered struggle for the League championship' in a 'slowly dying season'. Manchester United's Stan Pearson and John Carey marked the cards of Liverpool's Balmer for the outcome of their crucial encounter: 'Sorry Jack, but we're afraid you've had it today. We've made up our minds to top the league, so you needn't try too hard. It's in the bag.' Manchester United, fourteen points from eight games, could go top with a win. It was Liverpool's last home match and fittingly 48,800 welcomed the former King of Anfield, Matt Busby. Billy Liddell beat Carey 'all ends up for speed' to set up in-form Stubbins for a goal after twelve minutes: thereafter Manchester United 'produced some lovely football' against Liverpool's 'desperate defence' but lost 0-1.

Wolves now had 54 points (remaining games – three at home, one away); Stoke 52 (one at home, two away); Manchester United 51 (two at home, one away); Liverpool 50 (all four away from home).

WEEK 37: SATURDAY, 10 MAY

Jock Dodds reappeared. After his protest and short-lived sojourn in Ireland, Dodds had sparked Everton's recovery but was injured in the icy winter. Now Jock set up an early goal, and, although 'rampaging' Wolves promptly equalised, he harassed their defenders throughout and led the ageing Wolves captain Cullis 'a merry dance'. Dodds scored the second goal himself and laid on Wally Fielding's third. 'Just when it looked as though Wolves had given up the ghost' along came Dennis Westcott's 37th goal, a Wolves record. A rousing last ten minutes wasn't enough to save them. Wolves lost 2-3. The championship was wide open: 'Everton struck a note that will echo throughout the remaining weeks of the season to produce one of the most exciting finishes for years.'

Albert Stubbins' 'perfect hat-trick' enabled Liverpool to beat Cup holders Charlton 3-1 before 40,000 in the first of three away matches in London. Stoke won their seventh successive match.

WEEK 38: SATURDAY, 17 MAY
Wolverhampton Wanderers, now in 'agonies of apprehension', had a titanic battle with Blackburn Rovers. Wolves led 2-0 but Rovers fought on. The game entered a 'black phase' as Rovers played rougher, the referee lost control and the crowd abused both. Wolves lost their lead and leader, as Dennis Westcott exited the season injured. Then 'Cullis was knocked out for a minute, and a spectator dashing on to the field, took off his jacket and prepared to fight a Blackburn player.' The *Blackburn Times* was sceptical: that 'master showman Cullis took a particularly spectacular tumble and one of his over-zealous admirers dashed on to the field in sympathy, to be yanked off by the police.' Tom Galley's complaints gave the referee 'ample justification to send him off,' and at least three others could have gone – and were all subsequently suspended – in the ensuing rough house. Trailing 1-2 in the 44th minute, Rovers equalised, then went ahead. Eight minutes later, for all the numerous stoppages, Wolves still trailed 2-3 at home for the second successive week. Only ten men, their championship on the line. Then Galley equalised.

WEEK 39: SATURDAY, 24 MAY AND WHIT MONDAY, 26 MAY
Liverpool, now trailing by one point, were desperate for half-backs: as well as lacking Bob Paisley, Phil Taylor was injured playing for England. They chose two war heroes, Eddie Spicer and Bill Jones. Jones had been an unsung hero of Liverpool's season. He began as their centre-forward and scored two goals in September's 7-4 demolition of Chelsea. Displaced by Stubbins he filled in here and there, inside-forward, full-back, until Laurie Hughes broke an ankle. Jones was then centre-half through their long Cup run and championship revival. Now Jones occupied his sixth different position of the season. Liverpool dug in for another 'gruelling ordeal in sunshine'; Arsenal went ahead with a goal from their decorated war hero Ian McPherson, but Liverpool came back to win 2-1. On Whit Monday, Manchester United made a final effort, smashing Sheffield United 6-2, but could not overhaul Wolves' better goal-average: The top four could not be tighter:

TOP FOUR	P	For	Against	Points
1 Wolverhampton	41	97	54	56
2 Manchester United	42	95	54	56
3 Stoke	41	89	51	55
4 Liverpool	41	82	51	55

Manchester United's season was finished: they were out of it. Now there were three. However, Stoke's last match was not until 14 June, almost three weeks ahead. They could only await a head to head between Wolves and Liverpool and contemplate the permutations. If Liverpool beat Wolves and Stoke failed to win, Liverpool were champions. But if Stoke did win, they, founder members, could be Football League Champions for the first time. Likewise Wolves if they beat Liverpool. Billy Wright was back from England's tour and Jimmy Dunn, hardly able to play during the season because of Essential Work commitments, started for Wolves. His father, the former Wembley Wizard, came from Liverpool to watch.

WEEK 40: SATURDAY, 31 MAY

The 'unique' Wolves v Liverpool match decider in fact recalled the 1899 championship – then the winner of Aston Villa v Liverpool took the title: Villa won 5-0. More modern history was made when the loudspeaker announced that this would be Stan Cullis's last game. It was a 'duel in the sun'. Molineux was as hot as 'Melbourne Cricket Ground', an illusion supported by the match officials wearing white cricket shirts. Temperatures were in the 90s even before the 50,765 were let in (thousands more left outside), and found the traditional handkerchiefs-on-the-heads little defence against the blistering sun. Soon the grass verges were strewn with distressed spectators.

Jack Balmer showed 'mental coolness' in 'plentiful ration' as he skilfully put Liverpool ahead. Shots sailed over crossbar and past post as Wolves responded, but a clearance found Albert Stubbins on the halfway line. Stubbins won a thrilling struggle with Cullis and 'kept the ball under control admirably at top speed to finally steer it' past Bert Williams. 2-0. It was 'gruelling fare, too hot almost to think about football, never mind play it.' Wolves fought back: 'Sidlow came for a corner, failed to fist it far. It fell at Dunn's feet and he lobbed the ball over a group of players.' The goal inspired Wolves to attack with fresh fervour – 'while the ambulancemen were still carrying off dozens of women fainting' – but they broke their hearts hammering away in vain. Albert Stubbins remembered: 'wild were the scenes in our dressing room after the match.' Liverpool topped the table, and now had to wait for Stoke.

There were two weeks of tenterhooks before the season's final match would decide the championship, and two weeks of local tributes: 'this has been the finest season in the history of Liverpool FC.' A team thought more likely to struggle against relegation had nearly won the Double. Since 29 January they had won six and drawn two of their final eight away games. Despite almost constant journeying by manager George Kay – extraordinarily his scouting duties kept him from Liverpool's last few matches – the only newcomer had been Albert Stubbins – 'probably the finest centre-forward ever to wear their colours'. Jack Balmer's 'lustre' matched Stubbins' 24 goals and Billy Liddell supplied pace and power. Phil Taylor had been a passable imitation of irreplaceable Matt Busby and tireless Bob Paisley had been a revelation. But like all the clubs, Liverpool owed much to their rank and file pros. Twenty-six played, and among the occasional contributors was fourteen-year veteran Tom Bush. Tom's year began when he was summoned home from the American tour to tend to a dying infant daughter. Chairman Bill McConnell paid tribute: 'never have we had a finer lot of gentlemen, sportsmen and 100 per cent triers.' McConnell had first watched Liverpool 'with the tail of my shirt sticking out of the holes in the seat of my pants'. Now the owner of a chain of dockside canteens, he would not see them again: illness had dogged him throughout, and he died in August.

Stoke also received their share of tributes. Their success would represent the triumph of community in the English game. They would be the most inexpensive side to win the championship: nine of the eleven were locally born and none had required a conventional transfer fee.

WEEK 42: SATURDAY, 14 JUNE 1947
'The most important match Stoke City have ever played.' They would top the table if they won, and finish fourth if they did not. Opponents Sheffield United lacked Jimmy Hagan, while Jack Pickering had his first game: 22 years a pro, 1930s England international, champion of the player with another job. There were fears that summer conditions – a dry ground, light ball – might produce an arid goalless draw. No worries. This season of seemingly endless winter produced a fitting conclusion: 'A steady rain, a damp cold atmosphere and a small but highly excited 30,000 huddled together in what remains of the badly blitzed accommodation.'

Whilst the championship was being decided on the other side of the Pennines, full-strength Liverpool and Everton sides contested the Liverpool Senior Cup. One 'famous jolly' Liverpool player had to be smuggled in and out of the ground through an 'unusual exit': the income tax people had sent police to the players' entrance to 'collect' him for non-payment of bills. The kick-off was put back so the news and result at Sheffield could be known ... for good or ill: 'If "spitting on the ball" means anything I have done it. If Sheffield win, Duggie Livingstone, the trainer has promised to "snaffle" the ball for chairman Bill McConnell. If Stoke win, no-one in Liverpool will want so much as the lace.'

So the football publics of Sheffield, Liverpool and Stoke settled to the last match of 1946-47. Stoke rattles created the illusion of a cup-tie, but after two minutes Pickering's mis-hit shot 'meandered into the net', to goalkeeper 'King' Herod's 'obvious mortification'. Almost immediately United's goalkeeper Jack Smith (ever-present in both 1938-39 and 1946-47) stood flat-footed in the mud as Stoke winger Alex Ormston slashed a record twentieth goal into the far corner – 1-1.

'Latham legs Steele [of Stoke] in this match of tremendous speed and excitement and gives away a penalty, but the referee says no. Stoke are on top ... United are fighting like the Tykes they are ... Forbes with a vicious kick to clear, was so dangerous he well deserved a caution – a real dogfight ...'
'Sheffield's inspired tacklers remembered their mudlarking tradition ... three went temporarily off the field with injuries caused by their risk everything

efforts.' 'The rain is heavier than ever. The ball skids and spins … Pickering is the man of the match, a real General … another penalty appeal, but all that happens is that Smith comes out and picks up at his leisure … Now Sheffield are definitely on top.' Half-time. Soon after, Pickering's crossfield pass eluded a slipping and sliding defence and Sheffield's Walter Ricketts scored. Back at Anfield, 'the biggest cheer of all rent the skies when the scoreboard was changed to show Sheffield United beating Stoke 2-1.' 'Never can there have been a more thrilling league match. Drama in every moment … United play as though their lives depended on the result … Stoke are rattled, hurried, and quite out of their early stride. The ball is stopping dead in pools of water, but the pace is still a cracker … United are playing like champions … The Sheffield crowd roared itself hoarse as if everything was at stake – and not merely the joy of victory.'

Liverpool were the League Champions of 1946-47, and real football had come home.

TOMMY WALKER
Chelsea and Scotland

Likeable, quiet, good-looking Tommy Walker is a man with a mission. A different mission now, though. Once his ambition was to take Holy Orders. An educated, well-spoken young fellow, he planned to enter the Ministry. That wish governed his move from Tynecastle to London. He argued that any extra money his football talent could earn would meet his expenses until his theological studies were over. But the war shattered those hopes. After long service in the Royal Corps of Signals, much of it in the Far East, he changed his ambition. Now it is to become a newspaper sports writer and newsreel commentator, when his soccer days are over. At 32, he feels that those days are not so very far away. But at Stamford Bridge they laugh aside such pessimism. As Billie Birrell (himself once a player of the "Walker" type) puts it: "Chappies like Tommy go on for ever."

"*Which of you blokes keeps yelling at me to shoot?*"

The postwar boom in attendances meant an intense conflict between cash-rich clubs and the frustrated players, with the Government in the middle

Whiskers were growing on the football craft of 'Grand Old Men' Joe Mercer and Stan Cullis, but colossal sums (and cigarette card collections) were spent on transfer targets

Don Welsh led Charlton Athetic to an FA
Cup semi-final victory over Newcastle,
then applied to become United's manager

Burnley's FA Cup home replay with
Middlesbrough in March 1947 almost
saw a tragedy like that at Bolton in 1946

In an age of austerity, clubs appealed
for clothing coupons, and managers
sought homes for their players, even
when homeless themselves

FRANK SWIFT

Manchester City and England

See Frank Swift on the field. He's tall (6 ft. 3½ in.), quick to move into position, double-quick to intercept a centre or beat out a surprise shot. He has the greatest hand expansion recorded in the game—11½ in. Meet him off the field, maybe at Withington, the Manchester suburb, where he is the teetotal host of the " local." He is dark, good looking, well dressed, well spoken, and a witty conversationalist. Everyone in football likes Frank. Frank likes everyone in football—except one or two notoriously rugged centre-forwards !

Frank Swift criticised the monotonous, archaic training methods

England and Scotland had played at Maine Road in August 1946 in aid of the Bolton Disaster Fund. They met again in the Home Championships at Wembley in 1947. Note the pre-match entertainment

John Strachey, Minister of Food, was usually Public Enemy No 1,
but not when there were footballers to scream at

Football provided the perfect expression for the Government getting
knocked about following its crusade against midweek sport

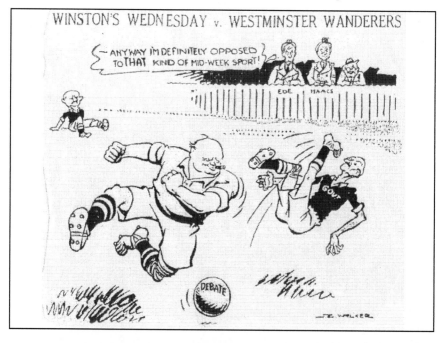

League Tables

1946-47: First Division

	P	W	D	L	F	A	Pts
1 Liverpool	42	25	7	10	84	52	57
2 Manchester U	42	22	12	8	95	54	56
3 Wolves	42	25	6	11	98	56	56
4 Stoke	42	24	7	11	90	53	55
5 Blackpool	42	22	6	14	71	70	50
6 Sheffield U	42	21	7	14	89	75	49
7 Preston	42	18	11	13	76	74	47
8 Aston Villa	42	18	9	15	67	53	45
9 Sunderland	42	18	8	16	65	66	44
10 Everton	42	17	9	16	62	67	43
11 Middlesbrough	42	17	8	17	73	68	42
12 Portsmouth	42	16	9	17	66	60	41
13 Arsenal	42	16	9	17	72	70	41
14 Derby	42	18	5	19	73	79	41
15 Chelsea	42	16	7	19	69	84	39
16 Grimsby	42	13	12	17	61	82	38
17 Blackburn	42	14	8	20	45	53	36
18 Bolton	42	13	8	21	57	69	34
19 Charlton	42	11	12	19	57	71	34
20 Huddersfield	42	13	7	22	53	79	33
21 Brentford	42	9	7	26	45	88	25
22 Leeds	42	6	6	30	45	90	18

LEADING SCORERS: IN ALL OFFICIAL GAMES, DOMESTIC AND INTERNATIONAL
41 Tommy Lawton (Chelsea)
38 Dennis Westcott (Wolves)
35 Stanley Mortensen (Blackpool)
34 Ronnie Rooke (Arsenal, including 13 goals for Fulham)
31 Wilf Mannion (Middlesbrough)
30 Albert Stubbins (Liverpool, including 1 goal for Newcastle)

1946-47: SECOND DIVISION

	P	W	D	L	F	A	Pts
1 Manchester C	42	26	10	6	78	35	62
2 Burnley	42	22	14	6	65	29	58
3 Birmingham	42	25	5	12	74	33	55
4 Chesterfield	42	18	14	10	58	44	50
5 Newcastle	42	19	10	13	95	62	48
6 Tottenham	42	17	14	11	65	53	48
7 West Brom	42	20	8	14	88	75	48
8 Coventry	42	16	13	13	66	59	45
9 Leicester	42	18	7	17	69	64	43
10 Barnsley	42	17	8	17	84	86	42
11 Nott'm Forest	42	15	10	17	69	74	40
12 West Ham	42	16	8	18	70	76	40
13 Luton	42	16	7	19	71	73	39
14 Southampton	42	15	9	18	69	76	39
15 Fulham	42	15	9	18	63	74	39
16 Bradford PA	42	14	11	17	65	77	39
17 Bury	42	12	12	18	80	78	36
18 Millwall	42	14	8	20	56	79	36
19 Plymouth	42	14	5	23	79	96	33
20 Sheffield Wed	42	12	8	22	67	88	32
21 Swansea	42	11	7	24	55	83	29
22 Newport	42	10	3	29	61	133	23

LEADING SCORERS: SECOND DIVISION
29 Charlie Wayman (Newcastle United)
28 David Walsh (West Brom)
26 George Lowrie (Coventry City)

1946-47: THIRD DIVISION (SOUTH)

		P	W	D	L	F	A	Pts
1	Cardiff	42	30	6	6	93	30	66
2	QPR	42	23	11	8	74	40	57
3	Bristol City	42	20	11	11	94	56	51
4	Swindon	42	19	11	12	84	73	49
5	Ipswich	42	16	14	12	61	53	46
6	Walsall	42	17	12	13	74	59	46
7	Bournemouth	42	18	8	16	72	54	44
8	Southend	42	17	10	15	71	60	44
9	Reading	42	16	11	15	83	74	43
10	Port Vale	42	17	9	16	68	63	43
11	Torquay	42	15	12	15	52	61	42
12	Notts Co	42	15	10	17	63	63	40
13	Northampton	42	15	11	17	72	75	40
14	Bristol Rov	42	16	8	18	59	69	40
15	Exeter	42	15	9	18	60	69	39
16	Watford	42	17	5	20	61	76	39
17	Brighton	42	13	12	17	54	72	38
18	Crystal Palace	42	13	11	18	49	62	37
19	Leyton Orient	42	12	8	22	54	75	32
20	Aldershot	42	10	12	20	48	78	32
21	Norwich	42	10	8	24	64	100	28
22	Mansfield	42	9	10	23	48	96	28

LEADING SCORERS: THIRD DIVISION (SOUTH)
36 Don Clark (Bristol City)
31 Stan Richards (Cardiff); Magnus McPhee (Reading)

1946-47: THIRD DIVISION (NORTH)

		P	W	D	L	F	A	Pts
1	Doncaster	42	33	6	3	123	40	72
2	Rotherham	42	29	6	7	114	53	64
3	Chester	42	25	6	11	95	51	56
4	Stockport	42	24	2	16	78	53	50
5	Bradford City	42	20	10	12	62	47	50
6	Rochdale	42	19	10	13	80	64	48
7	Wrexham	42	17	12	13	65	51	46
8	Crewe	42	17	9	16	70	74	43
9	Barrow	42	17	7	18	54	62	41
10	Tranmere	42	17	7	18	66	77	41
11	Hull	42	16	8	18	49	53	40
12	Lincoln	42	17	5	20	86	87	39
13	Hartlepools	42	15	9	18	64	73	39
14	Gateshead	42	16	6	20	62	72	38
15	York	42	14	9	19	67	81	37
16	Carlisle	42	14	9	19	70	93	37
17	Darlington	42	15	6	21	68	80	36
18	New Brighton	42	14	8	20	57	77	36
19	Oldham	42	12	8	22	55	80	32
20	Accrington	42	14	4	24	56	92	32
21	Southport	42	7	11	24	53	85	25
22	Halifax	42	8	6	28	43	92	22

LEADING SCORERS: THIRD DIVISION (NORTH)
41 Clarrie Jordan (Doncaster)
38 Walter Ardron (Rotherham)
36 Dick Yates (Chester)

Bibliography

NEWSPAPER REFERENCES: ALL 1946 AND 1947 UNLESS STATED

Accrington Observer and Times; Barnsley Chronicle and South Yorkshire News; Birmingham Sports Argus; Blackburn Times; Bolton Evening News; Bristol Evening Post; Burnley Express and Burnley News; Burton Football Mail; Chester Chronicle; Chronicle and Echo, Northampton; Coventry Evening Telegraph; Cumberland Evening News; Cumberland News; Daily Dispatch; Daily Express; Daily Graphic; Daily Herald; Daily Mail; Daily Mirror; Daily Record; Derby Evening Telegraph; Eastern Evening News, Norwich; Essex Chronicle; Evening Express, Liverpool; Evening Herald; Evening News, Glasgow; Evening Dispatch; Evening Sentinel, Stoke; Evening Standard, 1997; Exmouth Journal; Express and Echo, Exeter; Football Echo and Sporting Gazette, Southampton; Football Post, Nottingham; Football Star, Ipswich; The Green Un, Sports Edition of The Star, Sheffield [various years]; Grimsby News; Hull Daily Mail; Lancashire Daily Post; Leicester Evening Mail; Leicester Mercury; Liverpool Echo [various years]; Liverpool Daily Post; London Evening News; Luton News; Manchester Evening News; Middlesbrough Evening Gazette; Middlesex Chronicle; Midland Chronicle and Free Press; Newcastle Evening Chronicle; News Chronicle; Northern Daily Mail; Northern Echo; Oldham Evening Chronicle; The People; Plymouth Football Herald; Portsmouth Evening News [various years]; Reynolds News; Rochdale Observer; Sheffield Telegraph [various years]; South Shields Football Gazette; Sporting Buff; Sporting Chronicle; Sporting Pictorial; Stoke City Times [various years]; Sunday Chronicle; Sunday Dispatch; Sunday Empire News; Sunday Express; Sunday Mercury, Birmingham; Sunday Sun; Sunderland Echo; Swindon Evening Advertiser; The Times; Torbay Football Herald; Western Mail; West London Observer; Wolverhampton Express and Star; Wrexham Leader; Yorkshire Evening News; Yorkshire Sports and Football Argus.

OTHER REFERENCES:
When Saturday Comes, April 2000.
BBC 'Match of Their Day', November 1998
Comments by distinguished panelists at a Festival, 'A Celebration of the People's Game,' South Bank, London, 6 June 1998

BOOKS

Alston, I and Ward, A
Barnsley: a Study in Football 1953-58, Crowberry, 1981
Busby,M
My Story, Souvenir Press, 1957
Carter, H
Footballers' Progress: an autobiography, Sporting Handbooks, 1950
Cooper, L
'The Snoek Piquante,' in *The Age of Austerity*, eds M Sissons and
P French, Oxford University, 1986
Cullis, S
All for the Wolves, Rupert Hart Davis, London, 1960
Daniels, R
Blackpool Football: the Official Club History,' Hale, 1972
Doherty, P
Spotlight on Football, Arts and Educational Publishers, 1948
Duffy, M
Henry Purcell, Fourth Estate, 1995
Ellis, A
Refereeing Round the World, Hutchinson, 1954
Ford, T
I Lead the Attack, Stanley Paul, 1957
Franklin, N
Soccer at Home and Abroad, Stanley Paul, 1956
Glanvill, R
Sir Matt Busby A Tribute: the Official Authorised Biography, Andre
Deutsch, 1997
Glanville, B
'Britain Against the Rest,' in *The Age of Austerity*, eds M Sissons and
P French, Oxford University, 1986
Greaves, J, with Giller, N
*Don't Shoot the Manager: The Revealing Story of England's Soccer
Bosses*, Boxtree, 1994
Guthrie, J, with Caldwell, D
Soccer Rebel: the evolution of the professional footballer, Pentagon, 1976
Harding J
For the Good of the Game: the official history of the PFA, Robson Books,
1991
Hennessy, P
Never Again: Britain 1945-51, Vintage, 1993
Hewison, R
Culture and Consensus: England, art and politics since 1940, Methuen,
1995

Hutchinson, R
   The Toon: A Complete History of Newcastle United Football Club,
   Mainstream Publishing, 1997
Hurst, G
   The World Game, Stanley Paul, 1967
Kelly, S
   Bill Shankly It's Much More Important Than That: A Biography, Virgin
Books, 1996
Korr, C
   West Ham United: The Making of a Football Club, Duckworth, 1986
Lawton, T
   Football is My Business, Sporting Handbooks, 1946
Ledbrooke, A, and Turner, E
   Soccer from the Press Box, Nicholas Kaye, 1950
Matthews, S
   Feet First: autobiographical reminiscences, Ewen and Dale, 1948
Miller, D
   Stanley Matthews: the authorised biography, Pavilion, 1989
Moynihan, J
   The Chelsea Story, Arthur Barker, 1982
Paisley, B
   Bob Paisley: A Lifetime in Football, Arthur Barker, 1983
Paul, R
   A Red Dragon of Wales, Robert Hale, 1956
Ramsey, A
   Talking Football, Stanley Paul, 1952
Rollin, J
   Soccer at War – 1939-45, Collins, 1985
Seed, J
   The Jimmy Seed Story, Phoenix Sports Books, 1957
Shackleton, L
   Clown Prince of Soccer: His Autobiography, Nicholas Kaye, 1955
Sharpe, I
   40 Years in Football, Hutchinson's, 1952
Swift, F
   Football from the Goalmouth, Sporting Handbooks, 1948
Taylor, R, Ward, A, and Williams, J
   *Three Sides of the Mersey: An Oral History of Everton, Liverpool, and
   Tranmere Rovers*, Robson Books, 1993
Varley, N
   Golden Boy: A Biography of Wilf Mannion, Aurum Press, 1997
Walvin, J
   The People's Game: The History of Football Revisited, Mainstream, 1994
Watson, D
   Millmoor Personalities, 1946-86, Rotherham MBC, 1986

Wilkinson, G
  'At the Coal-Face of History: Personal Reflections on Using Newspapers as a Source,' in *Studies in Newspaper and Periodical History, 1995 Annual*, eds M Harris and T O'Malley, Greenwood Press, 1997
Wiltshire, J
  Play to the Whistle, WH Allan, 1948
Young, P M
  Football: facts and fancies, or the Art of Spectatorship, Dennis Robson, 1950
Young, P M
  Football in Sheffield, Sportsmans Book Club, 1964.

Index & Glossary
of personalities mentioned